T0312076

"Focusing on the interventions of sex work and prostitution third sector organizations in Africa, the Americas and Europe, this worthwhile scholarly contribution challenges and transforms third sector and civil society scholarship, development studies and the more critical work on humanitarianism. Going far beyond considering how the "rescue industry" affects sex workers, this volume offers an innovative perspective analyzing the factors that shape the interventions of organizations assembled around different understandings of sex for sale. It is an invaluable resource in order to critically reflect about these organizations' contribution to global circulation of discourses surrounding sex work and prostitution."

Adriana Piscitelli, *State University of Campinas, Brazil*

"An eye-opening account and refreshing acknowledgment of the complexities of sex work – even for institutions on the frontlines. This book surfaces the politics of survival in the industry and its impact on both sex workers and the institutions that care for them. In an industry that is often construed as being about survival for sex workers, survival is shown to be equally primal for TSOs. The book outlines the blindsiding challenges of self-reflection and personal truth-telling on the part of TSOs – challenges which must be embraced to effectively mediate the ideological 'messiness' of the field. In the current era of radical global change, this book is bound to propel the sex industry toward facing these challenges head-on, and becoming even more attentive to the voices of sex workers."

Chi-Chi Undie, *Population Council, Kenya*

"Most research on the sex industry focuses on workers and their customers or on state policies and law enforcement practices. Much less is known about nongovernmental organizations and service providers that have routine contact with sex workers. This remarkable book provides a unique comparative analysis of the diverse ways in which these organizations engage with individuals who work in the sex industry. Drawing from cases in Europe, Africa, and the Americas, the authors identify a host of contrasting approaches: in the groups' overall stance toward sex work, the resources available to them, relations with state agents, and engagement with sex workers on the ground. A terrific contribution to our understanding of third-party interventions in prostitution."

Ronald Weitzer, *George Washington University, US*

Third Sector Organizations in Sex Work and Prostitution

Third Sector Organizations in Sex Work and Prostitution is about sex work and prostitution third sector organizations (TSOs): nongovernmental and nonprofit organizations that provide support services to, and advocate for the well-being of people operating in the sex industries.

With a focus on three vast and extremely diverse regions, Africa, the Americas, and Europe, this book provides a unique vantage point that shows how interlinked these organizations' histories and configurations are. TSOs are fascinating research sites because they operate as zones of contestation which translate their understandings of sex work and prostitution into different support practices and advocacy initiatives. This book reveals that these organizations are not external to normative power but participate in it and are subject to it, conditioning how they can exist, who they can reach out to, where, and what they can achieve.

Third Sector Organizations in Sex Work and Prostitution is a resource for scholars, policymakers, and activists involved in research on, and work with third sector organizations in the fields of sex work and prostitution, gender and sexuality, and human rights among others.

Isabel Crowhurst is Senior Lecturer in Sociology at the University of Essex, UK.

Susan Dewey is Professor of Criminology and Criminal Justice at the University of Alabama, US.

Chimaraoke Izugbara directs the Global Health, Youth and Development program at the International Center for Research on Women (ICRW) headquartered in Washington, DC, US.

Interdisciplinary Studies in Sex for Sale

Interdisciplinary Studies in Sex for Sale is a new and exciting series emphasizing innovative work on the complexities of sex for sale, its practices, the policies designed to regulate it, and their effects. It covers both recent and historical developments with an aim to explore multidisciplinary and international perspectives, expand theoretical approaches, and analyze matters which are the subject of controversy and debate in this field.

We welcome submissions of single and co-authored books, as well as edited collections that address sex for sale, its practices and regulation, including those with a focus on: comparative analysis; multi-scalar approaches; methodological perspectives; cultural and economic contexts; and the policies concerned with the regulation of sex for sale.

This series emerges from, and intends to expand, the work of the European Concerted Research COST Action IS1209 "Comparing European Prostitution Policies: Understanding Scales and Cultures of Governance (*ProsPol*)", a European network funded under Horizon 2020 (www.prospol.eu).

Isabel Crowhurst is Senior Lecturer in Sociology and Criminology at the University of Essex, UK. Her research lies at the intersection of sociology, criminology, and critical social policy and centres on the regulation, social control, and lived experiences of commercial sex practices and of intimacy. She has researched and published on the regulation of commercial sex and of intimate citizenship in contemporary Europe.

Rebecca Pates, Professor of Political Theory at Leipzig University, Germany, is (co-)director of a number of grants for research projects on the micro-political regulation of prostitution and trafficking funded by the EU and the German Research Council. These research projects combined grounded theory with discourse analysis. She works on theories of the state, political anthropology and theories of policing. Besides publications on the regulation of sex work in Germany, she has edited a volume on the social construction of German ethnicities and is currently working on a monograph on policing in East Germany.

May-Len Skilbrei is Professor in Criminology at the University of Oslo, Norway, and Vice Chair of *Prospol*. She works within the fields of criminology, gender studies, and sociology of law, and does research on the formulation and implementation of legislation and welfare policies on prostitution nationally and regionally (the Nordic region) as well as on women's narratives of human trafficking. She has published broadly on prostitution and trafficking internationally. She is also an experienced editor, with four edited special issues to her name.

Erotic Performance and Spectatorship
Katy Pilcher

Prostitution Research in Context
Methodology, Representation and Power
Edited by May-Len Skilbrei and Marlene Spanger

Assessing Prostitution Policies in Europe
Edited by Hendrik Wagenaar and Synnøve Økland Jahnsen

Policing the Sex Industry
Protection, Paternalism and Politics
Edited by Teela Sanders and Mary Laing

Understanding Sex for Sale
Meanings and Moralities of Sexual Commerce
Edited by May-Len Skilbrei and Marlene Spanger

Women Who Buy Sex
Converging Sexualities?
Sarah Kingston, Natalie Hammond and Scarlett Redman

Sex Work and Human Dignity
Law, Politics and Discourse
Stewart Cunningham

Third Sector Organizations in Sex Work and Prostitution
Contested Engagements in Africa, the Americas and Europe
Isabel Crowhurst, Susan Dewey and Chimaraoke Izugbara

For more information, please visit: https://www.routledge.com/Interdisciplinary
-Studies-in-Sex-for-Sale/book-series/ISSS

Third Sector Organizations in Sex Work and Prostitution

Contested Engagements in Africa, the Americas and Europe

Isabel Crowhurst, Susan Dewey, and Chimaraoke Izugbara

Routledge
Taylor & Francis Group

LONDON AND NEW YORK

First published 2021
by Routledge
2 Park Square, Milton Park, Abingdon, Oxon OX14 4RN

and by Routledge
52 Vanderbilt Avenue, New York, NY 10017

Routledge is an imprint of the Taylor & Francis Group, an informa business

© 2021 Isabel Crowhurst, Susan Dewey and Chimaraoke Izugbara

British Library Cataloguing-in-Publication Data
A catalogue record for this book is available from the British Library

Library of Congress Cataloging-in-Publication Data
Names: Crowhurst, Isabel, author. | Dewey, Susan, author. | Izugbara, Chimaraoke O., author.
Title: Third sector organizations in sex work and prostitution: contested engagements in Africa, the Americas and Europe/Isabel Crowhurst, Susan Dewey and Chimaraoke Izugbara.
Description: Abingdon, Oxon; New York, NY: Routledge, 2021. | Includes bibliographical references and index.
Identifiers: LCCN 2020049583 (print) | LCCN 2020049584 (ebook) | ISBN 9780815354154 (hardback) | ISBN 9781351133753 (ebook)
Subjects: LCSH: Prostitution. | Prostitutes–Services for. | Nonprofit organizations.
Classification: LCC HQ118 .C76 2021 (print) | LCC HQ118 (ebook) | DDC 306.74–dc23
LC record available at https://lccn.loc.gov/2020049583
LC ebook record available at https://lccn.loc.gov/2020049584

ISBN: 978-0-8153-5415-4 (hbk)
ISBN: 978-0-3677-5388-7 (pbk)
ISBN: 978-1-351-13375-3 (ebk)

Typeset in Times New Roman
by Deanta Global Publishing Services, Chennai, India

Contents

Note on authors

Isabel Crowhurst is Senior Lecturer in Sociology at the University of Essex, UK. Her research is concerned with knowledge and practices produced around non-normative sexual practices and intimate lives and how they are negotiated in everyday lived experiences. Her more recent book is the co-authored *The Tenacity of the Couple Norm* (UCL Press, 2020).

Susan Dewey is Professor of Criminology and Criminal Justice at the University of Alabama, US, where she studies intersections between violence, poverty, and agency among criminalized women. She is author of over 100 papers and 11 books, including *Outlaw Women* (New York University Press, 2019).

Chimaraoke Izugbara directs the Global Health, Youth, and Development program at the International Center for Research on Women (ICRW). With over 20 years of experience working within and with research and academic institutes, he has driven research and programming related to the rights of marginalized people and communities in the Global South. He has authored over 120 papers and 3 books, including *Women's Health in Africa: Issues, Challenges and Opportunities* (Routledge, 2015).

Chapter 1

Introduction

*Isabel Crowhurst, Susan Dewey,
and Chimaraoke Izugbara*

Overview and aims

One day in Mwanza, a town on Malawi's western border with Mozambique, police officers arrested and charged 14 women with violating Section 146 of the Penal Code, which prohibits living off the proceeds of prostitution. With encouragement from the anti-prostitution and conservative third sector organizations (TSOs) that had reported the women to police, these officers forcibly tested the women for HIV and then read the results during the subsequent court hearing. The officers did so in a country where it is not illegal to sell sex and an estimated 20,000 women engage in sex work. Women who sell sex in Malawi are the target of a range of programs and interventions developed by TSOs that sometimes collaborate and at other times compete. In this instance, an alliance of sex worker-led TSOs and human rights lawyers immediately rose to the 14 women's defense by suing the police and the Government of Malawi for violating their rights. The court ruled in favor of the 14 women, holding that Section 146 of Malawi's Penal Code was in fact meant to protect, rather than criminalize, sex workers. Sex worker rights TSOs emerged victorious over the anti-prostitution and conservative TSOs that tried to weaponize prostitution's enduring stigma against them.

On any given day in a Caribbean TSO office, staff and volunteers confront the enduring legacy of colonialism as they ponder the vicissitudes of funding priorities dictated by the Global North in ways that will directly shape what they can accomplish with people in the sex industry. Should they focus their limited grant-writing time on developing proposals that emphasize public health, human rights, trafficking, or some other issue *du jour* deemed pressing by northern funders? Getting the answer wrong, they know, will potentially compromise their abilities to advocate for issues that are actually important to the people they serve, such as feeding families and making sure that children have access to education. Meanwhile, thousands of miles to the north in a major city in the United States, sex workers meet with civil rights attorneys to develop a set of principles regarding their right to be free from discrimination. They do so with full knowledge that their advocacy can publicly identify them as involved in illegal activity and accordingly make them targets for arrest and detention in a country that incarcerates more people than any other in the world.

Thousands of miles away in a Balkan country in Southeast Europe, TSO staff scramble to keep providing essential health and other harm reduction services to the marginalized people they serve. A major international funding program developed a new funding model and will suspend the grant that has been supporting their operations, including a project with Roma men and boys who sell sex. Soon the TSO staff will need to determine how long they can continue operations before ceasing their work entirely. Simultaneously in a Western European city, sex worker rights activists, university researchers, and police collaborate to design a technology that will protect people who sell sex from violence and exploitation. By working together, they hope, sex workers can be free from some of the harms associated with the exchange of sex for money in a partially criminalized environment.

Taken together, these vignettes exemplify the challenges facing TSOs in Africa, the Americas, and Europe. As both nongovernmental and nonprofit, third-sector organizations play a crucial role in the provision of a variety of support services to people operating in sex industries across the world and in advocating for their well-being. This book is about these organizations across three vast and extremely diverse geosocial regions: Africa, the Americas, and Europe. Our aim is to explore what we refer to as "sex work and prostitution third sector organizations" and how these groups shape their goals, activities, alliances, collaborations, and networks around different understandings of sex for sale, whilst navigating dynamic and context-specific sociocultural terrains of race, gender, and sexuality; prostitution-related laws and policies; performative powers associated with global agendas; and local operations of government, culture, and environment. The book's research questions are therefore concerned with the role that sex work and prostitution third sector organizations have in the provision of services to and advocacy for people who sell sex in a variety of different settings and modalities, and the factors that shape their interventions; they include: how do these organizations translate their values and approaches into practice? How does their ideological and functional diversity impact the work, services and/or advocacy they perform? What subjects do they produce and with what consequences? What contributions do they provide to their target population? How do they engage with governments and other local, national, and transnational institutions? How do they work with each other and challenge or reproduce discourses about sex work and prostitution? How are their activities impacted by and contributing to the global circulation of discourses surrounding sex work and prostitution?

Our starting point in addressing these questions is that third sector organizations operating in the field of sex work and prostitution are not external to normative power but participate in it and are subject to it, conditioning how they can exist, what they focus on, who and where they can reach out to, and what they can achieve. Far from being a power-free zone (Corry, 2011), third sector organizations are deeply embedded in their local and global contexts and are "an arena within which battles from society at large are internalized" (Clarke, 1996: 5). We do not wish to reduce them to passive tools in the hands of larger forces, but rather recognize that the power of dominant discourses, and related cultural, sociolegal and economic practices, are negotiated, responded to, and aided by these organizations which in turn can act as political actors of condescension, legitimization, contestation, dissidence, and/or subversion. Our analysis shows that sex work and prostitution third sector organizations have a generative role in producing and defining the subjects they aid and/or whom they represent, impacting the ways these subjects can enjoy (or not) the key elements of citizenship, "rights and responsibilities, belonging and participation" (Lister et al., 2007: 1). Moreover, far from being a homogeneous social force, in the three regions explored sex work and prostitution third sector organizations have historically been and continue to be deeply divided along fundamentally different understandings of prostitution which vary in both complexity and flexibility, with some constituted around rigid norms and abstract ideologies and others based on and responsive to the ever-shifting lived realities and needs of those who sell sex.

Third sector organizations that operate in the field of sex work and prostitution remain under-researched, despite their pivotal positions and roles in mediating the relationships between those who earn money from commercial sex, public authorities, governments, and the general population. The vast majority of published works on these organizations focus on country-specific practices and there is little scholarship that has examined the workings, discursive reconfigurations, and challenges faced by sex work and prostitution third sector organizations across national contexts, let alone across continents. The lack of such large-scale research may reflect the fact that the expansion of the field of sex industry studies in the past three decades has encompassed only a slowly developing body of research that takes a comparative and/or cross-national approach, and within it very little has been done at a cross-continental level. This is the case even though the governance of prostitution in policy and in practice is a matter of global concern, as evidenced by the increased attention given in recent decades to the subject in international law, national legislation, and city ordinances. We advance that third sector organizations are critical sites to examine precisely because of their complex connections to municipal, national, supranational, and international groups and ideologies and because of their unique position in establishing direct contact and relationships with the target populations of such measures and forces. Multiple financial, temporal, and ideological pressures, in tandem with the quotidian tasks of engagement with a marginalized group, do not always allow third sector organizations the time for critical reflection on the complex forces and flows that inevitably shape their work. Nevertheless, they are important social actors to analyze as a means to understand the complex sociolegal forces that constitute prostitution, its construction, and the means of engaging with it.

Of note is also how existing research on sex work and prostitution organizations is positioned for the most part within the rapidly expanding field of sex industry studies. Third sector and civil society scholarship, development studies, and the more critical work on humanitarianism that we review in the next section are still remiss in examining these important social and institutional actors in the field of sex work and prostitution. This book addresses this gap and aims to make a contribution to the different fields of studies listed above and beyond, hoping to disrupt knowledge, ideological and disciplinary silos that, perhaps conveniently, tend to compartmentalize and even exclude particularly fraught and contested subject matters, including sex work and prostitution.

Our interest in exploring the complex dynamics of sex work and prostitution third sector organizations emerges from our co-edited collection, the *Routledge International Handbook of Sex Industry Research* (Dewey, Crowhurst, and Izugbara, 2019b). As part of this project, we co-authored a chapter which examined discourses on the sex industry as they circulate globally and with a focus on the three regions we explore in this book: Africa, the Americas, and Europe (Dewey, Crowhurst, and Izugbara, 2019a). The *Handbook* showed that the complex contextual dynamics of "local" sex industry forms are linked to the global circulation of discourse related to governance, research, and the experiences of those who make their living within the sex industry. In what follows, we briefly outline some of the points we teased out in our *Handbook* chapter as they usefully outline the key contextual features in which this book is situated. First, historically marginalized groups who are overrepresented in the lowest-paid sex industry sectors are also more likely to suffer from criminalization, harm, punitive laws and policies, and societal stigma. This is the case in Africa, the Americas, and Europe, but ample research shows that such overrepresentation is indisputably a global state of affairs. Second, approaches that view prostitution as either reprehensible/immoral or as a form of gendered violence have existed in the three regions, mostly exported from Europe, for well over two centuries and remain strong and politically influential. In part, this is because these approaches claim to offer to put an end to a phenomenon, prostitution, which is constructed as an incumbent threat to deeply-held values, aspirations, and/or modes of existence. For example, the sex industry has been constructed as an attack on national aspirations for gender equality, cultural and moral values, ethnic and racial purity of an imagined community, and the lives and ambitions of women. Third, while sex worker rights groups have grown in the past four decades across the three regions and have built strong international networks and alliances, they remain either excluded or only partially consulted in policymaking and other initiatives which directly impact their professional and daily lives. Fourth, while the seller of sexual services is increasingly viewed as a victim in many European countries and in North America, the buyer/client has become either criminalized in law or attempts are made toward doing so. In Central and South America and in Africa this has not happened (yet), and clients are either mostly ignored in policies and in other prostitution-related interventions or are viewed, in Africa in particular, primarily as an at-risk group for public health action.

Interestingly, in both the chapter we wrote together and the whole *Handbook* of which the chapter was part, sex work and prostitution third sector organizations were only addressed to a limited extent. This book is, in part, our response to what we perceived as the need to pay more attention to these critical actors, and to do so through a vantage point that would enable us to identify inter-linked global developments. The scope of this investigation is certainly ambitious as it encompasses very large and diverse regions of the world. But it is the very breadth of the analysis we propose to carry out that we believe can reveal rich insights on interlinked and global patterns that transcend both the nation-state and more specific contingencies. An international analysis of Africa, the Americas, and Europe brings together contexts that are more frequently studied in the field, and others on which little remains known. Looking at Western Europe and North America, contexts on which most of sex industry scholarship focuses, alongside Africa, Latin America, and other parts of Europe, serves to de-center the "centers" of knowledge production and attention and thus open up further the "pathway to an internationalization of research" (Oyen, 2004: 287, cited in Hantrais, 2009: 4) in sex industry studies. Furthermore, we acknowledge that the geosocial entities we explore, and which we also refer to as "regions" in the book, are themselves social constructs whose boundaries or even existence as unitary entities are contested to this day. By looking at Africa, the Americas, and Europe we are not making a case for the existence of these regions as compact, clearly demarcated, with homogenous and distinct histories and sociopolitical features. Indeed, throughout the book we recognize and emphasize that each region is highly differentiated, carries histories of deep divisions, and confronts to this day endogenous and exogenous geopolitical and socioeconomic fractures and conflicts. However, the analysis we present, first through a historical outlook and then through the juxtaposition of three region-focused chapters, also allows us to tease out patterns that reveal specificities and continuities within each of these socially constructed entities.

In what follows, we first clarify the terminology used in the book and present a review of critical third sector scholarship followed by more specific studies on sex work and prostitution third sector organizations. We then outline the methodological approach underpinning the book and an overview of subsequent chapters.

Language and terminology

Coined in the 1970s, the term *third sector* was meant to identify various entities which are "separate from and balancing the state and the market, themselves considered separate sectors" (Corry, 2011: 11). Third sector scholarship has since engaged in animated debates[1] about what might be included and excluded from this "loose and baggy monster" term (Kendall and Knapp, 1995), whether it is indeed "third" (and not fourth, after state, market, clans and families), the extent to which it can travel cross-nationally and globally as a concept, and other potential ambiguities and limitations rendered even more obvious by its being "by nature unsuited to singular definitions" (Corry, 2011: 11).

We acknowledge the complexity and meaningfulness of this definitional and conceptual contestedness and we embrace its looseness, while explicitly opting for disengagement from debates and disagreements around the groupings covered (or not) by this term. Drawing on Jeremy Kendall (2009: 6), we define third sector as: "the ensemble of bodies that are neither constituted as for-profit bodies, nor owned and controlled by public authorities". This ensemble includes a variety of organizations that can be defined or self-identify as faith-based organizations, grassroots associations, nongovernmental organizations (NGOs), nonprofit organizations, social movement organizations, voluntary organizations, or voluntary groups.[2] Drawing on Kendall (2009) again, we use the term third sector as a point of departure (rather than an endpoint) which provides the analytical flexibility needed to observe and interpret processes that shift the configurations of these organizations locally and globally over time. Finally, the looseness of the term third sector is well suited to the complexity and diversity of contexts analyzed in this book because it encompasses the heterogeneity of organizations addressed and which we refer to as TSO(s) in shorthand.

As well as being diverse organizationally (i.e. in structure, goals and membership) and functionally (i.e. in the ways and levels at which they operate), TSOs are also characterized by ideological diversity (Fisher, 1997). Such diversity is particularly striking among TSOs concerned with commercial sex and informs our use of "sex work and prostitution TSOs" throughout the book, a term aimed at capturing the multiplicity of perspectives taken by the many different organizations we present and discuss. As we will expound in detail in the next chapters, these organizations occupy varying, often dynamic and changing positions on a complex and multidimensional continuum between two polarized perspectives that either regard transactional sex as a legitimate form of work or as an unacceptable social phenomenon, whether because it is viewed as immoral or as a gendered form of exploitation. The terminologies used in this fraught context are themselves contested, with linguistic disputes relating "to the terms used to describe the *practice* of commercial sex and the terms used to describe the *people* who sell sex" (Cunningham, 2020). Thus:

> Using the language of sex work entails making a political statement about the need to recognize and treat sexual labor as work with adequate labor rights, as opposed to a deviant and criminal activity. The term sex work also marks an ideological shift away from the "whore stigma" attached to the word prostitute and the gendered, racialized and classed assumption that a prostitute is a "bad woman" whose identity is exclusively predicated upon her involvement in prostitution. [...] For those who approach prostitution as a form of sexual slavery, the term sex work is an aberration. In its stead, the use of prostitution and prostituted women is advocated to emphasize what is considered to be the always exploitative sex industry which needs to be eliminated through criminal law.
>
> (Crowhurst and Garofalo Geymonat, 2020)

Our analysis shows that TSOs that take a sex worker rights approach often use the terms sex work and prostitution interchangeably, although sex work is most frequently adopted; likewise, they reject the term prostituted people which they view as a negation of sex workers' agency; they refer to people who sell sex as sex workers, although the term prostitute/s, hooker, whore, *puta*, and other similar appellations in different languages are also used when/if the appellation is explicitly chosen by the person/people who sell sex. Contrasting with these linguistic choices, organizations that view prostitution as immoral or as violent reject the term sex work and instead they generally adopt the terms prostitution, commercial sexual exploitation, and/or sexual slavery, and refer to people who sell sex as prostitutes, often as prostituted people, and/or survivors, when they have left prostitution.

What counts as sex work and/or prostitution and who is identified as a sex worker, a prostitute, or a prostituted person depends on a number of global and contingent factors that third sector organizations confront and respond to, including gendered and racialized constructions of sexualized behaviors, sociocultural perspectives on the intersection of sex and money, and designations of criminality and victimization. In the field of sex industry studies, the term "sex work and prostitution" (or "prostitution and sex work") is used increasingly (see for example: Kempadoo, 2009; Orchard, 2020) to account for the different positions within the field's political spectrum, not to dilute differences within it, but rather to encompass them. Sharing this understanding, we adopt the expression "sex work and prostitution TSOs" to refer to an ideologically and politically diverse constellation of organizations which operate in the field of sex work and prostitution, and whose different interpretations of and approaches to these very terms, and the understandings they subtend, will be explained and made further sense of in the forthcoming chapters.

But what does *operating* in the field of sex work and prostitution mean? What do the TSOs that we analyze actually do as part of their work aimed at people who make a living in the sex industry? In addressing these questions, we have favored looseness and flexibility instead of establishing rigid parameters about the activities of the organizations examined that could not easily be categorized within neatly sealed groupings such as service-oriented, human service, or advocacy organizations. Indeed, "it is becoming more and more difficult to classify NGOs in terms of traditional charity (service-providing) vs. advocacy organizations as many of the former have adopted rights-based philosophies and established advocacy branches" (Hahn and Holzscheiter, 2013: 502). Thus, our focus is on third sector organizations that provide a variety of support services directed exclusively at people who sell sex or at them among other populations, and third sector organizations that engage in advocacy activities, either exclusively or in conjunction with other support services, to promote the rights and well-being of those who sell sex.

Lastly, throughout the book, sex worker/s and people in prostitution are the terms we generally adopt to refer to those who sell sexual services; however, we also use the term prostitute/s and prostituted people to reflect the language used by others in a particular context and time.

Third sector: Critical perspectives

The role of third sector organizations, and especially of NGOs, has come under increasing scrutiny and criticism in scholarship from different disciplines. Writing in 1997, William Fisher lamented the fact that anthropological and other literature was still replete with generalizing, idealistic and optimistic statements about the potentials of NGOs for "doing good", "unencumbered and untainted by the politics of government or the greed of the market" (Fisher, 1997: 422). However, aware that "the power to do good is also the power to do harm" (ibid.), in the past two decades critical academic scholarship on the role and work of TSOs has started to flourish across different disciplines. Here we engage with three prevailing themes within this critical body of work to tease out arguments that will be returned to in subsequent chapters.

First, the notion of the third sector as separate from both state and market should not lead to assumptions of its separation from politics, power, and normative structures (Fisher, 1997). Challenges to the notion of third sector autonomy have been developed primarily within a poststructuralist approach which sees TSOs not as independent and detached from government, nor as passive objects to be acted upon, but as entities that are both object and subject of government (Sending and Neumann, 2006). Their "political significance resides both in their capacity to convey and mobilize preferences and concerns of individuals and communities, and in their capacity to carry out regulatory functions" (Sending and Neumann, 2006: 658). Victoria Bernal and Inderpal Grewal, writing from anthropological and women's studies perspectives, note that what they call the "NGO form" "derives power from working with the biopolitical logics of the state" (Bernal and Grewal, 2014: 8). For example, in the United States, NGOs are viewed very much as part of the privatization of social work pushed by neoliberal governments and thus act as enablers of the de-responsibilization of the state: "moving across what is included and excluded by the state also makes the NGO form key to neoliberal projects of privatization and state withdrawal" (Bernal and Grewal, 2014: 8). Social policy scholar Yeheskel Hasenfeld and analyst Eve Garrow (2012) argue that in the context of the current neoliberal regime, the US nonprofit sector, and within it human service organizations in particular, have had to conceptualize their clients as customers, as opposed to citizens, a shift that deprives poor and vulnerable populations of already precarious social rights and that diminishes these organizations' capacity to mobilize for social rights. Some scholars and activists have used the term nonprofit industrial complex to refer to the system of relationships between the state, the owning classes, foundations, and nonprofit/NGO social service and social justice organizations that enable the surveillance, derailment, and management of political movements (INCITE! 2020). They claim that the state uses nonprofits to:

> monitor and control social justice movements; divert public monies into private hands through foundations; manage and control dissent in order to make

the world safe for capitalism; redirect activist energies into career-based modes of organizing instead of mass-based organizing capable of actually transforming society; allow corporations to mask their exploitative and colonial work practices through "philanthropic" work; encourage social movements to model themselves after capitalist structures rather than to challenge them.

(INCITE! 2020)

The body of scholarship that is critical of these developments in the third sector maintains that the nonprofit industrial complex limits the typology and quality of services provided, and is "anathema to true social change" (Finley and Esposito, 2012: 6). Neoliberalism as a model of service provision sustains the status quo and "re-victimizes those who have been harmed by violence, as it pathologizes individual behavior" (Finley and Esposito, 2012: 7). While particularly evident in the North American context, as discussed further in Chapter 4 on the Americas, research shows that these processes are global, in part due to the increasing growth and transnationalization of TSOs globally, but also because of the globalization of neoliberal governance, with all its contingent manifestations (Carmody, 2007; Powell and Powell, 2007; Fischer, 2009; Obadare, 2013).

A second key point elaborated by this critical body of scholarship pertains to the consideration that "NGOs are powerful in part because they are a *recognized* form of public engagement that is legible to states, donors, other NGOs, and wider publics" (Bernal and Grewal, 2014: 9, emphasis added). However, not all NGOs – or TSOs, to reflect the term we adopt – are recognized as equal and legitimate political actors. Their inclusion in or exclusion from policymaking, funding, and collaborations are very much dependent on the extent to which their understanding and construction of the subjects they purport to aid are aligned (or not) with dominant discourses and understandings of the issues they address. In this context, some feminist organizations and coalitions have been accused of being complacently neoliberal in their advocacy and service provision and in the categories of "women" they produce through their work. By relying on constructions of pathologized, needy gendered, and racialized subjects that appeal to funders and that empower their aid efforts – often enforced through carceral practices of containment – they are blamed for failing to address the structural roots of social problems, an endeavor which would entail disrupting the neoliberal system itself (Finley and Esposito, 2012; Boyd, 2018; Halley et al., 2018). We return to the latter point of criticism in the next section in relation to sex work and prostitution TSOs specifically. Here, drawing on the concept of humanitarianism, we elaborate further on what alignment with dominant discourses might entail, not only in relation to the goals that third sector organizations set out for themselves but also in relation to the kind of subjects they produce (Bernal and Grewal, 2014).

Humanitarianism is "traceable both to various traditions of charity and philanthropy and to the so-called civilizing impulses of the Enlightenment and its subsequent manifestations in the expanses of empire" (Donini, 2008: 29), and is generally defined as a system of governance mobilized by the moral imperative to bring relief to those suffering and to save lives (Ticktin, 2006). But who is suffering? Who is a victim worth saving? Anthropologist Miriam Ticktin (2006) and others (for example: Fassin, 2001; Timmer, 2010) argue that NGOs and global civil society operate in a context that requires constructing and highlighting suffering, poverty, and discrimination while simultaneously evoking compassion, sympathy, and benevolence to justify their role in the "the global meritocracy of suffering" (Bob, 2002). This is done even though "many individual actors working within [these] organizations understand that the situation is exceedingly complex and that categorizing an entire people as 'in need' is, for the most part, counterproductive" (Timmer, 2010: 265). The needy subject is "best and most easily recognized by humanitarians when considered innocent – pure, outside politics, outside history, indeed, outside time and place altogether" (Ticktin 2017: 581). Similarly, political scientists Kristina Hahn and Anna Holzscheiter (2013: 499) argue that representational power is a forceful source of legitimacy for transnational advocacy NGOs which "often tend to perpetuate an identity of their constituency as particularly powerless, mute, and vulnerable in order to justify their own role as rightful representatives". And indeed, as they also advance, "conflict arises when the viewpoints held by these group of allegedly 'weak and voiceless' people contradict those their self-appointed advocates hold for them" (Hahn and Holzscheiter, 2013: 502). Thus, to exemplify, within this framework of understanding: a person in the sex industry who is victimized by a regime of criminalization and police brutality and who demands recognition of their rights as a worker may be viewed as too "political" and controversial to evoke compassion and humanitarian intervention. But if they fit the stereotypical victim subject (Kapur, 2002), i.e. a cis woman without agency, docile, "equated with passivity and apolitical corporeal existence" (Ticktin 2017: 582), then they are deserving of compassion and of rescue, and their saviors are deserving of the funds they need to rescue them.

Lastly, and crucially, the reduction of needy subjects to "pure victims" (Malkki, 1996), makes it "easier for them to be configured as objects of charity rather than of law" (Ticktin, 2006: 40). In other words, as pure victims identified solely as suffering bodies and not as right-bearing individuals, they are stripped of their legal personae, "as such, they cannot be protected by law; they are rendered politically irrelevant. And although they may be liberated from suffering, they are not liberated into full citizenship" (Ticktin, 2006: 44) – a problematic outcome that arises when NGOs and other actors mobilize empathy and compassion rather than the recognition of rights (Fassin, 2011).

Related to the arguments advanced above is the third main point we elaborate in this section: the fraught relationship between TSOs and sources of funding. Some organizations are determined to remain completely financially autonomous from public and private bodies and individuals in order to set an independent agenda, resist institutionalization, and prohibit external interference (Bernal and Grewal, 2014). In most of these cases, these organizations tend to stay small and operate locally. Others respond to preexisting funding calls that are defined by governmental institutions, national, regional, and/or local, as well as national and/or transnational donors, but doing so generally constrains the opportunities to pursue projects that they might be interested in and that they may deem more important than those set by the funder. TSOs' dependence on external funding often means that most of their work revolves around funding applications and fund-raising which end up being the primary purpose of their activities. Concerned more with their own preservation than their values and original goals, TSOs become not dissimilar from businesses (Brown, 2014), especially as these organizations – and the fields from which they draw advocacy workers – become increasingly more formalized and professionalized (Beckfield, 2003). The business-like structure and organization they create from within and the expectation that funders have that they abide by and operate within a business-like modus operandi tend to attract educated, middle-class, professional staff whose positions of socioeconomic, educational, and other intersecting forms of privilege are not always explicitly acknowledged, even though they can contribute to obscuring the views and voices of those whom they are meant to work with, represent, or otherwise aid (Brown, 2014; Costa, 2014). The key role of funders in keeping such organizations functional and active also means that TSOs are accountable primarily to these funders as opposed to their target group or wider society (Brown, 2014).

Also notable is the increasing influence of large TSOs and TSO networks, mostly from rich countries in the Global North, in setting the agenda and areas of intervention of TSOs in the Global South and in less wealthy, economically developing countries in the Global North. This channeling of resources is often made in the name of equal partnerships with local organizations (Pearce, 2010). However, as noted above, it is feared that in practice this discourse of collaboration may actually subordinate effective interventions to non-confrontational politics. Some critics argue that this subordinate effect is due to the fact that most TSOs operate locally, which "means that 'empowerment' never goes beyond influencing small areas of social life, with limited resources, and within the conditions permitted by the neoliberal state and macro-economy" (Petras, 1997: 14, cited in Pearce, 2010: 623). Anthropologist Aihwa Ong (2006: 241) is similarly critical in claiming that transnational NGOs "do not coalesce into a system of global governance that can actually safeguard the human rights of the globe's inhabitants". Situated constellations of political and ethical forces limit, she argues, what NGOs can actually deliver: contingent, specific, and temporary stop-gap measures.

Viewed as less constrained by the agendas and priorities of funders/donors and thus more "authentic" in their connections to the communities they serve are social movement organizations (Brown, 2014). However, even these organizations have not been immune to processes of institutionalization and professionalization. The need for them to gain legitimacy has meant "adopting market values and methods" (Eltanani, 2016: 60), including having to fight for a market share by engaging in competitive funding applications, a process which in turn has affected their internal structure, composition and priorities (ibid.). The effect of professionalization on these organizations might include dampening their reputation among their more radical members or peer organizations (Piven and Cloward, 1977; Anasti, 2017).

In conclusion, this section has presented some critical arguments from a broad, disciplinarily diverse body of scholarship that views third sector organizations as an expression of governmentality, i.e. as central features "of how power operates in late modern society" (Sending and Neumann, 2006: 652). The relevance of these arguments, and the extent to which they apply (or not) to the field of study addressed in this book, will be explored in the next chapters, and to an extent in the next section which reviews scholarship specifically on sex work and prostitution TSOs.

Sex work and prostitution TSOs: Overview of existing studies

We have already established that research on non-state organizations providing support to, and/or advocacy for, those who operate in the sex industry tends to focus on specific countries or regions and cities within them (see for example: Morgan Thomas, 2009; Hardy, 2010; Frame, 2017; Hounmenou, 2018; van Stapele, Nencel, and Sabelis, 2019), and in some cases on the dynamics within singular organizations (see for example: Longo, 1998; Pal et al., 1998; Coulibaly et al., 2014; Lam and Lepp, 2019). Studies with a more global scope generally examine transnational advocacy organizations (see for example: Limoncelli, 2006; Hahn and Holzscheiter, 2013). Many of these works are further engaged with in the region-specific chapters. Here the focus is primarily on those contributing to critical theorizations of sex work and prostitution TSOs that may emerge from empirical studies of specific locations, but that are to an extent unbound from any particular geographic context. We begin by examining how some of this literature has further elaborated the conceptual framework of humanitarianism.

In her study on the relationship between sex work and political economy in Vietnam, sociologist Kimberly Kay Hoang (2016) develops the concept of perverse humanitarianism to characterize how NGOs engage with local law enforcers to raid and rescue female sex workers and reclassify them from criminalized subjects to victims of sex trafficking. Hoang's research shows how the "rescued" women find themselves with the impossible choice of being "rehabilitated" or held against their will in a detention center. By looking at these processes and the role played by NGOs, Hoang (2016) argues that it is possible to extend Elizabeth Bernstein's notion of carceral feminism. With it, Bernstein describes the ways in which contemporary Western feminism has been facilitating the repressive and punitive arm of the state. Whereas previous feminist generations struggled for gender justice and sexual liberation, now, Bernstein argues, they demand more criminal justice support to end sexual violence against women (Bernstein, 2010, 2019). Hoang (2016) claims that NGOs are important actors that warrant inclusion in a more comprehensive understanding of how carceral feminism operates:

states deploy apparently benevolent nongovernmental entities that, under the guise of promoting freedom and women's rights effectively, implement practices that mirror incarceration. Ultimately, as sociologist Elena Shih relatedly argues by drawing on her US-based research, rescue projects do not increase the economic prospects of former sex workers on the longer term, rather "generate income for NGOs while privileging the perspective of cosmopolitan global activists" (Shih, 2015: 85). By becoming rescue vigilantes, Shih (2016) also advances, some non-state actors enforce state goals of surveillance whilst gaining influence, not through the authority of professional skills, but through the evocation of moral sex panics over trafficking and "anxieties about immigration, politics of border control, race, class, and gender inequalities" this phenomenon conjures (Shih 2016: 68).

Researchers across the globe note that such anxieties are widespread, with xenophobia and racism emerging as themes plaguing TSOs in diverse sites, including in interviews with social services providers in Puerto Rico who work with Dominican undocumented sex workers (Cabezas and Campos, 2016). The latter "are unlikely to receive any recognition other than as 'illegal aliens'" and are thus rendered unworthy of support and social protection (ibid.: 35). Anthropologist Sine Plambech's (2017) ethnographic work with women who aspired to migrate from Benin City, Nigeria, to Europe to earn money in the sex industry identifies an interconnected migration economy comprised of facilitation, remittances, deportation, and rescue, all of which is produced by a lack of work opportunities that pay a living wage. This study shows how European governments outsource their humanitarian responsibility to local NGOs, a dynamic that "changes the landscape of rescue in Benin because whereas the NGOs in Benin previously emerged as humanitarian or activist, they now appear as a response to the demand for outsourced services, increasingly providing humanitarianism on market terms" (Plambech, 2017: 153). Anthropologist Sealing Cheng shows that South Korean anti-prostitution activists who mobilize Korean nationalist historiography by using discourses of national suffering and redemption to oppose the sex industry neglect the difficult decisions that migrant sex workers must make: "prostituted women's suffering becomes an effective refrain in the vernacularization of the global anti-trafficking moment in South Korea" (2019: 14). Such investment in victimhood, Cheng argues, "individualizes both suffering and evil, encourages fears about female sexuality and promotes a strong criminal justice system as the solution to all injustices" (ibid.). In Mexico, feminist and queer studies scholar Jennifer Tyburczy (2019) reveals that TSOs' receipt of significant US donor aid is likewise contingent on espousing neoliberal narratives that erase the enduring impacts of neo-colonialism by cultivating empathy for individual actors victimized by individual perpetrators who trick their victims with promises of love and opportunity.

In their work on transnational advocacy organizations, Hahn and Holzscheiter (2013) explain how an emphasis on "needy subjects" and victimization operate to exclude sex worker–led organizations from decision making, policy formation, and large international events where important decisions, including definitional and policy-relevant ones, are and have been made in relation to prostitution and sexual exploitation. The authors note how, in these international fora, "images of the suffering, humiliated and helpless prostitute, incapable of self-determination or self-representation, have served as forceful ethical impetus for 'altruistic' NGOs advocating either abolition or alleviation of these women's situation" (Hahn and Holzscheiter, 2013: 516). The opposition brought about by the sex worker rights movement to these images of victimhood, they claim, presents a challenge to the legitimacy and authority of many international advocacy NGOs that rely on them in their central messages. Indeed, they conclude, the needy subject, powerless and victimized, serves to buttress advocacy NGOs' legitimacy and thus "may be compelled to keep their constituencies from claiming their own voice in international political forums" (Hahn and Holzscheiter, 2013: 520).

A striking aspect of the works reviewed here and in the preceding section is the emphasis on the harms and injustices caused and contributed to by what anthropologist Laura Agustín refers to as the "rescue industry", a complex, thriving sector comprising "social agents" or "social helpers" who construct their subjects as passive and helpless, deny them agency to justify and fund their actions, and thus achieve their main objective, "management and control: the exercise of governmentality" (Agustín, 2007: 8). But, as Maggie O'Neill asks in her review of Agustín's book,

> is it always the case that helping projects "benefit themselves rather than their less lucky sisters"? And, where there is power is there not also resistance? What are the ways and means in which helping projects manage, challenge, and resist hegemonic discourses and the dynamics and regimes of care/control?
>
> (O'Neill, 2008: 145)

These are important questions that, just as the critical points advanced by the literature presented so far, are at the forefront of our analysis.

Political scientist Samantha Majic's work has contributed to exploring and shedding light on practices of resistance, which she terms resistance maintenance, whereby social movement-borne nonprofit institutions (see endnote 2) operate "within the institutional constraints of non-profit status, grant agreements, and a political climate hostile to noncriminalizing approaches to prostitution [...to] foster and promote politically contentious ideas and challenge state policy inside and outside of their organizations" (Majic, 2013: 27). These organizations, Majic shows, can challenge hegemonic gender ideologies "even when they are located within an institutional nexus that appears to preclude this" (Majic, 2014: 468), as occurred with her case study sites at two California-based nonprofit organizations that provide health and education services to sex workers. Also US-based is sociologist Sharon Oselin's (2014) study of what she refers to as prostitute-serving organizations (PSOs), which are key agents of change in improving the lives of women in street sex work, whether they remain in it or embark on the complex journey to leave the sex industry. A number of other contributions have also presented the practices of resistance, through advocacy and various support activities, engaged in by sex worker–led organizations globally, highlighting the hostile societal and political environments in which they operate (Kempadoo and Doezema, 1998; Geymonat and Macioti, 2016; Mgbako, 2016). In particular, as legal scholar Chi Adanna Mgbako (2016: 183–184) states,

> the participation and leadership of Global South activists in the international [sex worker] movement challenge anti-prostitution activists' one-dimensional depiction of 'degraded Third World prostitutes' incapable of exhibiting agency. In fact, it is now sex worker activists from the Global South who are at the vanguard of the international movement.

We conclude this section by mentioning one of the few studies that carried out a mapping of different sex work and prostitution TSOs and attempted to create a typology that categorizes them in different clusters. In their US- and Canada-based study, sociologists Sharon Oselin and Ronald Weitzer (2013) identify four types of PSOs – radical feminist, sex work, youth oriented, and neutral – and align them with three different ideological perspectives on prostitution: the oppression paradigm, the empowerment paradigm, and the polymorphous paradigm, based on Weitzer's (2009) categorization. They argue that radical feminist PSOs align with the oppression paradigm "which depicts all types of sex work as exploitative and harmful because of patriarchal conditions" (Oselin and Weitzer, 2013: 446). Sex work PSOs align with the empowerment paradigm, "which holds that sex work has the potential to enhance the lives of those who engage in it" (Oselin and Weitzer, 2013: 447), while youth-oriented and neutral PSOs are closer to the polymorphous paradigm, an approach that is sensitive to the individual and structural contexts that shape the many different experiences, power relations, and occupational arrangements of those operating in prostitution (Weitzer, 2009). The authors' findings suggest "that local context does not significantly influence the various missions of the organizations, […] instead we found patterns across locations that did not seem to be context dependent" (Oselin and Weitzer, 2013: 462), although the local setting and institutional forces certainly influence how these organizations organize their specific operations.

Methodology

We begin this section by stressing the methodology that we did *not* apply: this is not a comparative book. We have not set out to systematically compare sex work and prostitution third sector organizations across the three regions. Rather, we engage in a transnational analysis that explores social actors and phenomena that "do not belong exclusively to one place or another and can therefore only be understood by analyzing *linkages between places*" (Bowling, 2011: 363, emphasis in the original). What do we gain by taking such a broad outlook, one that encompasses three vast and diverse continents? We are able to see the "globality" of sex work and prostitution TSOs and how interlinked their historical and contemporary configurations are. We use globality here with reference to the meaning that Göran Therborn (2004) provided in his book on the history of the family across the world. Globality, he writes, is about the "connectivity, variability and inter-communication of social phenomena", and more specifically it refers to "connections between different forces and events in different parts of the globe", to "the worldwide variability of causal processes as well as of institutional forms and outcomes", and to "communication between actors on different continents" (Therborn, 2004: 10).

What do we lose by taking such a broad outlook? We are not able to retain the analytical depth of studies that focus on a single site or country, and thus lose out on making sense of cultural specificities and geopolitical contingencies. We may also risk making generalizations about commonalities within the three regions. To avoid this, we refrain from advancing claims about quintessential and uniform characteristics of African, American, or European sex work and prostitution TSOs. Nevertheless, we do look for and identify continuities, variabilities, and intersections within each of the three regions and across them.

The regional chapters (3, 4, and 5) derive from content analysis of a variety of documentary data accessed via desk-based research, including websites of relevant TSOs, their social media pages (Facebook and Twitter) when websites were not available, and the many reports they produce and which are available from either their individual websites or those of coalitions to which they belong. TSOs, to borrow from Troy Glover's words on grassroots associations, "are institutional contexts in which collective identities are forged through the social practice of storytelling" (Glover, 2004: 48). We looked at these organizations' websites/ social media as spaces of "storytelling" about themselves, and through which they present – to their target population, the general public, funders, other organizations, researchers like ourselves, and interested parties – their own identity and history as well as the identity and history of the subjects they reach out to and/or represent.

We navigated online resources which are to a large extent available in English but also relied, where we could, on our knowledge of other languages, and where we could not, on online translation websites, being well aware of their limitations and therefore on the restrictions this had on our own understandings. Also important to note is that not all TSOs have easy and reliable access to the internet and to the funds and skills required to build and maintain an online interface. Some of the websites we looked at were of the highest quality and presentation and were regularly updated. Others were more basic and some not always up to date. In some instances, weblinks were not working any longer, and some organizations had instead moved to free social media platforms or had no online presence at all. Some organizations have also ceased to exist and their websites are no longer accessible. Resources on these TSOs were sought out in published research, reports, and on the websites of other organizations to ensure, as much as possible, that not having an online interface would not exclude them from our analysis.

The research and writing of the regional chapters were also informed by our own experiences with TSOs in different capacities over more than two decades. Isabel worked for a Hungarian sex work and prostitution TSO in the early 2000s and later did her PhD on the role of TSOs in providing support services to migrant sex workers in Italy, a project that entailed fieldwork with over 15 of these organizations. She continues to be involved in research with TSOs in the field in different European countries. Susan has worked for most of her professional life in the United States with TSOs that engage with people facing challenges such as intimate partner violence, substance use disorder and other forms of compromised mental health, homelessness, and incarceration. She founded and directed a nonprofit organization that provided incarcerated people with the opportunity to attend free courses for college credit and worked *pro bono* for many years at a transitional housing facility for women who had experienced the multiple forms of structural and interpersonal violence associated with street prostitution in the United States. For over two decades, Chimaraoke has researched prostitution in a number of African contexts, particularly Nigeria and Kenya. In Kenya, he conducted extensive research with both Kenyan sex workers and transnational sex workers from the Democratic Republic of Congo, Ethiopia, Burundi, Uganda, Tanzania, and Rwanda. He has also advised and worked with sex work and prostitution TSOs in Africa, supporting them in fundraising, proposal development, and engagement with policy actors. In sum, we came to this collaborative project after decades of independent research in each of the three global regions, and built upon it to develop our analysis.

Structure of the book

This book explores how sex work and prostitution TSOs operate as zones of contestation, how they translate their understanding of sex work and prostitution into practice, and the ways in which their influence and activities co-constitute and are co-constituted by interconnected and historically configured global forces. Doing so offers important insights with respect to how understandings of human rights, gender, sexuality, and labor circulate within and among third sector organizations.

Chapter 2 traces some of the major historical developments and conjunctures in the shaping of contemporary understandings of commercial sex globally, with a focus on the three regions specifically. It highlights some of the most significant shifts that have informed the emergence and diversification, ideological and functional, of third sector organizations in the field. The chapter sets the scene for a deeper understanding of the region-specific chapters that follow and presents the interlinked histories and contemporary landscapes of the three regions as mutually shaped by colonialism, postcolonial imperialism, global migrations, unfettered neoliberalism, a pandemic, and other geopolitical events.

Chapters 3, 4, and 5 are the region-specific chapters focusing on Africa, the Americas, and Europe, respectively. Each of these chapters is independently written by one of this book's three co-authors. We elected not to frame these chapters around the same sub-headings to avoid being constrained by a super-imposed homogeneous structure and to emphasize the unique themes that the authors identified as better reflecting the complexities at work in each of the specific landscapes presented. The regional chapters are to an extent descriptive in nature, with the broader aim of presenting a very diverse body of organizations that differ in size, aims, and typologies of services provided. Each of the chapters also maintains a tight focus on how the most pressing contemporary global issues related to the subject manifest in each of these region's sex work and prostitution TSOs.

More specifically, in Chapter 3 on Africa, we situate sex work TSOs within four primary approaches: anti-prostitution, sex worker rights, prostitution exit support, and sex worker legal assistance; we find both overlaps and differences in their approaches, alliances, challenges, and impacts. We argue that these TSOs, taken together, are part of the global weaponization of charitable funding by competing powerful Western interests and networks seeking to advance their distinctive agendas and strategic ideologies. Not only are the activities of these TSOs and their financers frustrating efforts to respond systematically to sex work and sex workers' issues in Africa, their contradictory ideologies promote incompatible models that hamper the emergence of a decisive agenda for transforming the lives of sex workers in the region. In Chapter 4 we utilize a fourfold typological framework to analyze how TSOs in the Americas engage with people in the sex industry: the scope of the neoliberal nonprofit industrial complex, cultural values of individualism, self-help, and self-actualization, criminalization and militarization, and outlaw politics. In Chapter 5 we identify three main clusters of TSOs in Europe and their alternating fortunes vis-à-vis access to funding and political and policy-making inclusion. Divisiveness in the field is particularly acute at the present time and it is playing out around contested "policy models" that reveal the strengthening of neo-abolitionist views and TSOs in the region on the one hand, and the weakening of any opportunities for collaborations, much-needed mapping exercises, and the sharing of best practices among TSOs on the other.

In Chapter 6, the concluding chapter, we engage in analytical work to make sense of the links, continuities, and differences between the three different regions. We return to the key questions raised in the introduction and emphasize how a multidimensional analysis sheds light on the complexity, dynamicity, and diversity between and within these organizations.

Notes

1 For an overview of these debates, see Salamon and Sokolowski (2016).
2 Definitions around these terms are also not clear-cut and there are many overlaps between them. *Faith-based organizations* "are religious, faith-based groups, and/or faith-inspired groups which operate as registered or unregistered non-profit institu-

tions" (UNFPA, 2009). *Grassroots associations* are generally understood to be self-organized, volunteer-based, nonprofit groups with a low degree of formality pursuing common interests that have a broader purpose than those of self-help groups, community-based organizations or neighborhood associations (Radu and Radišić, 2012). *NGOs* are usually described as self-governing nonprofit organizations typically involved in development/humanitarian work and who generally receive funds from national or international institutions, private and public, to carry out their activities (Brown, 2014). *Nonprofit organization* is a term that has been mostly used in the US context to identify nongovernmental organizations positioned "in relation and opposition to the private corporate sector" (Bernal and Grewal, 2014: 7). For *social movement organizations* we use Majic's (2014: 5) definition of what she terms the social movement-borne nonprofit organization: "created by activists involved in oppositional social movements that capitalized on resource incentives to continue 'the work' of their movement through service provision". *Voluntary organizations and groups* are nonprofit, more or less formalized, self-governing, and involving meaningful voluntary participation in activities and management as well as private, voluntary donations (Casey, 2016).

References

Agustín, L.M. 2007. *Sex at the Margins: Migration, Labour Markets and the Rescue Industry*. London: Zed Books.

Anasti, T. 2017. "Radical professionals? Sex worker rights activists and collaboration with human service nonprofits." *Human Service Organizations: Management, Leadership and Governance* 41(4): 416–437.

Beckfield, J. 2003. "Inequality in the world polity: The structure of international organization." *American Sociological Review* 68(3): 401–424.

Bernal, V., and I. Grewal 2014. "Introduction. The NGO form." In: *Theorizing NGOs. States, Feminism and Neoliberalism*, edited by Bernal and Grewal, 1–18. Durham, NC: Duke University Press.

Bernstein, E. 2010. "Militarized humanitarianism meets carceral feminism: The politics of sex, rights, and freedom in contemporary antitrafficking campaigns." *Signs: Journal of Women in Culture and Society* 36(1): 45–72.

——— 2019. *Brokered Subjects: Sex, Trafficking, and the Politics of Freedom*. Chicago: University of Chicago Press.

Bob, C. 2002. "Merchants of morality." *Foreign Policy* 129: 36–45.

Bowling, B. 2011. "Transnational criminology and the globalization of harm production." In: *What Is Criminology?*, edited by Bosworth and Hoyle, 361–379. Oxford: Oxford University Press.

Boyd, K. 2018. "Stop thinking properly: Feminist activism and coalescing with history." *Feminist Formations* 30(2): 40–64.

Brown, T. 2014. "Negotiating the NGO/social movement dichotomy: Evidence from Punjab, India." *Voluntas: International Journal of Voluntary and Nonprofit Organizations* 25(1): 46–66.

Cabezas, A.L., and A.A. Campos 2016. "Trafficking discourses of Dominican women in Puerto Rico." *Social and Economic Studies* 65(4): 33–56.

Carmody, P. 2007. *Neoliberalism, Civil Society and Security in Africa*. New York: Springer.

Casey, J. 2016. *The Nonprofit World: Civil Society and the Rise of the Nonprofit Sector*. Sterling, VA: Kumarian Press.

Cheng, S. 2019. "Echoes of victimhood: On passionate activism and 'sex trafficking'." *Feminist Theory*. doi: 10.1177/1464700119881303.

Clarke, G. 1996. *Non-Governmental Organisations (NGOs) and Politics in the Developing World*. Swansea: Centre for Development Studies, University of Wales.

Corry, O. 2011. "Defining and theorizing the third sector." In: *Third Sector Research*, edited by Taylor, 11–20. New York: Springer.

Costa, L.M. 2014. "Power and difference in Thai Women's NGO activism." In: *Theorizing NGOs. States, Feminisms and Neoliberalism*, edited by Bernal and Grewal, 166–192. Durham, NC: Duke University Press.

Coulibaly, A., B. Dembelé Keita, E. Henry, and E. Trenado 2014. "Facilitating access to care for most-at-risk populations: The Bamako night sexual health clinic experience (Mali)." *Sante Publique* 26 (1 Suppl): S67–70.

Crowhurst, I., and G. Garofalo Geymonat 2020. "Sex work." *Dicionário Alice*. Accessed 8th June 2020. https://alice.ces.uc.pt/dictionary/index.php?id=23838&pag=23918&entry=24542&id_lingua=2.

Cunningham, S. 2020. *Sex Work and Human Dignity: Law, Politics and Discourse*. Abingdon: Routledge.

Dewey, S., I. Crowhurst, and C.O. Izugbara 2019a. "Globally circulating discourses on the sex industry." In: *Routledge International Handbook of Sex Industry Research*, edited by Dewey, Crowhurst and Izugbara, 186–197. London and New York: Routledge.

——— 2019b. *The Routledge International Handbook of Sex Industry Research*. London: Routledge.

Donini, A. 2008. "Through a glass, darkly." In: *Capitalizing on Catastrophe: Neoliberal Strategies in Disaster Reconstruction*, edited by Gunewardena and Schuller, 29–46. Lanham, MD: Rowman and Littlefield.

Eltanani, M.K. 2016. ""But it comes with a price": Employment in social movement organizations." PhD. The University of Edinburgh. https://era.ed.ac.uk/bitstream/handle/1842/30997/Kandlik%20Eltanani2016.pdf?sequence=2&isAllowed=y.

Fassin, D. 2001. "The biopolitics of otherness: Undocumented foreigners and racial discrimination in French public debate." *Anthropology Today* 17(1): 3–7.

——— 2011. *Humanitarian Reason: A Moral History of the Present*. Berkeley, CA: University of California Press.

Finley, L., and L. Esposito 2012. "Neoliberalism and the non-profit industrial complex: The limits of a market approach to service delivery." *International Journal of Peace Studies* 5(3): 4–26.

Fischer, E.F. 2009. *Indigenous Peoples, Civil Society, and the Neo-Liberal State in Latin America*. London: Berghahn Books.

Fisher, W.F. 1997. "Doing good? The politics and antipolitics of NGO practices." *Annual Review of Anthropology* 26(1): 439–464.

Frame, J. 2017. "Exploring the approaches to care of faith-based and secular NGOs in Cambodia that serve victims of trafficking, exploitation, and those involved in sex work." *International Journal of Sociology and Social Policy* 37(5/6): 311–326.

Geymonat, G.G., and P.G. Macioti 2016. "Sex workers speak: Who listens?" *Open Democracy 'Beyond Trafficking and Slavery'* Issue.

Glover, T.D. 2004. "Narrative inquiry and the study of grassroots associations." *Voluntas: International Journal of Voluntary and Nonprofit Organizations* 15(1): 47–69.

Hahn, K., and A. Holzscheiter 2013. "The ambivalence of advocacy: Representation and contestation in global NGO advocacy for child workers and sex workers." *Global Society* 27(4): 497–520.

Halley, J., P. Kotiswaran, R. Rebouche, and H. Shamir 2018. *Governance Feminism*. Minneapolis, MN: University of Minnesota Press.

Hardy, K. 2010. "Incorporating sex workers into the Argentine labor movement." *International Labor and Working-Class History* 77(1): 89–108.

Hasenfeld, Y., and E.E. Garrow 2012. "Nonprofit human-service organizations, social rights, and advocacy in a neoliberal welfare state." *Social Service Review* 86(2): 295–322.

Hoang, K.K. 2016. "Perverse humanitarianism and the business of rescue: What's wrong with NGOs and what's right about the 'johns'?" In: *Perverse Politics? Feminism, Anti-Imperialism, Multiplicity*, edited by Orloff, Ray and Savci, 19–43. Bingley, UK: Emerald Group Publishing Limited.

Hounmenou, C. 2018. "Policy response and service provision to child victims of commercial sexual exploitation in the West African region." *Journal of Human Trafficking* 4(4): 336–361.

INCITE! 2020. "Beyond the non-profit industrial complex." Accessed 12th June 2020. https://incite-national.org/beyond-the-non-profit-industrial-complex/.

Kapur, R. 2002. "The tragedy of victimization rhetoric." In: *Erotic Justice: Law and the New Politics of Postcolonialism*, 129–131. London: Glasshouse.

Kempadoo, K. 2009. "Prostitution and Sex Work Studies." In: *A Companion to Gender Studies*, edited by Essed, Goldberg and Kobayashi, 255–265. Malden, MA: Blackwell.

Kempadoo, K., and J. Doezema 1998. *Global Sex Workers: Rights, Resistance, and Redefinition*. New York: Routledge.

Kendall, J. 2009. "Terra incognita: Third sectors and European policy processes." In: *Handbook on Third Sector Policy in Europe*, edited by Kendall, 3–20. Cheltenham, UK: Edward Elgar.

Kendall, J., and M. Knapp 1995. "A loose and baggy monster: Boundaries, definitions and typologies." In: *An Introduction to the Voluntary Sector*, edited by Smith, Rochester and Hedley, 65–94. London: Routledge.

Lam, E., and A. Lepp 2019. "Butterfly: Resisting the harms of anti-trafficking policies and fostering peer-based organising in Canada." *Anti-Trafficking Review* 12(12): 91–107.

Limoncelli, S.A. 2006. "International voluntary associations, local social movements and state paths to the abolition of regulated prostitution in Europe, 1875–1950." *International Sociology* 21(1): 31–59.

Lister, R., A. Anttonen, U. Gerhard, J. Bussemaker, and F. Williams 2007. *Gendering Citizenship in Western Europe: New Challenges for Citizenship Research in a Cross-National Context*. Bristol, UK: Policy Press.

Longo, P.H. 1998. "The Pegacao program: Information, prevention and empowerment of young male sex workers in Rio de Janeiro." In: *Global Sex Workers*, edited by Kempadoo and Doezema, 231–239. New York and London: Routledge.

Majic, S. 2013. *Sex Work Politics: From Protest to Service Provision*. Philadelphia, PA: University of Pennsylvania Press.

——— 2014. "Beyond 'victim-criminals': Sex workers, nonprofit organizations, and gender ideologies." *Gender and Society* 28(3): 463–485.

Malkki, L.H. 1996. "Speechless emissaries: Refugees, humanitarianism, and dehistoricization." *Cultural Anthropology* 11(3): 377–404.

Mgbako, C.A. 2016. *To Live Freely in This World: Sex Worker Activism in Africa*. New York: New York University Press.

Morgan Thomas, R. 2009. "From 'toleration' to zero tolerance: A view from the ground in Scotland." In *Regulating Sex for Sale: Prostitution Policy Reform in the UK*, edited by Phoenix, 137–158. Bristol: Policy Press.

O'Neill, M. 2008. "Book review: Laura María Agustín, Sex at the Margins: Migration, labour markets and the rescue industry." *European Journal of Women's Studies* 15(2): 142–145.

Obadare, E. 2013. *The Handbook of Civil Society in Africa.* New York: Springer.

Ong, A. 2006. "Experiments with freedom: Milieus of the human." *American Literary History* 18(2): 229–244.

Orchard, T. 2020. "Sex work and prostitution." In: *Encyclopedia of Sexuality and Gender,* edited by Lykins. New York: Springer.

Oselin, S.S. 2014. *Leaving Prostitution: Getting Out and Staying Out of Sex Work.* New York: New York University Press.

Oselin, S.S., and R. Weitzer 2013. "Organizations working on behalf of prostitutes: An analysis of goals, practices, and strategies." *Sexualities* 16(3–4): 445–466.

Oyen, E. 2004. "Living with imperfect comparisons." In: *A Handbook of Comparative Social Policy,* edited by Kennett, 276–291. Cheltenham: Edward Elgar.

Pal, M., S. Mukherji, M. Jaiswal, and B. Dutta 1998. "Wind of change is whispering at your door: The Mahila Samanwaya Committee." In: *Global Sex Workers,* edited by Kempadoo and Doezema, 200–203. New York and London: Routledge.

Pearce, J. 2010. "Is social change fundable? NGOs and theories and practices of social change." *Development in Practice* 20(6): 621–635.

Petras, J. 1997. "Imperialism and NGOs in Latin America." *Monthly Review* 49(7): 10.

Piven, F.F., and R.A. Cloward 1977. *Poor People's Movements: Why They Succeed, How They Fail.* New York: Pantheon.

Plambech, S. 2017. "Sex, deportation and rescue: Economies of migration among Nigerian sex workers." *Feminist Economics* 23(3): 134–159.

Powell, F., and F.W. Powell 2007. *The Politics of Civil Society: Neoliberalism or Social Left?* Bristol, UK: Policy Press.

Radu, R., and J. Radišić 2012. "Well-being reconsidered: Empowering grassroots organizations." *Open Society Foundation.* Accessed 8th July 2020. https://www.ope nsocietyfoundations.org/uploads/de7781bb-c2a5-4f1a-84ca-7143447ad2e6/grassr oots_08022012.pdf.

Salamon, L.M., and S.W. Sokolowski 2016. "Beyond nonprofits: Re-conceptualizing the third sector." *Voluntas: International Journal of Voluntary and Nonprofit Organizations* 27(4): 1515–1545.

Sending, O.J., and I.B. Neumann 2006. "Governance to governmentality: Analyzing NGOs, states, and power." *International Studies Quarterly* 50(3): 651–672.

Shih, E. 2015. "The anti-trafficking rehabilitation complex: Commodity activism and slave-free goods." In: *Beyond Trafficking and Slavery Short Course,* edited by Okyere and Kotiswaran. OpenDemocracy. Accessed 12th December 2020. https://www.ope ndemocracy.net/en/bts-short-course-table-of-contents/.

——— 2016. "Not in my "backyard abolitionism": Vigilante rescue against American sex trafficking." *Sociological Perspectives* 59(1): 66–90.

Therborn, G. 2004. *Between Sex and Power: Family in the World 1900–2000.* New York: Routledge.

Ticktin, M. 2006. "Where ethics and politics meet." *American Ethnologist* 33(1): 33–49.

——— 2017. "A world without innocence." *American Ethnologist* 44(4): 577–590.

Timmer, A.D. 2010. "Constructing the "needy subject": NGO discourses of Roma need." *PoLAR: Political and Legal Anthropology Review* 33(2): 264–281.

Tyburczy, J. 2019. "Sex trafficking talk: Rosi Orozco and the neoliberal narrative of empathy in post-NAFTA Mexico." *Feminist Formations* 31(3): 95–117.

UNFPA 2009. "Global forum of faith-based organisations for population and development." *UNFPA*. Accessed 8th July 2020. https://www.unfpa.org/sites/default/files/pub-pdf/global_forums_fbo.pdf.

van Stapele, N., L. Nencel, and I. Sabelis 2019. "On tensions and opportunities: Building partnerships between government and sex worker-led organizations in Kenya in the fight against HIV/AIDS." *Sexuality Research and Social Policy* 16(2): 190–200.

Weitzer, R. 2009. "Sociology of sex work." *Annual Review of Sociology* 35(1): 213–234.

Chapter 2

Sex for sale and service provision in Africa, the Americas, and Europe

Contexts, historical developments, and contemporary landscapes

Isabel Crowhurst, Susan Dewey, and Chimaraoke Izugbara

Introduction

As a dense gendered signifier through which social anxieties are expressed (Phoenix, 2017), the prostitute subject has been stigmatized and *her* identity spoiled across time and space (Scoular, 2015). This chapter historically and geo-politically situates the roles and functions of third sector organizations (TSOs) operating in the provision of services to those involved in the sex industry by reviewing some of the most significant developments that have shaped contemporary understandings of and responses to sex for sale. Three chronologically ordered sections capture major political, socioeconomic, and ideological shifts and continuities: the nineteenth and early twentieth centuries; the central decades of the twentieth century; and, finally, recent developments that have unfolded since the 1990s. Since our three subsequent region-specific chapters contextualize some of the events and temporal-ideological configurations discussed in this chapter, here we focus on the emergence and exchange of discourses and practices between and among geographical locations.

Regulationism, rescue, and resistance

Europe

We begin our overview with a focus on nineteenth-century Europe, where prostitution's regulation underwent "a revolution of massive proportions" (Harsin, 1985: xv) with global reverberations that resonated across Africa and the Americas. It is during this time that women in prostitution, who had been traditionally viewed as sinful and outcasts, became redefined as a social problem and a threat to public health (Scoular, 2015). Spurred by the characteristically nineteenth-century European optimism about the effectiveness of regulationism (Levine, 2003), state officials made prostitution the object of dedicated governance by implementing policy models that imposed strict policing measures and medical testing requirements on women in prostitution. This approach originated in France, where "administrators, motivated by a new sense of responsibility for the well-being of the citizenry, rationalized the control of prostitution to a remarkable degree"

(Harsin, 1985: xv), giving rise to what can still be observed in and beyond the three geosocial regions we explore in this book: the state's concern, even obsession, with the containment and regulation of prostitution (Wagenaar, 2018). Regulationism imposed numerous conditions on women in prostitution, including compulsory registration and licensing for women and the brothels in which they worked, and mandatory regular medical testing (alongside state-enforced treatment) for venereal diseases, all enforced through intensified policing in public spaces and the creation of a dedicated "morals police" (Howell, 2004; Limoncelli, 2006). The regulation of prostitution through such an extensive, intrusive apparatus of disciplinary surveillance coincided and became deeply entangled with the changing dynamics of power accompanying the formation and consolidation of modern European nation-states (Howell, 2004; Scoular, 2015).

The example of Italy is particularly telling in this respect, as it was in the very midst of the wars of unification of 1860 that the first law on prostitution for a nation that was still in the making was passed (Gibson, 1986). A country that had not yet been unified was already establishing codes regularizing prostitution in order for the ruling classes and new bourgeoisie to consolidate their political and moral hegemony by keeping the "dangerous classes" under strict surveillance (Gibson, 1986). In line with dominant beliefs about public health developed by powerful epidemiologists and doctors of the time, women in prostitution, despite being singled out as the most prominent representatives of the "dangerous classes", were not treated as criminals. Prevailing gendered beliefs characterized male sexuality as uncontrollable and women in prostitution as a necessary "safety valve" that preserved social equilibrium by diverting men's aggressive sexual desires away from "honest" women who did not sell sex. Any attempt to eliminate prostitution through criminalization was accordingly regarded as impractical and inadequate. While the visibility of streetwalkers offended the moral sensibilities of the middle and upper classes, "enclosure prevented both the moral and physical pollution of society by contact with prostitutes" (Gibson, 1986: 32). The fragile, nascent Italian state thus extended its powers into new social terrain by using the figure of the prostitute to impose centralized legislation and homogenize the Italian population around the construction of shared norms and morals (Werth, 1994).

Nineteenth-century European optimism about regulationism's effectiveness signaled a new enthusiasm for state surveillance and intervention into the lives of the "unrespectable poor" at home and of those viewed as unworthy-of-self-rule in the colonies (Walkowitz, 1982; Levine, 2003). Such regulation in colonial territories additionally took a marked racialized dimension through the reinforcement of strict social boundaries at the very foundation of the racist, sexist, and classist colonial order (Tracol-Huynh, 2010). As Philip Howell puts it (2004: 231), "the disciplinary modernity of the state, its medicalization of power and construction of sexual deviance are all inseparable from the history of imperialism, the role of colonial medicine and the discursive and material significance of racial difference".

Africa

In Africa, the era of regulation coincided with the widespread socioeconomic disruption initiated and maintained through European colonialism. Surveillance and intervention took different forms throughout Africa, with French colonies focused on preventing the spread of sexually transmitted infections among the French soldiers responsible for enforcing the colonial project (Harries, 2016) and segregating brothels to prevent sex between people of different races (Darley et al., 2017). Five of the thirteen brothels operating in 1899 Algiers were strictly *indigenes* [staffed by local women] and confined to segregated neighborhoods home only to Algerians, reflecting the system that underpinned colonial society (Dunne, 1994). The United Kingdom's Contagious Diseases Acts, which aimed to prevent the spread of sexually transmitted infections among soldiers in the 1860s, were enforced in virtually every British colonial territory until independence, underlying the concern over prostitution's threat to Britain's alleged racial superiority (Bryder, 1998).

Colonial responses to prostitution in Africa involved a multiplicity of factors, including sexual morality, public health, and colonial economic interests (Naanen, 1991; Aderinto, 2012; Muchomba, 2014). Racist social constructions of a "dark continent" mired in immorality, animalistic promiscuity, social and technological backwardness, and in need of civilization and redemption loomed large in European colonial discourses about Africa (Harlan, 1966). Colonial authorities understood that the imperial gendered social organization of labor created prostitution in the colonies while simultaneously using the existence of prostitution as evidence of indigenous Africans' moral immaturity, sexual depravity, or oppressive family structures (Nkwi, 2016). A 1944-commissioned report on Social Welfare in the Colony and Protectorate of Nigeria exemplifies this paradox in noting that economic opportunities "are denied to the Nigerian girl, and if she wants to escape from [the] close grip of the family, prostitution is almost the only alternative open to her [due to…] the idea of woman as a mere household drudge and sleeping partner" (Aderinto, 2010: 24). Colonial administrators' stance "that prostitution was loathsome" (Aderinto 2015a: 89) resulted in campaigns emphasizing its backwardness and harmful effects on the family and public decency. African elites, especially educated women, reiterated the colonial narrative while additionally depicting prostitution as an "un-African" practice that fostered incivility and irresponsibility, obstructing the consolidation of an African society of "civilized" men and women (Aderinto, 2010).

Economic interests also weighed heavily on colonial responses to prostitution, and in African colonial contexts where administrators perceived prostitution as key to the colonial economic interest, it was permitted, gently regulated, or ignored (Naanen, 1991; White, 2009; Muchomba, 2014). Yet in African contexts where colonial administrators construed prostitution as a threat to security, labor supply and colonial profit motives, it was criminalized or outlawed (Jackson and Manktelow, 2015; Kufakurinani, 2015). One example of soft colonial regulation of prostitution took place in 1930s Kenya, where European social constructions of male sexuality as hydraulic (requiring "release") led administrators to regard prostitution as serving British colonial interests by meeting the "needs" of African male labor migrants who were forced to leave their wives and children in their rural homes (White, 1984, 1986, 2009). Nairobi's colonial Municipal Native Office observed how prostitution, particularly *malaya* prostitution, with its associated services of cooking and other care-work, facilitated significant cost-savings on housing for Africans "because the needs of eight men may be served by the provision of two rooms for the men and one for [...] prostitutes" (Davis, 1939: 14). Conversely, colonial officials in Nigeria's Cross-River Delta regarded widespread prostitution as a "serious evil" largely because women's emigration depopulated villages and reduced the number of taxable adults (Naanen, 1991), resulting in laws and edicts punishing anyone who lived off the proceeds of prostitution or facilitated women's entry into prostitution. In another example of colonial authorities condemning prostitution when it did not serve their economic interests, those who were frustrated with the high cost of treating sexually transmitted infections in Southern Rhodesia (Zimbabwe) subjected single African women or suspected women in prostitution to arrest and compulsory medical screening (Jackson and Manktelow, 2015; Kufakurinani, 2015). Concerns about public health were also apparent in colonial approaches to regulating prostitution in Africa, such as in Lesotho, where the High Commissioner criminalized prostitution to reduce the prevalence of sexually transmitted infections and substance abuse, thereby ensuring a regular supply of healthy male workers (Maloka, 1997). In colonial Sierra Leone, and indeed in most of colonial West Africa, similar concerns with venereal diseases led to the prohibition of prostitution (Richard Phillips, 2005).

The Americas

As occurred in Africa, historical developments during the age of regulation in the Americas closely resemble those that happened simultaneously in Europe because colonialism exported continental debates and anxieties about prostitution alongside its systems of governance. Public health concerns regarding the spread of syphilis and other venereal diseases that emerged in Europe, for example, were transposed to and took hold in Argentina and Mexico, where they played a pivotal role in the introduction of a system of strict regulation in 1875 and 1867, respectively (Rivera-Garza, 2001). In British colonies all over the world, regulationist contagious diseases laws even predated its "domestic cousin", with examples from the Americas, including Quebec and Ontario in 1865, Jamaica in 1867, Barbados in 1868, and Trinidad in 1869 (Levine, 2003). Colonial administrative practices in the Americas supplanted diverse sexual norms among Indigenous peoples, on whose land Europeans settled, and among Africans transported against their will into the shackles of plantation labor. Slavery, colonialism, and genocide created and naturalized inequalities of race, class, and gender that shaped social relations in newly colonized countries of the Americas in ways that extend well beyond the state's purview. For example, practices such as concubinage, in which free women of color were financially supported by wealthy white men, reflected the gendered sexual-economic order of plantation slavery for generations after slavery was abolished (Kempadoo, 2004).

Approaches to regulating prostitution in the Americas during this era, however, remained uneven and emblematic of "rogue colonialism", a conglomeration of tenuous alliances between the nascent state, free-market capitalism, and outlaws making a living on the margins of society (Dawdy, 2009). Prior to the Progressive Era (1880–1920), prostitution in the United States was largely practiced without state regulation although migrant women and women of color were overrepresented among those punitively targeted by state authorities (Lucas, 1995). Significantly larger numbers of men relative to women – sometimes with a ratio as high as 20 to 1 (MacKell and Collins, 2009) – in regions dominated by resource extraction industries, such as mining, along with very limited options for women to earn a living, resulted in prostitution being the single largest – and often the most lucrative – occupation for women, as was the case in the silver ore mining towns of nineteenth-century northwestern Nevada (Goldman, 1981). Throughout the post–Civil War American West, women in prostitution largely led transient lives as they relocated from one frontier community to another, paying taxes and fines that enriched these new communities even as they faced growing stigma (Butler, 1985).

As many American nations began their first faltering attempts to form a shared identity in the late nineteenth and early twentieth centuries, prostitution became an increased focus of public debate regarding newly consolidated states' roles in regulating individual sexual behavior. These debates were part of deeply rooted anxieties about state control over individual autonomy, as well as the relationship between morality and politics. Historian Jeffrey Nichols' (2002) analysis of public debates regarding prostitution and polygynous marriage among Mormons in nineteenth- and early twentieth-century Salt Lake City, for example, finds that such debates had at their core a battle for political dominance between Mormons and non-Mormons. It is from debates like these, which took place in various forms throughout the countries of the Americas, that contemporary perspectives on prostitution began to take shape.

Organizing around prostitution

With ideologies and practices based on an understanding of prostitution as a social problem travelling "within and between metropole and empire" (Kozma, 2017: 2), policies and controversies surrounding prostitution were already global in the nineteenth century. An example of the geographical expansion and ramification of debates and strong positioning on how to address the phenomenon is the internationalization of movements that opposed regulationism and sought to abolish prostitution (hence referred to as "abolitionist") globally. Abolitionist campaigns led by middle-class women, evangelicals, and radical workers gathered increasing public and political support for their anti-regulationist approach across and beyond Europe in the late nineteenth century. Abolitionists cast "fallen women" in prostitution as objects of care and concern to be rescued and civilized, a mission that empowered them as the moral custodians of the disenfranchised (Scoular, 2015). Attempts to rescue "fallen women" began in the second half of the eighteenth century but rose to prominence as an "important arena of public philanthropy amongst women in the nineteenth century" (Luddy, 1997: 494). The "rescuers" viewed women in prostitution as intemperate lower-class women destroyed by sexual experience, and they never accepted that, even in countries that provided few employment opportunities for women, "women could choose prostitution as a viable means of earning or supplementing an income" (Luddy, 1997: 493).

Lay and religious refuge homes, also called Magdalene asylums in honor of the biblical character Mary Magdalene, formed part of the rescue apparatus' attempts to eradicate prostitution by isolating and reforming those involved in it and preventing younger women and girls from "falling into vice" (Luddy, 1997: 53). Consider the following vivid portrait of these institutions in Ireland, which

> sought to inculcate in the penitent the correct attitudes and behavior expected of women in this period. Penitents were trained in deference and subordination, the world was protected from them as possible sites of contamination, and they were shielded from the world, the source of possible temptation. The women who entered these refuges were held responsible for their actions and rescue workers stressed the importance of personal discipline to their salvation. Within these asylums the women were not expected to display any individual expression of personality or sexuality. Judging from the large numbers of women who left these refuges voluntarily, it is obvious that these standards were unacceptable to many.
>
> (Luddy, 1997: 498)

Similar rescue and rehabilitation homes opened throughout Western Europe, Australia, Canada, and the United States during the nineteenth century, with the goal of simultaneously preventing prostitution and morally reforming the working-class women who resided there (Stevenson, 2004; Scoular, 2015). Abolitionists were a heterogeneous group with different opinions regarding the state's appropriate role in controlling prostitution and on how women in prostitution should be, or the extent to which they could be, redeemed (Hunt, 1999). Josephine Butler, for example, the founder of the British anti-prostitution movement, cautioned her abolitionist peers in 1897 against including "purity workers in our warfare" because such workers believed that coercive and degrading treatment could force a person into adopting moral beliefs associated with a social purity agenda (Walkowitz, 1982: 252).

Butler's warning did not prevent the social purity movement from gaining strength, a development rising from the moral panic about what was known in the nineteenth century as the White Slave Trade. Having emerged in Britain in the latter parts of the nineteenth century as an "offshoot of abolitionism" (Gibson, 1986), the White Slave Trade referred to the abduction by foreign men of hapless, passive European and North American white women for sale into prostitution abroad to be sexually exploited by greedy men (Gibson, 1986; Levine, 2003; Doezema, 2010). Sensationalistic reports explained how white women, particularly minors, were attracted with offers of lucrative employment and then transported to foreign countries and forced to work in "houses of debauchery". Despite very little evidence to support its existence, the White Slave Trade aroused public concern internationally, which bolstered the abolitionist stance that regulationism was little more than state-sanctioned exploitation of innocent victims. Abolitionist organizations' expanding influence led to the formation of international voluntary associations that contributed to early twentieth-century international agreements aimed at restricting women's migration to protect them from the "evil of prostitution" (Berman, 2003; Limoncelli, 2006). By feeding "the flames of the most prurient social-purity elements" (Walkowitz, 1982: 215), the anti-White Slave Trade campaigns contributed to greater social control of women through rescue institutions, policing, and other repressive measures (Walkowitz, 1982; Gibson, 1986; McCormick, 2018). In Italy, for example, the rhetoric of white slavery was used to justify further state control over prostitution by establishing collaborations with abolitionist groups that could provide "precious information, confidential reports, and circumspect surveillance" in aid of the police and the justice system (Gibson, 1986: 71).

Xenophobia, sexism, and classism significantly shaped dominant cultural responses to prostitution across the Americas during the Progressive Era, and it is no coincidence that moral panics about "White Slavery" emerged simultaneously (Odem, 1995; Donovan, 2010). Women's migration from Western Europe to Argentina during this time period sparked widespread concern on both sides of the Atlantic that young unmarried women would be forced into prostitution, often in ways that reflected a strong public desire to regulate and restrain female sexuality (Guy, 1991). In the Americas between the end of the nineteenth and the first half of the twentieth century, prostitution became a scapegoat for social ills of concern to Progressive Era reformers, including large-scale rural-to-urban migration and shifting gendered socioeconomic norms. Growing numbers of young people leaving rural areas in search of the city's tantalizing promises of upward mobility, alongside unprecedented migration from Europe to the Americas, raised fundamental questions for reformers regarding how these new arrivals would impact urban life after being untethered from their rural traditions of social control (Clement, 2006). The resulting reform movement – often referred to as the "social hygiene" or "social purity" movement – endeavored to create what its proponents regarded as a morally just society free of sexually transmitted infections and the sexual double standard by encouraging young people to abstain from sex prior to marriage and to practice monogamy after marriage (Luker, 1998). In its focus on maintaining the Victorian sexual norms familiar to earlier Anglo migrants, the social purity movement bolstered nationalism in early twentieth-century

English-speaking Canada (Valverde, 2008), as well as elsewhere in the Americas. For many of these Progressive Era reformers, "prostitution remained a moral problem that symbolized the shaky state of the nation's soul" (Rosen, 1982: 13). It is perhaps not surprising, then, that League of Nations measures, passed in the 1920s in response to extensive lobbying by reformers, encouraged police investigators to focus their energies on international cases and third parties rather than women deemed "insufficiently pure", with shifts almost immediately occurring in policing practices in both colonial India and West Africa (Tambe, 2005; Aderinto, 2015a, 2015b).

In Africa, most political processes organizing around prostitution took the form of moral campaigns led by colonialists and local elite men and women who sought to preserve a moral order rooted in notions of essential Africanness (Naanen, 1991; Aderinto, 2010; Muchomba, 2014; Nkwi, 2016). Local African elites supported colonial venereal diseases laws that emphasized the vision of a clean colonial society free from the moral threat posed by so-called undesirable women (Aderinto, 2010). Colonial authorities frequently collaborated with elite women and urban ethnic associations comprised of migrants to mount morality-focused anti-prostitution campaigns and to support women who wanted to leave prostitution (Aderinto, 2010; Adesina, 2018). Anti-prostitution campaigners distributed leaflets, published newspaper articles, and conducted outreach to both rural and urban households and families that emphasized morality, family values, appropriate gender expectations, and the dangers of prostitution (Naanen, 1991; Aderinto, 2006, 2010; Carotenuto, 2012).

In some colonial contexts, African landlords were frequently pressured by ethnic associations, local newspapers, and African community leaders not to rent houses to unmarried or single urban women without identifiable livelihoods (Aderinto, 2015a, 2015b). Local newspapers played a particularly visible role in the colonial anti-prostitution movement. In Kenya, Matthew Carotenuto (2012) notes that the newspaper *Ramogi,* sponsored by the Luo Union, published several articles on the dangers of prostitution, the need for stricter control of urban unattached women, and the possibility of wider use of the Luo Union to chase away "suspected prostitutes" from colonial towns throughout East Africa. One 1950 *Ramogi* editorial admonished parents to send their city-dwelling daughters back home, rather than let them learn immoral city manners, including prostitution (Carotenuto, 2012).

In colonial Ghana, local organizing against prostitution involved informal community efforts to prevent women from selling sex, stigmatizing women who did, and attacked those perceived as prostitutes, particularly migrant women from neighboring Togo and Nigeria (Naanen, 1991). Condemnation and punishment for women in prostitution, or suspected ones, were pervasive in colonial Kenya. Often these women were hunted down, forcibly stripped, and their heads shaved before being paraded "in a gunny sack to be humiliated by the court of public opinion" and then forcibly repatriated back to their rural homeland (Carotenuto, 2012: 9–10). Carotenuto (2012) links these violent acts of gendered surveillance by urban men to emerging masculine anxieties regarding gender, loss of control of female sexuality, and politics of belonging in a colonial social order that left them with deep feelings of disempowerment. Male youth were very active in colonial anti-prostitution activism. In colonial West Africa, the male-dominated Nigerian Youth Association in Sekondi, Ghana, wrote to its Nigerian Branch Association in Lagos in 1939, lamenting that prostitution was "soiling the image of the Nigerian nation" in Ghana (Nkwi, 2016: 101).

Religious organizations, particularly Christian missions, were not left out of anti-prostitution organizing in colonial Africa. Using their close links to local communities, they coordinated community-based anti-prostitution campaigns and local resistance against colonial efforts to legalize or ignore prostitution. Nils Oermann (1999), writing about Southwest Africa under German Colonial rule, notes that the Rhenish Missionary Society (RMS) was vocal in anti-prostitution organizing in colonies such as Namibia. The anti-prostitution stance of churches and Christian missions in colonial Africa had its own internal logic and contradictions. Deborah Gaitskell (1979) argues that colonial missionaries were clearly apprehensive of the relative freedom of African townswomen from patriarchal or official restraints. Curbing their freedoms paralleled success in the Christianizing mission. When German colonial authorities proposed to permit white sex workers to operate under state control to meet the growing demand for prostitutes among white people in Namibia, the RMS opposed it, not on grounds of morality but because they believed that the policy would undermine the position of white women before Africans (Hartmann, 2007).

Before moving on to explore further developments in the twentieth century, we want to emphasize that women in prostitution across the three regions did not passively submit to the coercive policies and practices presented above. Instead, where possible, women mobilized against them and/or found ways of challenging and subverting rules and of negotiating their enforcement to alleviate its degrading effects on their lives. Examples cited by historians are many and we will return to some of them in later sections of the chapter. Records show that Nigerian women operating in prostitution in colonial Ghana and Togo, and Cameroonian women in prostitution in Nigeria and Gabon, resorted to bringing their male relatives to live with them in the countries they worked (Naanen, 1991; Nkwi, 2016; Ekpootu, 2017). Rising economic fortunes meant that these women could easily bribe their ways out of arrest or detention by local police or pay fines for contravening the laws against prostitution, freeing them to continue their business (Naanen, 1991). Algerian women in prostitution conspired to avoid what they regarded as demeaning requirements such as registration and mandatory medical testing by signing fake marriage contracts that allowed them to claim status as "respectable" women (Dunne, 1994), and Italian women similarly avoided compulsory registration by paying bribes to state officials (Sapio, 2007). While their acts of resistance were generally ephemeral and localized, women in prostitution also mobilized and protested more formally, including a 1790 anti-police protest in Paris, a 1907 strike against New Orleans rent increases, unionization in several

German cities in the 1920s, and use of printed media in 1930s Argentina to call for improved working conditions (García, van Voss, and van Nederveen Meerkerk, 2017; Dziuban and Stevenson, 2018). It was not until the 1970s that organized national and international sex worker movements formed alongside systems and structures aimed at supporting sex workers in ways that vastly differed from the rescue-based organizations presented so far. Many changes had to take place, however, for these developments to unfold, as discussed below.

Moving toward a pluralism of (conflicting) approaches

Europe

Between the end of the nineteenth and the first half of the twentieth century, European countries that had promoted a strict regulationist approach to prostitution gave in to abolitionist campaigns, with regulationism abolished in the United Kingdom in 1886, Norway in 1888, Denmark in 1906, the Netherlands in 1911, Sweden in 1918, Germany in 1927, France in 1946, Spain in 1956, and Italy in 1958.[1] Regulationism's repeal put an end to its sovereign power as a system inscribed in and proscribed by law, but the normative power of regulation and the surveillance it entailed kept (and keeps) persisting (Scoular, 2015). Moreover, "while regulation as a practice lost more and more support over the years, the assumption of a direct link between promiscuity and disease, and between sexual desire and racial characteristics, remained stable" (Levine, 2003: 323). State and municipal agents in European countries and colonized territories continued to subject women in prostitution to compulsory medical inspections aimed at managing sexually transmitted infections well into the mid-twentieth century (Taraud, 2003). Even institutions such as Magdalene asylums, reformatories and refuge homes that allegedly fought vice and protected the vulnerable, continued working as they had before to keep those activities in check rather than to challenge the causes of women's vulnerability. Abolitionism simply took on new forms following regulationism's demise, with German abolitionist Anna Pappritz noting in 1927 that "the motto is now: to continue to work for our aims with fresh courage and tough energy, to pursue the campaign against the 'double standard' of morality so that later generations can profit from our endeavors" (Wolff, 2008: 234).

Coercive sexual surveillance practices targeting women continued unabated in early twentieth-century Britain, "marked by a shadowy mix of formal and informal, statutory and charitable, and recorded and unrecorded measures" (Cox, 2007: 113). Central to this was the charitable rescue sector, a network of very diverse organizations that operated at the margins of the law, slipped in and out of an emerging public sector audit culture, and therefore remained historically invisible (Cox, 2007). The assumption underpinning long-held disciplinary practices whereby "sexual deviants" are better kept under some form of institutional control can be observed to this day, with many contemporary prostitution policy regimes subjecting street sex workers to criminal sanctions, whereas private/brothel sex workers face less state scrutiny "if they embrace the public health model of self-care and harm reduction" (Scoular, 2015: 47). Yet "the prostitute", as a socially sanctioned signifier of deviance, and prostitution, as a social problem in need of control, became the target of new specific criminal justice policies throughout the twentieth century. The expansion of this punitive dimension took shape through either *repressive* policy regimes aimed at eradicating "sex work in order to protect society and/or those selling sex from harm", or *restrictive* regimes aimed at imposing limits on "the sex work sector in order to protect society and/or those selling sex from harm" (Östergren, 2017: 17).

Examples of such developments can be found in the socialist regimes of what became known as the Eastern bloc, where prostitution was viewed as a bourgeois phenomenon to be repressed and criminalized. In Slovenia, this resulted in the implementation of a system of criminalization that made all prostitution illegal (Sori and Pajnik, 2018). Czechoslovakia's Communist regime regarded prostitution as a crime of parasitism because it contravened "socialist morality" by shirking honest labor (Havelková 2018) and instituted public health laws which authorized that "any prostitute taken into custody would be subjected to involuntary medical examinations and treatment" (Havelková 2016: 172). While Slovenia, Slovakia, and the Czech Republic changed these policy approaches at the end of the century, in Albania and Romania the criminalization of prostitution (and specifically of selling sexual services) introduced in 1945 and 1949, respectively, remains to this day. In other European countries, regulationism was replaced by restrictive systems of partial criminalization, whereby the sale and purchase of sex *per se* was/is not a crime, but most prostitution-related behaviors were/are criminalized, including advertising, soliciting, loitering, and profiting from the prostitution of others. Referring to the UK context, Jo Phoenix comments that "one of the unintended consequences of such partial criminalization has been the relative over-policing of women's prostitution activities and the under-policing of the crimes committed against them" (Phoenix, 2009: 15–16), a state of affairs also evident across many other European countries (see Jahnsen and Wagenaar, 2018).

After the slow economic recovery of the post-war years, the expansion of the consumer economy west of the Iron Curtain coupled with a loosening of sexual mores set the foundation for the development of the modern sex industry. With the prosperity of Western Europe, sex tourism to countries in South East Asia boomed, and the domestic Western European scene underwent a dramatic revolution with sex phone lines, sex clubs, and escort services catering to increasingly affluent men (Roberts, 1992; Outshoorn, 2004a).

Events that took shape in France during the 1960s and 1970s provide an example of further shifts that started occurring in many parts of Europe, especially in relation to how changes in prostitution policies contributed to increasing the role of TSOs in the provision of services in the field. From 1960 to 1965, the French government set out a number of policies to establish a regime based on the institution of a new criminal justice framework aimed at fighting all forms of exploitation in prostitution and a social policy framework aimed at rehabilitating individuals in prostitution. As part of these measures, the government put in place statutory organizations dedicated to providing support to individuals in prostitution, those at risk of becoming involved, and those wishing to exit it (St. Denny, 2016). The lack of financial and institutional support from the government, however, made these newly created instruments largely inoperative (Mazur, 2004). The gap in service delivery that was thus created was quickly filled by third sector abolitionist organizations that established themselves as key service providers in the field (Mathieu, 2001, 2004; St. Denny, 2016). This development reinforced the already dominant abolitionist approach and its underpinning assumption that those tasked with supporting people involved in prostitution are endowed with a moral guardianship that "legitimizes their claim to be in a better position than the prostitutes themselves to define the best way for them to lead their lives" (Mathieu, 2004: 155).

The Americas

In the Americas, state responses to prostitution generally favored criminalization during the twentieth century, as is true today, yet such legislation and enforcement were anything but smooth or uniform. Revolutionary social reform that swept Mexico from 1910 through 1940 depicted prostitution as symbolic of corruption and decay, although efforts to legally regulate or abolish prostitution failed due to entrenched norms that endorsed the sexual double standard and regarded prostitution as a stigmatized but necessary social role (Bliss, 2001). Mobilizing for sex worker rights occurred even in regulationist regimes such as Argentina, where in 1922 sex workers refused to serve soldiers who massacred civilians; in doing so, the women prompted a strike for better wages and conditions for all workers across Patagonia (Hardy, 2010). While the sex worker rights movement is often described as originating in the Global North, mobilizations such as the one that occurred in Argentina took place across Latin America and the Caribbean throughout the early twentieth century. Sex workers organized in support of their rights in Mexico City and Havana during the 1920s and 1930s, including by founding a newspaper, *La Cebolla* (*The Onion*), financed by affluent sex workers as an outlet for sharing news and anti-government sentiments among the diverse group of women who worked in Havana's red-light district (Cabezas, 2000).

Migration to engage in sexual labor continued to be a prominent feature across the Americas throughout this time period. The largest brothel in the Caribbean, Campo Alegre (Camp Happy) opened in 1949 in a converted military barracks in Curaçao to serve Dutch and US soldiers as well as oil and gas workers and is still in existence today. Founded and operating using a logic of containment and regulation also practiced in neighboring countries such as Aruba, the Dominican Republic, Colombia, and St. Maarten, local women were forbidden from working at Campo Alegre, which instead employed sex workers – primarily from the Dominican Republic, Colombia, and Haiti – who applied for three-month work permits through the state and then registered with immigration, health, and police departments (Kempadoo, 2004). Migration also continued to play a role in the Global North's sex industry, with many sexually oriented businesses (e.g., sex shops) in Canada and elsewhere owned by migrant men who were otherwise excluded from doing less stigmatized business with the established Anglo elite (Ross, 2009).

Regional dynamics and relationships significantly contributed to the organization of prostitution in this era. For example, most Caribbean countries received independence during the 20 years between the early 1960s and 1980s, during which tourism was widely touted by global economic authorities as the solution to the region's economic reliance on monocrop agriculture, such as sugarcane, coffee, and cacao, that had been its mainstay under colonialism. Yet, instead of being a panacea to the region's economic problems, tourism across Latin America and the Caribbean became "a theater for playing out colonialism's unfinished business" (Fusco, 1998: 152). The intersections of racialized sexual stereotypes, the neocolonial dynamics of tourism, and enduring gendered socioeconomic inequalities contributed to the formation of what anthropologist Mark Padilla terms the "Caribbean pleasure industry" (Padilla, 2007). Despite (and perhaps in response to) these entrenched social problems, the revolutions of the 1960s throughout the Americas led to significant changes to women's roles in society alongside the emergence of movements for LGBTQ+ rights, all of which resulted in greater global visibility for sex worker rights activists (Cabezas, 2000).

Africa

Independence from colonial rule significantly shifted the cultural and socioeconomic landscape surrounding prostitution and its regulation in Africa (Homaifar, 2008). Stories of the limitless social and economic opportunities offered by cities and towns in newly independent African countries proved an irresistible lure for many rural people, occasioning a boom in rural-urban migration (Caldwell, 1969; Jonathan Baker et al., 1995). Where they existed, men were the major beneficiaries of these new opportunities because they had higher levels of education and were also considered more suitable for the manual labor jobs that were emerging in post-independence urban Africa (Herbert, 2016). Focusing on Uganda, Christine Obbo (1980) argues that many single women migrants to cities in early post-independence Africa sought to escape rural drudgery, limited opportunities, and personal dissatisfaction with rural life, only to find prostitution the most lucrative option in urban spaces where men control most economic sectors.

The dynamic forms of and responses to prostitution in early post-colonial Africa were not dramatically different from the situation in the colonial period (Homaifar, 2008). Urban single women and women in prostitution remained major sources of political, nationalist, and moral anxieties (Brennan, 2002) and were often described as immoral and sinful in nationalist discourse and political speeches. Attitudes publicly espoused by the earliest post-independence African leaders and politicians paralleled the attitudes of the African colonial elite of the previous decade, bordering on puritanism and characterizing prostitution as an "un-African" vice. For instance, under Juvénal Habyarimana, who ruled for 20 years beginning in the late 1970s, Rwanda prevented peasants and single women from entering Kigali and detained large numbers of unmarried Kigali-based women, some of whom engaged in prostitution, in jails and rehabilitation camps (Chrétien, 1991; Prunier and Hoffman, 1999; Verwimp, 2006). In the 1970s and 1980s, presidential pronouncements in Africa regularly excoriated both prostitution and the moral laxity associated with Western fashions such as miniskirts (Horn, 1979). Idi Amin, who led Uganda from 1971 to 1979, frequently and publicly acknowledged the moral threat of prostitution to his country and on many occasions mandated the country's policy and military to deal ruthlessly with women in prostitution as part of efforts to return the country to a moral, godly path. Amin nonetheless publicly solicited political support from women in prostitution by asking them to provide information about their clients who opposed his government, noting that "even prostitutes can do some work, reporting subversives" (Semakula and Masaba, 2014).

The economic crisis that began to plague African states in the mid-1970s laid the foundation for policies resulting in massive job losses, inflation, high rates of poverty, unemployment, and many other social problems, including pervasive repression and political instability (De Vries, Timmer, and De Vries, 2015). Women were among the worst hit by these trends (Emeagwali, 1995), with prostitution representing a survival strategy (Haram, 1995; Hunter, 2002), which was nevertheless condemned as immoral and antithetical to local cultural traditions.

African governments generally responded to the sex trade boom during the 1970s either by ignoring the issue entirely or by continuing to depict women in prostitution as folk devils through calls for national self-restraint, moderation, discipline, piety, and moral regeneration as solutions to their economic problems (Nwahunanya, 2011). Women in prostitution thus remained common targets of political, moral, and nationalist rhetoric by African political elites who attempted to shift blame for declining economic fortunes onto citizens (Brennan, 2002). Pervasive political turmoil and instability during the 1970s further compounded the problems facing women in prostitution through wars, coups, peacetime violence, political instabilities, displacement of persons, and forced migration. It was in this context that transcontinental prostitution began to take firm roots in Africa as girls and women in the region began to move in large numbers into the Asian and European sex industries (Ejalu, 2006), with several thousand African women reported to be selling sex in Europe alone by 1985 (Aghatise, 2004).

Sex worker rights and harm reduction

Third sector scholarship has advanced different theories to explain TSOs' progressive growth over the last decades of the twentieth century while simultaneously emphasizing the importance of accounting for context-specific contingencies that inform general trends and factors contributing to these developments. In Western Europe and North America, these include the decline in manufacturing and the expansion of the service economy, new policies based on partnerships between government and third sector organizations, and the shrinking role of the state leading to a reallocation of responsibilities between the state and society (Anheier, 2004). The fact that so many "ordinary people" worldwide have opted to "take matters into their own hands and organize to improve their conditions or seek basic rights" (Salamon, 1994: 121) has also expanded the number of TSOs, and in Latin America, Africa and other economically developing regions in particular, outside pressures from religious bodies, private donor organizations, and official aid agencies have also contributed to what Lester Salamon (1994) refers to as a global "associational revolution".

In tandem with the expansion in the relevance and roles of TSOs around the world, the scope, advocacy, and type of services provided by non-state organizations in the field of sex work and prostitution underwent an equally global revolution in the latter decades of the twentieth century. Throughout the 1970s, TSOs remained active in the field, albeit still limited in numbers (especially in Africa and Latin America) and with their functions largely focused on the rescue and rehabilitation of women in prostitution. This approach was not fully challenged until the early 1980s when newly formed sex worker and third sector health-based organizations began to emerge.

The fervent political activism around sex and sexuality in the 1970s and 1980s provided the backdrop for the emergence and growth of sex worker rights movements. With the famous slogan of "outlaw poverty, not prostitutes", the sex worker rights movement was in full swing by the 1970s in the United States, having been founded in the early 1970s as part of Whores, Housewives, and Others, the group that later became the sex worker rights organization COYOTE, an acronym for "Call Off Your Old Tired Ethics" (Leigh, 1997). This era in the United States produced its own vibrant body of literature that connected global economic flows, sexism, the feminization of poverty, and other major concerns; many of the canonical works in this body of literature were produced or strongly influenced by the voices of sex workers themselves (Delacoste and Alexander, 1987; Pheterson, 1989; Bell, 1994; Kempadoo and Doezema, 1998).

Such social justice activism in movements for socio-sexual liberation prompted reactionary responses from nations across the Americas, including in Canada where the "state was forced to take an increasingly active role to maintain its hegemony in the face of movements for social and sexual liberation" (Brock, 1998). In a number of countries throughout the Americas, a growing intolerance for rights-based repression in any form led to increasingly radical activism and the formation of transnational networks, particularly in Latin America. Consider, for instance, sex worker rights activists' account of a protest led by the Association of Independent Female Sex Workers in Ecuador's El Oro Province:

> In 1984 we called a strike that gained national attention. We closed down the brothels, cut the telephone lines, padlocked the rooms and made sure that those who profited from our work were unable to do anything during those

days, from the boys who fetched water, to the cleaning staff, to the taxi drivers. There was full radio coverage during the strike. Authorities were held hostage in the place where the association operates until the demands were met.

(Abad et al., 1998)

Throughout the mid- to late 1980s, sex worker rights activism made tremendous progress in Latin America and the Caribbean by obtaining social security and health benefits in Uruguay, forming the national Brazilian Network of Prostitutes, and hosting the first Latin American Congress of Sex Workers (Sanders, O'Neill, and Pitcher, 2018; Cabezas, 2019). This era also established a transnational network of sex worker rights activists connecting 15 countries across the region, the Network of Female Sex Workers in Latin America and the Caribbean (RedTraSex) (Koné, 2016).

In Europe, the occupation by sex workers of a church in Lyon, France, in 1975, to publicly demonstrate against police repression and the protests that ensued across the country were a defining moment in the evolution of the sex workers' movement (Mathieu, 2001; Scoular, 2015), spurring the formation of the first national sex worker organizations. Sex workers' mobilizations across and between North America and Europe also led to the organization of two World Whores' Congresses, in 1985 in Amsterdam and in 1986 in Brussels, culminating in the development of the first international instrument for sex workers' rights, the World Charter for Prostitutes' Rights, and the founding of the International Committee for Prostitutes' Rights. These congresses and related initiatives demonstrate that by the 1980s, "the movement was officially more organized, recognized, and stronger than ever. Communication among prostitutes from around the world galvanized determination to demand respect as human beings, rights as workers, and representation as taxpayers and citizens" (Sanders, O'Neill, and Pitcher, 2018: 135).

By the mid- to late 1980s, newly formed sex workers-led organizations had to reconsider their activities, agendas, and priorities in light of the HIV/AIDS epidemic. The alarm that accompanied the pandemic brought attention to the intersection of prostitution and public health and, as was the case throughout Africa, prompted the emergence of new TSOs that campaigned for sex work's decriminalization (Mgbako, 2016). Public health experts internationally began to regard sex workers as a group at higher risk of contracting HIV/AIDS due to structural factors including poverty, violence, and the effects of criminalization, and widespread stigma, all of which discourage them from utilizing health services (Dourado et al., 2019). Such "risk group" status soon doubly stigmatized sex workers all over the world as vectors of the virus and people who sell sex (Sanders, O'Neill, and Pitcher, 2018). As Ruth Morgan Thomas wrote in 1992:

"Prostitutes spread AIDS" seems to be a statement accepted without question or thought, whereas "Prostitutes prevent AIDS" is an unacceptable or challenging concept for many. ... The buck apparently stops with the sex worker, as being the person ultimately responsible for infecting "decent" people, regardless of the source of her own infection.

(Morgan Thomas, 1992: 72)

Organizations that previously campaigned for the recognition and protection of sex workers as equal citizens very quickly took on board the additional risks involved in advocacy work around the new sexually transmitted disease and by organizing education and prevention programs targeted at sex workers facilitated to a large extent by the funds made available locally, nationally, and transnationally to support HIV/AIDS-related initiatives (Morgan Thomas, 1992). Non-sex worker-led governmental and nongovernmental organizations received funding during the latter part of the century to address health-related matters among individuals at higher risk of contracting HIV/AIDS, including sex workers. New grassroots sex worker organizations were also formed across the three regions in direct response to the HIV/AIDS emergency, with most that still operate today having expanded the provision of services to areas beyond public health.

In the Americas, nearly all of the sex worker rights organizations founded in the 1980s and early 1990s included HIV/AIDS awareness and prevention within their portfolio of activities, including Women with a Vision (New Orleans), COIN and MODEMU in the Dominican Republic, and the Stichting Maxi Linder Association in Suriname (Cabezas, 2019). Another example is the innovative partnership between COYOTE, the Exotic Dancers' Alliance, and the San Francisco Department of Health that in 1999 founded the San Francisco-based St. James Infirmary, the first clinic to provide peer-led services to sex workers (Lutnick, 2006). In the unique case of Brazil, sex worker rights groups took the lead as political actors – rather than mere "peer educators" – in acting as equal partners in state responses to the pandemic (Murray, Kerrigan, and Paiva, 2019).

The emergence of HIV/AIDS in Africa facilitated more public health and state engagement with prostitution, as research conducted in the very early years of the pandemic put sex work at the center of its spread. For instance, in 1985, Clumeck and Van Pierre (cited in Clarke and Potts, 1988: 245) noted the following characteristics of their study participants living with HIV/AIDS:

[W]ith healthy controls matched for sex, age, geographic, ethnic origin, and annual income, the patients had significantly higher median number of different heterosexual partners per year and also had more frequent contact with prostitutes. ... [I]n addition, of the 42 African women in whom AIDS or AIDS-related complex had been diagnosed in Brussels and Kigali, 10 were professional prostitutes.

Many studies on HIV/AIDS in Africa made similar claims in subsequent years, leading to widespread moral panic about women in prostitution in the 1980s and 1990s (D'Costa et al., 1985). The anxieties caused by these early studies prompted efforts to incorporate sex workers in health promotion interventions, an approach that continues today in many African policy responses that include sex workers in the fight against HIV/AIDS, albeit with mixed results. For instance, in Senegal, where prostitution has been legal since 1966, the HIV/AIDS pandemic led to new requirements for sex workers to register with authorities, be over 21 years old, undergo regular medical screenings, and present a valid and current medical report card to the police upon request, yet there are still equivalent numbers of unregistered and registered women selling sex (Foley and Nguer, 2010). Many HIV/AIDS education, care, and services interventions have been developed and implemented among sex workers in countries across Africa since the early 1990s, including the South African Sex Workers Education and Advocacy Taskforce (SWEAT, founded in 1990), Côte D'Ivoirean Espace Confiance (founded in 1992), and the Senegalese Association of Women at Risk of AIDS (founded in 1993). In countries as wide ranging as Kenya, Nigeria, Uganda, and South Africa, there has been greater donor engagement with sex worker collectives, supporting them to demand decriminalization, increased state protection, and more access to resources, with some efforts made to reduce violence and stigma while improving relationships between police and sex workers (Ardayfio, 2012; Odhiambo undated).

Since the 1980s, harm reduction has been a central focus of work with sex workers in Africa specifically in relation to HIV/AIDS and as part of an approach focused on shifting attention away from moralizing debates. Such efforts have also sought to develop ways of ending violence, stigma, and discrimination against sex workers, to strengthen sex workers' access to resources and service, and to create public awareness on and support for ending violence against sex workers. Sex workers in Africa continue to be common targets of programs that aim to improve condom use, enhance capacity to negotiate safe sex with clients, and increase utilization of formal health care systems (Ngugi et al., 2012). Sex workers' clients have also been targeted with interventions and programs that emphasize sex workers as a risk group, condom use, and the importance of formal health facilities use in the early identification and prevention of sexually transmitted infections (Voeten et al., 2002; Lowndes et al., 2007).

Harm reduction's nonjudgmental public health approach of minimizing risks to improve the health and well-being of people selling sex was new to most European countries. Equally novel was the purely voluntary involvement of sex workers in the services provided (Phoenix, 2017), a notable contrast to the often forceful "rescue" co-optations carried out by voluntary organizations in previous decades, as observed earlier. Such initiatives' flourishing reveals how the HIV/AIDS pandemic, with all the global devastation of human lives that it entailed, has been "the most successful catalyst for sex worker organizing" (Sanders et al, 2018: 136). At the 1992 International AIDS Conference in Amsterdam, for example, the Global Network of Sex Work Projects (NSWP)[2] was launched as a result of the networking activities of a group of sex worker rights activists who met at the Paris International AIDS Conference two years earlier. As stated on its website, since its founding, "NSWP has conducted activities in partnership with other organizations, and has influenced policy and built leadership among sex workers and facilitated the development of regional and national networks of sex workers and sex work projects" (NSWP, 2019).

The discursive approaches and activities of many TSOs involved in HIV/AIDS programs with sex workers were and still are built around a compassionate and pragmatic approach aimed at reducing the harms associated with behaviors and lifestyles perceived as "risky", as opposed to focusing on sex workers as "risky people" (Collins et al., 2012; Phoenix, 2017). In light of this, abolitionist organizations, in and beyond the three regions we examine, have criticized what they identify as the limited scope of harm reduction initiatives because they refuse to denounce prostitution altogether (Barrows, 2008). Overall, the global expansion of harm reduction work, whether carried out by bottom-up grassroots organizations, by top-down public health initiatives, or both, marked a rupture with the past by introducing a completely novel framework of understanding and related practices whereby sex workers are not identified and treated as victims or deviants but as individuals with specific needs that they can be peer workers in helping to meet. Although not unchallenged, as stated above, this approach contributed to a shift in dominant perspectives on and responses to prostitution. Furthermore, the activities carried out by harm-reduction services enabled the unprecedented collection of new and rich information that contributed to a more nuanced knowledge about sex workers' lives (Phoenix, 2008). This had repercussions for increased awareness, facilitated by the contemporaneous growth of the sex worker rights movement, of the specific needs and exclusions faced by male and transgender sex workers who had been ignored in policies, laws, and by support services (Bimbi and Koken, 2014).

Trafficking, sex workers' rights, and selective resources allocation

In this final section, we identify and discuss developments that unfolded in the 1990s through the second decade of the 2000s.

In the Americas, prevailing legislative and ideological stances on sex work have shifted since the 1990s, when labor, harm reduction, and human rights took center stage, to focus on risk, vulnerability, and victimization, often in ways that conflate sex work with sex trafficking (Orchard et al., 2020). This shift stems in part from research indicating that many sex workers' abilities to make choices are limited by oppressions that are both structural, such as sexism and other intersectional harms, and interpersonal, such as substance abuse and struggles with mental health (Porras et al., 2008). Yet this shift to a focus on victimization is particularly troubling because it occurred in tandem with the rise of the nonprofit industrial complex, which, as seen in Chapter 1, refers to the "incorporation of pro-state liberal and progressive campaigns and movements into a spectrum of government-proctored non-profit organizations" as a means to surveil and control activism throughout the Americas (Rodriguez, 2007: 21). Particularly in the United States, the result has been a proliferation of organizations that medicalize sex for sale as the result of a cycle of traumatization and a condition from which women can only emerge through a process of healing assisted by social workers and other state-sponsored bureaucrats (Lerum, 1998).

Some TSOs led by women who identify as former prostitutes have also embraced the language of "survivor", as is the case with the SAGE (Standing Against Global Exploitation) Project, a San Francisco organization that provides mental health and trauma therapy while engaging in peer counseling and harm reduction (Hotaling et al., 2004). Today, the long history of coercive interventions by social workers in the lives of people in the sex industry is considerably complicated across the Americas, and particularly in the United States, by competing discourses, which include state-endorsed abolitionism, the sex worker rights stance of decriminalization, and harm reduction principles prioritized by more progressive social services providers (Anasti, 2018). The Sex Workers Outreach Project (SWOP) Chicago is just one example of how even in a political environment hostile to sex worker rights activism, sex worker-led groups can succeed; SWOP Chicago maintains a network of sex worker-friendly social services nonprofits, partners with a legal clinic, and provides its own services to sex workers (Anasti, 2017).

In many ways, the shifting tide from rights to risks was the culmination of an irreconcilable split that occurred between feminists and other activists concerned with prostitution beginning in the 1980s as part of what was known as "the sex wars". These battles focused on whether women could ever truly consent to prostitution in cultural and economic contexts characterized by men's continued dominance over women, and are well-chronicled in literature that documents these struggles from a sex worker rights organizing perspective (Chapkis, 1997; Oakley, 2007; Ditmore, Levy, and Willman, 2013). The US Congress passed the Trafficking Victims Protection Act (TVPA) of 2000, which subsequently enshrined trafficking as the major discursive framework for understanding and interpreting sexual labor and allocating funding to combat it. This development did not bode well for the future of sex worker rights organizing when combined with the significant stress, limited funding, and lack of meaningful support for frontline services providers to sex workers (Phillips et al., 2012), nor did the allocation of significant US financial resources to combat trafficking under this federal statute, which quickly changed the way that many organizations and national governments throughout the Americas responded to trafficking.

The TVPA authorized millions of dollars to support what the US Department of State termed "the three P's: prosecution, protection, and prevention". This approach prioritized criminal justice responses irrespective of a national government's ability to fairly and impartially enforce the law, threatened significant US donor aid sanctions in the event of failure to comply, and enjoyed strong support from the powerful Evangelical Christian political lobby (Bernstein, 2010). US government funding made available through the Leadership Against HIV/ AIDS, Tuberculosis, and Malaria Act subjected organizations globally to an anti-prostitution clause that required endorsing a stance that conflates prostitution with sex trafficking (Ditmore and Allman, 2013); this stance was required from 2003 until the US Supreme Court judged it to be a violation of the right to free speech enshrined in the US Constitution.

The TVPA also led to the creation of coalitions across multiple professional fields of practice throughout the Americas and across a wide range of fields with the goal of identifying victims and providing services to them, including among health care providers (Schwarz et al., 2016), residents in cities hosting global sporting events (Mitchell, 2016), law enforcement raid and rescue measures conducted in the name of national security (Soderlund, 2005), and various other disparate entities. Funding streams authorized by the TVPA resulted in the exponential growth of TSOs across Latin America (Guinn, 2008) and elsewhere in the Americas. Some countries throughout the Americas have rejected US aid because of the powerful strings attached, most notably in the case of Brazil's famous rejection of over 40 million dollars (Blanchette and Da Silva, 2012). Yet such rejection is far from the norm, particularly as a majority of Latin American and Caribbean nations are "downsized states" in which the provision of basic services falls to TSOs, many of which promote the "performance of victimhood when strategic and beneficial" to the organization and those it serves (Rivers-Moore, 2018: 852). Despite the continued shift toward political conservatism in the Americas, particularly in the United States and Brazil, sex worker rights organizing continues to challenge prevailing anti-trafficking discourse, and harm reduction groups continue to prioritize meeting sex workers "where they are at". Yet, as is further addressed in Chapter 4, it is arguable that such political shifts have in fact quelled radical sex worker rights activism in the Americas.

In Africa, sex workers entered global development discourse and action in the 1980s (Mgbako, 2016) through a combination of forces, including critical feminist theory's influence on African development discourse, the intensification of transcontinental sex work, the rise in democratization, the HIV/AIDS pandemic, and increased attention to gender-based violence against women in the Global South (Scheepers and Lakhani, 2020). Multifocal engagement during this period included efforts to support sex worker organizing and collectivization, provision of direct services, fostering legal reform and advocacy, and building intersectional and regional movements to reject the stigmatization of sex work and demand the realization and protection of African sex workers' dignity, human rights, labor rights, and the recognition of sex work as a legitimate profession within the broader framework and larger agenda of African women's rights movement (Wojcicki, 2003; Mgbako and Smith, 2009; Chipamaunga, Muula, and Mataya, 2010; Richter, 2012; Mgbako, 2016).

A key feature of this recent era has also been the involvement of multinational organizations such as the UNFPA (United Nations Population Fund) and WHO (World Health Organization) in calls to end violence, stigma, and discrimination against sex workers; the strengthening of legal and health support systems for sex workers; and the creation of partnerships for sex workers' rights (Chipamaunga,

Muula, and Mataya, 2010). High-level political support for the sex worker rights movement simultaneously emerged in Mozambique, Namibia, South Africa, and, more recently, Nigeria. However, backlash against sex worker rights and other liberal movements has also become pervasive in Africa as a growing number of women formerly involved in sex for sale, women's groups, churches, and political leaders continue to call for the criminalization of prostitution (Wojcicki, 2003; Msibi, 2011).

As far as Europe is concerned, the last three decades have been characterized by a growing influx of migrant populations involved in the sex industry, with migrants taking a major role in modifying the composition and organization of the region's sex markets. The presence of migrant sex workers from Asia, Latin America, and Northern Africa in Western and Southern European countries had already increased during the time of the post-war economic boom, but even larger movements of sex workers, this time from Central and Eastern Europe, occurred as a result of the fall of the Iron Curtain in the 1990s. By 1998, the number of nationalities in the European sex markets had risen to 25 from 10 in the early 1990s (TAMPEP, 2007). More recently, the 2004 and 2007 enlargements of the European Union (EU) led to further migration flows of sex workers from new EU member-states toward the rest of the Union, and in the 2010s, some asylum seekers and refugees fleeing from Africa, Western and South Asia, the Caucasus, and the Middle East have been resorting to selling sexual services for their survival in Europe (ICRSE, 2016).

As increasingly large numbers of migrants occupied positions in European sex industries, existing and newly formed TSOs were initially unprepared to respond to their needs and the services provided during these early stages were accordingly still very tentative (Brussa, 1999). In Italy, during the early 1990s, for example, the phenomenon of "foreign prostitution", as it was called, was so new and unknown in its various manifestations that different methods of intervention attempted by TSOs occasionally had negative repercussions. Some women were beaten by their pimps for having accepted free condoms from TSOs' outreach projects, while others used two condoms for increased protection because they were unaware of the risks of increased breakage (Crowhurst, 2007). TAMPEP[3] was the first project to research migrant prostitution in Europe from the early 1990s, and to develop, in collaboration with migrant sex workers and with projects already active in the field of prostitution, more effective strategies of support and intervention (Brussa, 1999) that are now widely used by TSOs in and beyond Europe.

The increased presence of migrants in European sex industries caused prostitution and trafficking to reoccupy a prominent position on the political agenda of many countries and supranational institutions (Outshoorn, 2004a). The so-called sex wars mentioned earlier defined the tones of the debates centered around whether all migration in the sex industry should count as exploitation. Following passionate lobbying from both abolitionist activists, as exemplified by the US-based Coalition Against Traffic king in Women (CATW), and sex worker rights activists, exemplified by the Thailand-based Global Alliance Against the Traffic in Women (GAATW), these battles culminated in the passage of a globally influential legal instrument: the United Nations Protocol to Suppress, Prevent, and Punish Trafficking in Persons, Especially Women and Children (Doezema, 2005). The UN attempted to find consensus on these trafficking debates in issuing this international measure to halt trafficking (Outshoorn, 2004a; FitzGerald, 2008), yet the protocol retained many definitional ambiguities, for example, over what constitutes trafficking itself. As Anne Gallagher (2017: 85) states, such definitional issues have served and continue to serve

> as a proxy for infinitely more complicated debates around difficult issues such as prostitution and irregular migration … [and] provide ammunition for all those with a particular position to advance or defend and have contributed to ensuring that such tensions remain unresolved.

Indeed these very tensions were reproduced at the EU level, where the "controversy between abolitionism and the sex work position influenced events and resolutions" (Outshoorn, 2004a: 12). Starting in the late 1980s and early 1990s, EU institutions launched a series of initiatives to combat human trafficking aimed at involving various tiers of governance for a more effective response. For measures to be taken specifically by national governments, in 1997 the European Council of Ministers formulated a joint action on trafficking, which "obliged [EU] member states to penalize the trafficking of persons, to pass measures to prosecute those profiting from trafficking and to confiscate their profits, and to support and protect victims of trafficking" (Outshoorn, 2004a: 12). The ensuing focus on sex trafficking impacted the priorities of local, national, and supranational funding bodies across the region, resulting in fewer resources devoted to supporting victims of other forms of trafficking and to sex worker rights groups.

It is in the context of international calls to put an end to sex trafficking that many governments in Europe (and beyond) responded by attempting to abolish prostitution by way of punitive measures, leading to what Teela Sanders et al. have identified as the third major period of legislative activity on prostitution (Sanders, O'Neill, and Pitcher, 2018). As Phoenix (2017: 694) explains, we are now witnessing

> an apparent reversal in the declared trajectory of regulation. … Now, the main stated targets are predatory and powerful males, "sexual abusers", "pimps", "traffickers", and "organized criminal gangs" because of the threats of abuse and exploitation that they pose to "society", "the vulnerable", and "the victimized".

Sweden was the first country to promote this approach and to introduce, in 1998, a new law that criminalizes the purchase, but not the sale, of sexual services, and similar policy approaches and laws were subsequently introduced in Finland (2006), Iceland (2009), Norway (2009), Northern Ireland (2015), France (2016), and Ireland (2017). What problematically became known as the "Nordic model"[4] was also supported by the European Parliament in 2014 in a nonbinding resolution, despite vigorous opposition by sex workers organizations and researchers, and in stark contrast to the long-standing approach of EU institutions to avoid interference on matters related to national-level policies on prostitution.

The criminalization of clients has also been introduced in other European countries, for example, in Lithuania in 2005 and in Serbia in 2016. Interestingly in these cases, the criminalization of sex workers already inscribed in law has been retained, thus defying the underlying principle of the "Nordic model", i.e., the decriminalization of the "victim". These developments reveal a shift to increasingly punitive and repressive policies, whether specifically addressing prostitution or in other policy domains, such as migration, licensing laws, or taxation, which have exclusionary effects on sex workers. Even in countries that have adopted a form of regulated and legalized prostitution, such as Austria, Germany, Greece, Hungary, Latvia, and the Netherlands, sex workers are targeted through restrictive zoning ordinances, mandatory registration, and health checks in the name of preventing or combating sex trafficking. Nonetheless, international organizations, including Amnesty International and the WHO, continue to express their support for decriminalization because of overwhelming evidence that suggests decriminalization supports sex workers' health, well-being, and rights (World Health Organization, 2012; Amnesty International, 2016).

Conclusion

In this chapter, we provided a chronological overview of some of the most significant geopolitical and socioeconomic developments that unfolded around sex for sale in Africa, the Americas, and Europe since the nineteenth century. We outlined some of the impacts they had on the construction of and responses to prostitution and the roles that TSOs have played in these processes. Many of the themes and issues that emerged from this contextualization will be explored in more detail in the region-specific chapters; nevertheless, here we identify three key threads that run throughout the book.

First, while recent years have witnessed an upsurge in TSOs providing support to people operating in the sex industries, these activities by nonstate actors have deep roots that defy what Salamon (1994: 121) calls the myth "'of immaculate conception', the notion that nonprofit organizations are essentially new in most parts of the world". Indeed, the outlook on the three regions reveals the interconnectedness of these historical roots across the three regions and, spurred by direct colonial rule and/or economic imperialism, the gendered, racialized, and classed ideologies of rescue, salvation, and reform underpinning them. Second, TSOs, both contemporary and historical, do not operate outside of social, political, cultural, and economic contexts but rather they internalize, respond to, and navigate them. They hold more or less power depending on their capacity to respond to, and willingness to embrace, dominant priorities, discourses, and the funds attached to them. A related third and final point in the context of increased competition for TSO funding is the expansion of nascent sex workers' collectives and organizations. The shifting cultural and political climate of the 1960s and 1970s and the catalyst effect of the HIV/AIDS pandemic enabled the unprecedented unification and recognition (to an extent) of sex workers and their initiatives to provide various forms of support to those operating in the sex industry. While many of their activities continue, more recent ideological changes, the focus on sex trafficking, and the increased and diffused anti-prostitution punitivism present challenges to the impact of their advocacy and in many cases to their long-term existence.

Notes

1 There are of course always exceptions to general trends. Greece, for example, has kept a regulationist system to this day.
2 Registered in Scotland in 2008 as the Global Network of Sex Work Projects is a not-for-profit private company limited by guarantee.
3 The TAMPEP project originated in 1993 in Italy, Germany, and the Netherlands, and later extended to Austria, but currently it operates in 24 European countries with funds from the European Commission, national governmental, and nongovernmental organizations, see also Chapter 5.
4 As Skilbrei and Holmström (2013) argue, there is no homogenous "model" across the Nordic countries as each of the approaches implemented by each country presents substantial differences in objectives and application.

References

Abad, A., M. Briones, T. Cordero, R. Manzo, and M. Marchán 1998. "The association of autonomous women workers, Ecuador: '22nd June'." In: *Global Sex Workers*, edited by Kempadoo and Doezema, 172–177. London: Routledge.

Aderinto, S.A. 2006. "'The girls in moral danger': Child prostitution and sexuality in Colonial Lagos, Nigeria, 1930s to 1950." *Journal of African History* 46: 115–137.

——— 2010. *Sexualized Nationalism: Lagos and the Politics of Illicit Sexuality in Colonial Nigeria, 1918–1958*. Austin, TX: University of Texas at Austin, Texas, PhD Dissertation.

——— 2012. "'The problem of Nigeria is slavery, not white slave traffic': Globalization and the politicization of prostitution in southern Nigeria, 1921–1955." *Canadian Journal of African Studies/La revue Canadienne des études africaines* 46(1): 1–22.

——— 2014. *When Sex Threatened the State: Illicit Sexuality, Nationalism, and Politics in Colonial Nigeria, 1900–1958*. Urbana-Champaign, IL: University of Illinois Press.

——— 2015. "Journey to work: Transnational prostitution in colonial British West Africa." *Journal of the History of Sexuality* 24(1): 99–124.

Adesina, O.A. 2018. "State and cross-border sex trade in colonial and post-colonial Nigeria." In: *Routledge International Handbook of Sex Industry Research*, edited by Dewey, Crowhurst and Izugbara, 485–494. London: Routledge.

Aghatise, E. 2004. "Trafficking for prostitution in Italy: Possible effects of government proposals for legalization of brothels." *Violence Against Women* 10(10): 1126–1155.

Amnesty International 2016. "Amnesty international policy on state obligations to respect, protect and fulfil the human rights of sex workers." Accessed 3rd July 2020. https://www.amnesty.org/download/Documents/POL3040622016ENGLISH.PDF.

Anasti, T. 2017. "Radical professionals? Sex worker rights activists and collaboration with human service nonprofits." *Human Service Organizations: Management, Leadership & Governance* 41(4): 416–437.

———— 2018. "Survivor or laborer: How human service managers perceive sex workers?" *Affilia* 33(4): 453–476.

Anheier, H.K. 2004. "The third sector in Europe: Five theses." In: *Strategy Mix for Nonprofit Organisations*, edited by Zimmer and Stecker, 285–299. Boston, MA: Springer.

Ardayfio, R. 2012. "UNFPA Ghana. Ghana Police service partners with UNFPA to reduce HIV stigma of female sex workers." Accessed 12th June 2020. http://ghana.unfpa.org /news.php?dd=242.

Baker, J., and T.A. Aina 1995. *The Migration Experience in Africa*. Uppsala, Sweden: Nordic Africa Institute.

Barrows, J. 2008. "An ethical analysis of the harm reduction approach to prostitution." *Ethics & Medicine* 24(3): 159.

Bell, S. 1994. *Reading, Writing, and Rewriting the Prostitute Body*. Bloomington, IN: Indiana University Press.

Berman, J. 2003. "(Un)popular strangers and crises (un)bounded: Discourses of sex-trafficking, the European Political Community and the Panicked State of the Modern State." *European Journal of International Relations* 9(1): 37–86.

Bernstein, E. 2010. "Militarized humanitarianism meets carceral feminism: The politics of sex, rights, and freedom in contemporary antitrafficking campaigns." *Signs: Journal of Women in Culture and Society* 36(1): 45–72.

Bimbi, D.S., and J. Koken 2014. "Public health policy and practice with male sex workers." In: *Male Sex Work and Society*, edited by Minichiello and Scott, 199–222. New York: Harrington Park Press.

Blanchette, T.G., and A.P. Da Silva 2012. "On bullshit and the trafficking of women: Moral entrepreneurs and the invention of trafficking of persons in Brazil." *Dialectical Anthropology* 36(1–2): 107–125.

Bliss, K.E. 2001. *Compromised Positions: Prostitution, Public Health, and Gender Politics in Revolutionary Mexico City*. University Park, PA: Penn State Press.

Brennan, J.R. 2002. *Nation, Race and Urbanization in Dar es Salaam, Tanzania, 1916– 1976*. Evanston, IL: Northwestern University, PhD Dissertation.

Brock, D.R. 1998. *Making Work, Making Trouble: Prostitution as a Social Problem*. Toronto, ON: University of Toronto Press.

Brussa, L. 1999. *Health Migration & Sex Work: The Experience of TAMPEP: Transnational AIDS/STD Prevention Among Migrant Prostitutes in Europe*. Amsterdam, The Netherlands: TAMPEP International Foundation.

Bryder, L. 1998. "Sex, race, and colonialism: An historiographical review." *The International History Review* 20(4): 806–822.

Butler, A.M. 1985. *Daughters of Joy, Sisters of Misery: Prostitutes in the American West, 1865–90*. Urbana, IL: University of Illinois Press.

Cabezas, A.L. 2000. "Legal challenges to and by sex workers/prostitutes." *Cleveland State Law Review* 48: 79–91.

Cabezas, A.L. 2019. "Latin American and Caribbean sex workers: Gains and challenges in the movement." *Anti-Trafficking Review* 12(12): 37–56.

Caldwell, J.C. 1969. *African Rural-Urban Migration: The Movement to Ghana's Towns*. Canberra, ACT: Australian National University Press.

Carotenuto, M. 2012. "Repatriation in colonial Kenya: African institutions and gendered violence." *The International Journal of African Historical Studies* 45(1): 9–28.

Chapkis, W. 1997. *Live Sex Acts: Women Performing Erotic Labor*. New York: Routledge.

Chipamaunga, S., A.S. Muula, and R. Mataya 2010. "An assessment of sex work in Swaziland: Barriers to and opportunities for HIV prevention among sex workers." *SAHARA-J: Journal of Social Aspects of HIV/AIDS Research Alliance* 7(3): 44–50.

Chrétien, J.-P. 1991. "Presse Libre et propagande raciste au Rwanda." *Politique Africaine* 42(1): 109–120.

Clarke, L.K., and M. Potts 1988. *The AIDS Reader*. Wellesley, MA: Branden Books.

Clement, E.A. 2006. *Love for Sale: Courting, Treating, and Prostitution in New York City, 1900–1945*. Chapel Hill, NC: University of North Carolina Press.

Collins, S.E., S.L. Clifasefi, D.E. Logan, L.S. Samples, J.M. Somers, and G.A. Marlatt 2012. "Current status, historical highlights, and basic principles of harm reduction." In: *Harm Reduction: Pragmatic Strategies for Managing High-Risk Behaviours*, edited by Marlatt, Larimer and Witkiewitz, 2nd edition, 6–10. New York: Guildford Press.

Cox, P. 2007. "Compulsion, voluntarism, and venereal disease: Governing sexual health in England after the Contagious Diseases Acts." *Journal of British Studies* 46(1): 91–115.

Crowhurst, I. 2007. "The 'foreign prostitute' in contemporary Italy: Gender, sexuality and migration in policy and practice." PhD, Sociology. London School of Economics.

D'Costa, L.J., F.A. Plummer, I. Bowmer, L. Fransen, P. Piot, A.R. Ronald, and H. Nsanze 1985. "Prostitutes are a major reservoir of sexually transmitted diseases in Nairobi, Kenya." *Sexually Transmitted Diseases* 12(2): 64–67.

Darley, M., M. David, V. Guienne, L. Mathieu, and G. Mainsant 2017. "France." In: *Assessing Prostitution Policies in Europe*, edited by Jahnsen and Wagenaar, 92–106. Abingdon, UK: Routledge.

Davis, E.S.A. 1939. "Some problems arising from the conditions of housing and employment of natives in Nairobi." Confidential report 18.

Dawdy, S. 2009. *Building the Devil's Empire. French Colonial New Orleans*. Chicago, IL: University of Chicago Press.

De Vries, G., M. Timmer, and K. De Vries 2015. "Structural transformation in Africa: Static gains, dynamic losses." *The Journal of Development Studies* 51(6): 674–688.

Delacoste, F.D.R., and P. Alexander 1987. *Sex Work: Writings by Women in the Sex Industry*, 1st edition. Pittsburgh, PA: Cleis Press.

Ditmore, M.H., and D. Allman 2013. "An analysis of the implementation of PEPFAR's anti-prostitution pledge and its implications for successful HIV prevention among organizations working with sex workers." *Journal of the International AIDS Society* 16(1): 17354.

Ditmore, M.H., A. Levy, and A. Willman 2013. *Sex Work Matters: Exploring Money, Power and Intimacy in the Sex Industry*. London: Zed Books.

Doezema, J. 2005. "Now you see her, now you don't: Sex workers at the UN trafficking protocol negotiation." *Social & Legal Studies* 14(1): 61–89.

——— 2010. *Sex Slaves and Discourse Masters: The Construction of Trafficking*. London: Zed Books.

Donovan, B. 2010. *White Slave Crusades: Race, Gender, and Anti-Vice Activism, 1887–1917*. Urbana, IL: University of Illinois Press.

Dourado, I., M.D.C. Guimarães, G.N. Damacena, L. Magno, P.R.B. de Souza Júnior, C.L. Szwarcwald, and The Brazilian FSW Group 2019. "Sex work stigma and non-disclosure to health care providers: Data from a large RDS study among FSW in Brazil." *BMC International Health & Human Rights* 19(1): 8.

Dunne, B.W. 1994. "French regulation of prostitution in nineteenth-century colonial Algeria." *The Arab Studies Journal* 2(1): 24–30.

Dziuban, A., and L. Stevenson 2018. "Reflecting on labour exploitation in the sex industry." In: *Routledge International Handbook of Sex Industry Research*, edited by Jahnsen and Wagenaar, 405–417. Abingdon, UK: Routledge.

Ejalu, W.A. 2006. "From home to hell: The telling story of an African woman's journey and stay in Europe." In: *Trafficking and the Global Sex Industry*, edited by Beeks and Amir, 165–186. Oxford, UK: Oxford University Press.

Ekpootu, M.U. 2017. "Sexualizing the city: Female prostitution in Nigeria's Urban Centres in a historical perspective." In: *Selling Sex in the City: A Global History of Prostitution, 1600s–2000s*, edited by García, van Voss and van Nederveen Meerkerk, 306–328. Leiden, The Netherlands: Brill.

Emeagwali, G.T. 1995. *Women Pay the Price: Structural Adjustment in Africa and the Caribbean*. Trenton, NJ: Africa World Press.

FitzGerald, S.A. 2008. "Putting trafficking on the map: The geography of feminist complicity." In: *Demanding Sex: Critical Reflections on the Regulation of Prostitution*, edited by Munro and Della Giusta, 99–120. Aldershot: Ashgate.

Foley, E.E., and R. Nguer 2010. "Courting success in HIV/AIDS prevention: The challenges of addressing a concentrated epidemic in Senegal." *African Journal of AIDS Research: AJAR* 9(4): 325–336.

Fusco, C. 1998. "Hustling for dollars: Jineterismo in Cuba." In: *Global Sex Workers: Rights, Resistance, and Redefinition*, edited by Kempadoo and Doezema, 151–166. Abingdon, UK: Routledge.

Gaitskell, D. 1979. "'Christian compounds for girls': Church hostels for African women in Johannesburg, 1907–1970." *Journal of Southern African Studies* 6(1): 44–69.

Gallagher, A. 2017. "The international legal definition of 'trafficking in persons': Scope and application." In: *Revisiting the Law and Governance of Trafficking, Forced Labor and Modern Slavery*, edited by Kotiswaran, 83–111. Cambridge, UK: Cambridge University Press.

García, M.R., L.H. van Voss, and E. van Nederveen Meerkerk 2017. *Selling Sex in the City: A Global History of Prostitution, 1600s–2000s*. Leiden: Brill.

Gibson, M. 1986. *Prostitution and the State in Italy, 1860–1915*. New Brunswick, NJ: Rutgers University Press.

Goldman, M.S. 1981. *Gold Diggers & Silver Miners: Prostitution and Social Life on the Comstock Lode*. Ann Arbor, MI: University of Michigan Press.

Guinn, D.E. 2008. "Defining the problem of trafficking: The interplay of US law, donor, and NGO engagement and the local context in Latin America." *Human Rights Quarterly* 30(1): 119–145.

Guy, D.J. 1991. *Sex & Danger in Buenos Aires: Prostitution, Family, and Nation in Argentina*. Lincoln, NE: University of Nebraska Press.

Haram, L. 1995. "Negotiating sexuality in times of economic want: The young and modern Meru women." In: *Young People at Risk: Fighting AIDS in Northern Tanzania*, edited by Klepp, Talle, and Biswalo, 31–48. Oslo, Norway: Scandinavian University Press.

Hardy, K. 2010. "Incorporating sex workers into the Argentine labor movement." *International Labor & Working-Class History* 77(1): 89–108.

Harlan, L.R. 1966. "Booker T. Washington and the white man's burden." *The American Historical Review* 71(2): 441–467.

Harries, A. 2016. "Faire le bordel: The regulation of urban prostitution in French Morocco." Oxford University. http://frenchhistorysociety.co.uk/forms/Alex%20Harries%20Faire %20le%20Bordel.pdf.

Harsin, J. 1985. *Policing Prostitution in Nineteenth-Century Paris*. Princeton, NJ: Princeton University Press.

Hartmann, W. 2007. "Urges in the colony. Men and women in colonial Windhoek, 1890– 1905." *Journal of Namibian Studies: History Politics Culture* 1: 39–71.

Havelková, B. 2016. "Blaming all women: On regulation of prostitution in state socialist Czechoslovakia." *Oxford Journal of Legal Studies* 36(1): 165–191.

——— 2018. "Czech Republic." In: *Assessing Prostitution Policies in Europe*, edited by Jahnsen and Wagenaar, 272–286. Abingdon, UK: Routledge.

Herbert, J. 2016. "Masculinity and migration: Life stories of East African Asian men." In: *Gendering Migration*, edited by Ryan and Webster, 201–216. Abingdon, UK: Routledge.

Horn, A. 1979. "Uganda's theatre—The exiled and the dead." *Index on Censorship* 8(5): 12–15.

Homaifar, N. 2008. "The African prostitute: An everyday debrouillard in reality and African fiction." *Journal of African Cultural Studies* 20(2): 173–182.

Hotaling, N., A. Burris, B.J. Johnson, Y.M. Bird, and K.A. Melbye 2004. "Been there done that: SAGE, a peer leadership model among prostitution survivors." *Journal of Trauma Practice* 2(3–4): 255–265.

Howell, P. 2004. "Race, space and the regulation of prostitution in colonial Hong Kong." *Urban History* 31(2): 229–248.

Hunt, A. 1999. *Governing Morals: A Social History of Moral Regulation*. Cambridge, UK: Cambridge University Press.

Hunter, M. 2002. "The materiality of everyday sex: Thinking beyond prostitution." *African Studies* 61(1): 99–120.

ICRSE 2016. "Surveilled. Exploited. Deported. Rights violations against migrant sex workers in Europe and Central Asia." https://www.sexworkeurope.org/sites/default/f iles/resource-pdfs/icrse_briefing_paper_migrants_rights_november2016.pdf.

Jackson, W., and E. Manktelow 2015. *Subverting Empire: Deviance and Disorder in the British Colonial World*. New York: Springer.

Jahnsen, S.Ø., and H. Wagenaar 2018. *Assessing Prostitution Policies in Europe*. Abingdon, UK: Routledge.

Kempadoo, K. 2004. *Sexing the Caribbean: Gender, Race and Sexual Labor*. New York: Routledge.

Kempadoo, K., and J. Doezema 1998. *Global Sex Workers: Rights, Resistance, and Redefinition*. New York: Routledge.

Koné, M. 2016. "Transnational sex worker organizing in Latin America: RedTraSex, labour and human rights." *Social & Economic Studies* 65(4): 87–108.

Kozma, L. 2017. *Global Women, Colonial Ports: Prostitution in the Interwar Middle East*. Albany, NY: SUNY Press.

Kufakurinani, U. 2015. "Empire and sexual deviance: Debating white women's prostitution in early 20th century Salisbury, Southern Rhodesia." In: *Subverting Empire*, 205–225. New York: Springer.

Leigh, C. 1997. "Inventing sex work." In: *Whores and Other Feminists*, edited by Nagle, 225–231. New York: Routledge.

Lerum, K. 1999. "Twelve-step feminism makes sex workers sick: How the state and the recovery movement turn radical women into useless citizens." *Sexuality & Culture* 2: 7–36.

Levine, P. 2003. *Prostitution, Race, and Politics: Policing Venereal Disease in the British Empire*. New York: Routledge.

Limoncelli, S.A. 2006. "International voluntary associations, local social movements and state paths to the abolition of regulated prostitution in Europe, 1875–1950." *International Sociology* 21(1): 31–59.

Lowndes, C.M., M. Alary, A.-C. Labbe, C. Gnintoungbè, M. Belleau, L. Mukenge, H. Meda, M. Ndour, S. Anagonou, and A. Gbaguidi 2007. "Interventions among male clients of female sex workers in Benin, West Africa: An essential component of targeted HIV preventive interventions." *Sexually Transmitted Infections* 83(7): 577–581.

Lucas, A.M. 1995. "Race, class, gender, and deviancy: The criminalization of prostitution." *Berkeley Women's Law Journal* 10: 47–60.

Luddy, M. 1997. "'Abandoned women and bad characters': Prostitution in nineteenth-century Ireland." *Women's History Review* 6(4): 485–504.

Luker, K. 1998. "Sex, social hygiene, and the state: The double-edged sword of social reform." *Theory & Society* 27(5): 601–634.

Lutnick, A. 2006. "The St. James Infirmary: A history." *Sexuality & Culture* 10(2): 56–75.

MacKell, J., and J.M. Collins 2009. *Red Light Women of the Rocky Mountains*. Albuquerque, NM: UNM Press.

Maloka, T. 1997. "Khomo Lia oela: Canteens, brothels and labour migrancy in colonial Lesotho, 1900–40." *The Journal of African History* 38(1): 101–122.

Mathieu, L. 2001. *Mobilisations de prostituées*. Paris: Belin.

——— 2004. "The debate on prostitution in France: A conflict between abolitionism, regulation and prohibition." *Journal of Contemporary European Studies* 12(2): 153–163.

Mazur, A.G. 2004. "Prostitute movements face elite apathy and gender-biased universalism in France." In: *The Politics of Prostitution: Women's Movements, Democratic States and the Globalisation of Sex Commerce*, edited by Outshoorn, 123–143. Cambridge: Cambridge University Press.

McCormick, L. 2018. "The dangers and temptations of the street: Managing female behaviour in Belfast during the first World War." *Women's History Review* 27(3): 414–431.

Mgbako, C.A. 2016. *To Live Freely in This World: Sex Worker Activism in Africa*. New York: New York University Press.

Mgbako, C.A., and L.A. Smith 2009. "Sex work and human rights in Africa." *Fordham International Law Journal* 33: 1178.

Mitchell, G. 2016. "Evangelical ecstasy meets feminist fury: Sex trafficking, moral panics, and homonationalism during global sporting events." *GLQ: A Journal of Lesbian & Gay Studies* 22(3): 325–357.

Morgan Thomas, R. 1992. "HIV and the sex industry." In: *Working with Women and AIDS: Medical, Social, and Counselling Issues*, edited by Bury, Morrison and Mclachlan, 71–84. London: Routledge.

Msibi, T. 2011. "The lies we have been told: On (homo) sexuality in Africa." *Africa Today* 58(1): 55–77.

Muchomba, F.M. 2014. "Colonial policies and the rise of transactional sex in Kenya." *Journal of International Women's Studies* 15(2): 80–93.

Murray, L.R., D. Kerrigan, and V.S. Paiva 2019. "Rites of resistance: Sex workers' fight to maintain rights and pleasure in the centre of the response to HIV in Brazil." *Global Public Health* 14(6–7): 939–953.

Naanen, B.B. 1991. "'Itinerant gold mines': Prostitution in the cross river basin of Nigeria, 1930–1950." *African Studies Review* 34(2): 57–79.

Ngugi, E.N., E. Roth, T. Mastin, M.G. Nderitu, and S. Yasmin 2012. "Female sex workers in Africa: Epidemiology overview, data gaps, ways forward." *SAHARA: Journal of Social Aspects of HIV/AIDS Research Alliance* 9(3): 148–153.

Nichols, J.D. 2002. *Prostitution, Polygamy, and Power: Salt Lake City, 1847–1918.* Urbana, IL: University of Illinois Press.

Nkwi, W.G. 2016. "Prostitution in Colonial Lagos and Accra: Evidence from the National Archives Buea, Cameroon, c. 1930s–1950s." *Vestiges: Traces of Record* 2(1): 89–109.

NSWP 2019. "History." Accessed 23rd January 2020. https://www.nswp.org/history.

Nwahunanya, C. 2011. "Jagua nana's children: The image of the prostitute in post colonial African literature." *UJAH: Unizik Journal of Arts & Humanities* 12: 339–356.

Oakley, A. 2007. *Working Sex: Sex Workers Write about a Changing Industry.* Seattle, WA: Seal Press.

Obbo, C. 1980. *African Women: Their Struggle for Economic Independence.* London: Zed Books.

Odem, M.E. 1995. *Delinquent Daughters: Protecting and Policing Adolescent Female Sexuality in the United States, 1885–1920. Gender & American Culture.* Chapel Hill, NC: University of North Carolina Press.

Odhiambo, T. n.d. *Collaborative Documentation: A Model of Sex Worker—Police Cooperation in Kenya Submitted for Open Society Institute Panel. Remaking Law Enforcement: Strategies for Harm Reduction in Policing.* London: Open Society Foundation.

Oermann, N.O. 1999. *Mission, Church and State Relations in South West Africa under German Rule (1884–1915)*, 5. Stuttgart, Germany: Franz Steiner Verlag.

Orchard, T., A. Murie, K. Salter, H.-L. Elash, M. Bunch, C. Middleton, and C. Benoit 2020. "Balance, capacity, and the contingencies of everyday life: Narrative etiologies of health among women in street-based sex work." *Qualitative Health Research* 30(4): 518–529.

Östergren, P. 2017. "From zero-tolerance to full integration: Rethinking prostitution policies." *DemandAT Working Paper.* Accessed 24th February 2020. http://www.demandat.eu/si tes/default/files/DemandAT_WP10_ProstitutionPoliciesTypology_June2017_0.pdf.

Outshoorn, J. 2004a. "Introduction: Prostitution, women's movements and democratic politics." In: *The Politics of Prostitution-Women's Movements, Democratic States and the Globalisation of Sex Commerce*, edited by Outshoorn, 1–20. Cambridge: Cambridge University Press.

Outshoorn, J. 2004b. "Pragmatism in the polder: Changing prostitution policy in the Netherlands". *Journal of Contemporary European Studies* 12(2): 165–176.

Padilla, M. 2007. *Caribbean Pleasure Industry: Tourism, Sexuality, and AIDS in the Dominican Republic. Worlds of Desire.* Chicago, IL: The University of Chicago Press.

Pheterson, G. 1989. *A Vindication of the Rights of Whores.* Seattle, WA: Seal Press.

Phillips, R. 2005. "Heterogeneous imperialism and the regulation of sexuality in British West Africa." *Journal of the History of Sexuality* 14(3): 291–315.

Phillips, R., C. Benoit, H. Hallgrimsdottir, and K. Vallance 2012. "Courtesy stigma: A hidden health concern among front-line service providers to sex workers." *Sociology of Health & Illness* 34(5): 681–696.

Phoenix, J. 2008. "Be helped or else! Economic exploitation, male violence and prostitution policy in the UK." In: *Demanding Sex: Critical Reflections on the Regulation of Prostitution*, edited by Munro and Della Giusta, 35–50. Aldershot, UK: Ashgate.

———— 2009. *Regulating Sex for Sale: Prostitution Policy Reform and the UK*. Bristol, UK: Policy Press.

———— 2017. "Prostitution and sex work." In: *The Oxford Handbook of Criminology*, edited by Liebling, Maruna and McAra, 6th edition, 685–703. Oxford: Oxford University Press.

Porras, C., M. Sabidó, P. Fernández-Dávila, V.H. Fernández, A. Batres, and J. Casabona 2008. "Reproductive health and healthcare among sex workers in Escuintla, Guatemala." *Culture, Health & Sexuality* 10(5): 529–538.

Prunier, G., and T. Hoffman 1999. "The Rwanda crisis: History of a genocide." *Queen's Quarterly* 106(1): 93.

Richter, M. 2012. "Sex work as a test case for African feminism." *BUWA!: A Journal of African Women's Experiences* (October): 62–69.

Rivera-Garza, C. 2001. "The criminalization of the syphilitic body: Prostitutes, health crime and society in Mexico City, 1867–1930." In: *Crime and Punishment in Latin America: Law and Society Since Late Colonial Times*, edited by Dalvatore, Aguirre, and Joseph, 147–180. London and Durham, NC: Duke University Press.

Rivers-Moore, M. 2018. "We fight with God's weapons: Sex work and pragmatic penance in neoliberal Costa Rica." *Signs: Journal of Women in Culture & Society* 43(4): 851–876.

Roberts, N. 1992. *Whores in History*. London: HarperCollins.

Rodriguez, D. 2007. "The political logic of the non-profit industrial complex." In: *The Revolution Will Not Be Funded: Beyond the Non-Profit Industrial Complex*, edited by INCITE! Women of Color Against Violence, 21–40. Boston, MA: South End Press.

Rosen, R. 1982. *The Lost Sisterhood: Prostitution in America, 1900–1918*. Baltimore, MD: JHU Press.

Ross, B. 2009. *Burlesque West: Showgirls, Sex and Sin in Postwar Vancouver*. Toronto, ON and Buffalo, NY: University of Toronto Press.

Salamon, L.M. 1994. "The rise of the nonprofit sector." *Foreign Affairs* 73(4): 109–122.

Sanders, T., M. O'Neill, and J. Pitcher 2018. *Prostitution: Sex Work, Policy & Politics*. London, UK: Sage.

Sapio, R. 2007. *Prostituzione: Diritto e società*. Rimini: NdA Press.

Scheepers, E., and I. Lakhani 2020. "Caution! Feminists at work: Building organisations from the inside out." *Gender & Development* 28(1): 117–133.

Schwarz, C., E. Unruh, K. Cronin, S. Evans-Simpson, H. Britton, and M. Ramaswamy 2016. "Human trafficking identification and service provision in the medical and social service sectors." *Health & Human Rights* 18(1): 181.

Scoular, J. 2015. *The Subject of Prostitution: Sex Work, Law and Social Theory*. Abingdon, UK: Routledge.

Semakula, J., and J. Masaba 2014. "Uganda at 52: Interesting quotes of Ugandan presidents." Accessed 12th June 2020. https://www.newvision.co.ug/news/1311943/uganda-quotes-ugandan-presidents.

Skilbrei, M.-L., and C. Holmström 2013. *Prostitution Policy in the Nordic Region: Ambiguous Sympathies*. London: Ashgate.

Soderlund, G. 2005. "Running from the rescuers: New US crusades against sex trafficking and the rhetoric of abolition." *NWSA Journal* 17(3): 64–87.

Sori, I., and M. Pajnik 2018. "Slovenia." In: *Assessing Prostitution Policies in Europe*, edited by Jahnsen and Wagenaar. Abingdon, UK: Routledge, 228–242.

St. Denny, E. 2016. "Explaining the emergence and gradual transformation of policy regimes: the case of contemporary French prostitution policy (1946–2016)." PhD. Nottingham Trent University.

Stevenson, K. 2004. "Fulfilling their mission: The intervention of voluntary societies in cases of sexual assault in the Victorian criminal process." *Crime, Histoire & Sociétés* 8(1): 93–110.

Tambe, A. 2005. "The elusive ingénue: A transnational feminist analysis of European prostitution in colonial Bombay." *Gender & Society* 19(2): 160–179.

TAMPEP 2007. "Final report." Accessed 5th January 2021. https://tampep.eu/wp-content/uploads/2017/11/report_tampep_7.pdf.

Taraud, C. 2003. *La prostitution coloniale: Algerie, Tunisie, Maroc (1830–1962)*. Paris: Payot.

Tracol-Huynh, I. 2010. "Between stigmatisation and regulation: Prostitution in colonial Northern Vietnam." *Culture, Health & Sexuality* 12(Suppl 1): S73–S87.

Valverde, M. 2008. *The Age of Light, Soap, and Water: Moral Reform in English Canada, 1885–1925*. Toronto, ON: University of Toronto Press.

Verwimp, P. 2006. *Peasant Ideology and Genocide in Rwanda under Habyarimana*. New Haven, CT: Yale University Press.

Voeten, H.A., O.B. Egesah, M.Y. Ondiege, C.M. Varkevisser, and J.D.F. Habbema 2002. "Clients of female sex workers in Nyanza province, Kenya: A core group in STD/HIV transmission." *Sexually Transmitted Diseases* 29(8): 444–452.

Wagenaar, H. 2018. "Introduction. Prostitution policy in Europe: An overview." In: *Assessing Prostitution Policies in Europe*, edited by Jahnsen and Wagenaar, 1–28. Abingdon, UK: Routledge.

Walkowitz, J.R. 1982. *Prostitution and Victorian Society: Women, Class, and the State*. Cambridge: Cambridge University Press.

Werth, P.W. 1994. "Through the prison of prostitution: State, society and power." *Social History* 19(1): 1–15.

White, L. 1984. "A history of prostitution in Nairobi, Kenya, c. 1900–1952." Unpublished PhD thesis. Cambridge: University of Cambridge.

——— 1986. "Prostitution, identity, and class consciousness in Nairobi during World War II." *Signs: Journal of Women in Culture & Society* 11(2): 255–273.

——— 2009. *The Comforts of Home: Prostitution in Colonial Nairobi*. Chicago, IL: University of Chicago Press.

Wojcicki, J.M. 2003. "The movement to decriminalize sex work in Gauteng Province, South Africa, 1994–2002." *African Studies Review* 46(3): 83–109.

Wolff, K. 2008. "Herrenmoral: Anna Pappritz and abolitionism in Germany." *Women's History Review* 17(2): 225–237.

World Health Organization (WHO) 2012. "Prevention and treatment of HIV and other sexually transmitted infections for sex workers in low-and middle-income countries: Recommendations for a public health approach." *World Health Organization*. Accessed 8th July 2020. https://www.who.int/hiv/pub/guidelines/sex_worker/en/.

Chapter 3

Sex work and prostitution third sector organizations in Africa

Chimaraoke Izugbara

Introduction

Africa, the world's largest and second most populous continent, comprises 54 sociopolitically and economically diverse countries. The West African country of Nigeria was a British colony and is now, two decades after emerging from protracted military dictatorship, home to the region's largest economy, a population of over 190 million and 340 distinct languages and ethnicities. Namibia, in Southern Africa, first colonized by Germany and later by South Africa, has 12 ethnic groups, 2.1 million people, and a stable electoral democracy since its independence in 1990. Africa's economic diversity is also striking; it includes some of the world's richest countries by commodity wealth as well as the world's poorest countries. The Democratic Republic of Congo has an estimated $54 trillion in untapped mineral deposits, and South Africa, more than $2.5 trillion in mineral reserves. However, 21 of the world's 25 poorest countries are African (Chandy, 2017). The legacy of weak democratic structures, political instability, rapid urbanization, reliance on development aid, the dominance of received laws developed in other countries, and a persistent crisis of basic civil liberties and human rights are common features across the region (Elias, 2018; Michalopoulos and Papaioannou, 2020). African countries share a historical legacy of exploitative colonial policies that dispossessed and displaced local people and communities, underdeveloped indigenous productive capacities, and destroyed critical local social institutions (Lonsdale, 2016). Currently, they generally depend on Western aid for development, resulting in policies and programs that exacerbate poverty by undermining local productive capacities, ignoring national priorities, and otherwise advancing a neocolonial agenda (Asongu and Nwachukwu, 2016).

Two main prostitution policy regimes exist in Africa. In the first, sex work itself, and sex work-related activities (such as soliciting and pimping) are criminalized, as is the case in Angola, Equatorial Guinea, Eritrea, Gabon, Ghana, Guinea, Kenya, Liberia, Mozambique, Namibia, Rwanda, Somalia, South Africa, Tanzania, Uganda, and Zambia. In the second, sex work is not proscribed, but procurement and solicitation of sex are prohibited in public places, as in Burkina Faso, Cape Verde, the Central African Republic, Côte d'Ivoire, Ethiopia, Lesotho,

Madagascar, Malawi, Sierra Leone, Swaziland, and Zimbabwe (Mgbako and Smith, 2009; Ngugi et al., 2012). There is no African country where sex work is an entirely licit vocation, free of regulation. Even in Senegal, the only African country where prostitution is legal, regulations still apply (Foley, 2018; Mgbako, 2016). Sex workers in Senegal must be over 21, register with the government, and undergo mandatory monthly health check-ups. Whatever the legal framework around sex work in Africa, there is large-scale stigma and discrimination as well as public anxiety toward sex workers and sex work (UNAIDS, 2014).

Notwithstanding variations in its legality in countries in the region, prostitution remains widespread in Africa and surrounded by fierce debates and contestations (Albertyn, 2016). For instance, even in African countries where prostitution is formally illegal or prohibited, new legal interpretations based on court cases involving suspected sex workers have challenged existing legal codes (Buzsa et al., 2017). And in contexts where sex work is legal or not proscribed, pressures and movements to explicitly criminalize it continue to build. Sex work is illegal in Zimbabwe, for example, but a 2015 court ruling banned the police from arresting suspected sex workers, heralding reports that sex workers were free to operate (Busza et al., 2017). On the other hand, in Senegal where sex work is legal, anti-prostitution campaigners have called for its criminalization on grounds that it promotes child sexual exploitation and trafficking. Bop (2008) reports that organizations such as the Islamic Committee for Senegalese Family Code Reform (CIRCOFS), known for its fiery speeches against the "enemies of religion and moral values in Senegal", have called for the prohibition of sex work on grounds that it destroys the "Senegalese family".

As described in the previous chapter, modern prostitution and its rapid rise in contemporary Africa are rooted in colonialism which, together with the accompanying processes of urbanization, industrialization, callous dispossession, and proletarianization, set the socioeconomic stage for the emergence of contemporary sex work in Africa (Naanen, 1991; White, 1984, 1986, 2009; Aderinto, 2012, 2010). In several parts of Africa, non-indigenous words are used to describe sex workers, indicating the lack of fit of the Western-type notion of a "prostitute" with indigenous sexual economies. Max Marwick (1965) observes that the Malawian Chichewa word for prostitute (*hule*) is a corruption of the Afrikaans expression, *hoer*; Chichewa words do not often begin with an "h". Popular Nigerian terms used to describe sex workers, such as "*ashawo*" and "*akwuna*", also only emerged in the context of colonialism (Naanen, 1991; Aderinto, 2015a, 2015b). As we showed in Chapter 2, prostitution in colonial Africa resulted from limited opportunities for women to earn money in the highly masculinized colonial economy, the presence of large numbers of male soldiers, and new patterns of male labor migration instigated by exploitative colonial industrialization processes (Akyeampong, 1997; Pankhurst, 1974; Muchomba, 2014). Colonial regulation of prostitution in the 20th century was often lax until World War II, when administrators became concerned about the spread of sexually transmitted infections among European troops and officials stationed in Africa (Mgbako, 2019), echoing previous concerns about imperial soldiers' fitness in the 1800s (Van Heyningen, 1984).

In Africa, policies and discourses about sex work were originally informed largely by a focus on health, culture, violence, and morality. It was only in the early 1990s that *rights* became a key part of the discourse on sex work across the continent. The criminalization of sex work in most colonial and postcolonial African states was therefore often justified on grounds of protecting the African family, public morality, national image, African women and men, and local culture (Homaifar, 2008). In the region, competing discourses variously depict the sale of sex as degrading and oppressive to women and men, an assault on womanhood and manhood and morality (Connelly, 2018; Fayemi, 2009; Hofmann, 1997; Udeh, Uduka and Mbah, 2019; Wojcick, 2003); an essentially violent practice with negative health consequences (Farley, Cotton, Lynne et al., 2004; Raymond, 2004); a profession of last resort (Pickering et al., 1992); and a potentially legitimate work with development implications (Overall, 1992).

African leaders also often publicly depict prostitution as incompatible with African culture, which emboldens public attacks, client abuses, regular raids, arrests, police harassment, and detention of (suspected) sex workers (Currier and McKay, 2017). President Paul Kagame of Rwanda, in his 2015 International Women's Day speech, described prostitution as un-African and demeaning. He cautioned Rwandans who engaged in it "to go to other countries where the vice is accepted" (Mgbako and Smith, 2009). Also, although sex workers were included in former Ghanaian President Kwame Nkrumah's efforts to promote workers' associations in the 1960s, his government neither legally recognized its members as workers nor repealed the section of the Criminal Code on soliciting (Bindman, 1997).

As was the case in colonial times, sex workers continue to be rather anxiously viewed as wayward, depraved, and morally compromised vectors of disease. This perception, among other things, leaves them voiceless, defenseless, stigmatized, and with little recourse to justice. Many attacks on, or murders of, sex workers in the region never result in consequences for the perpetrators (Hodgskiss, 2004; Izugbara, 2012; Mgbako, 2016). These problems are further complicated by the silence of many African women's rights organizations on issues of sex worker rights, even in the face of a burgeoning sex worker rights movement across the region (Mgbako, 2009). The contemporary African sex industry is diverse, comprising various venue-based and virtual economies shaped by a vast array of local and global processes (Igbinovia, 1984; Hassan, 2015; Bidemi, 2017; Foley, 2019), including access to technology (Longe et al., 2009; Dlamini and Nzama, 2019). Other major sources of influence on Africa's sex work industry include legal and policy discourses regarding the state's role in regulating sexual behavior, human rights, social media debates, health-related developments, urbanization and economic dynamics that facilitate particular forms of sexual exchanges and labor, and migration (Luiz and Roets, 2000; Achebe, 2004; Vanyoro, 2019).

The history and context of prostitution, like the individual circumstances of each sex worker, are unique in each African state, yet the major drivers of entry into prostitution include widespread poverty, gender inequality, violence, and lack of quality livelihood opportunities (Achebe, 2004; Ngugi et al., 2012). Most African sex workers are women and girls, although men, boys, transgender, and intersex persons are also increasingly visible in the sector (Teunis, 2001; Richter and Massawe, 2009, 2010; Ngugi et al., 2012; Richter, 2012; Richter et al., 2013; Scorgie, 2013, Longo et al., 2017). The social organization of sex work and demographic characteristics of sex workers also vary significantly across Africa. Sex workers in the region range in age, relationship status, the degree to which they rely on their sex work earnings to support themselves, and labor arrangements negotiated with third parties and other sex workers. As is the case globally, sex work in Africa can be a part-time or full-time vocation; sex workers can also work independently or through intermediaries. They can work as escorts, solicit their clients from a variety of venues, and provide services in street-based settings, indoors at bars/pubs, brothels, hotels, their own homes, rented rooms, webcams, or other online media. There are also sex workers whose operations cut across venues (Pitpitan et al., 2013).

African sex workers' transnational migration has historically occurred both within the region and beyond. Marwick (1965) writes that women in colonial Malawi regularly moved to the Zambian Copperbelt to sell sex. The main road leading to Zambia was thus nicknamed *mtengamahule* (conveyor of prostitutes). In 2016 alone, an estimated 80% of the 11,100 Nigerian women who arrived in Sicily, Italy, became sex workers and were largely bonded or indentured (Wallis, 2019). In Abidjan, capital city of Côte d'Ivoire, women from Ghana, Mali, Nigeria Senegal, Togo and other parts of West Africa sell sex (Anarfi, 1990, 1995; Vuylsteke, 2001; Ditmore, 2006). Reminiscent of colonial times when "continental women" from Europe and Asia operated as sex workers in African cities (Van Heyningen, 1984), up to 18,500 Chinese prostitutes currently work across the region, from Cameroon to Uganda (Ndjio, 2009, 2017). Substantial numbers of Ugandan, Ethiopian, Tanzanian, Rwandan, and Congolese sex workers operate in Kenya (Izugbara, 2011), while migrant sex workers in South Africa come from Eswatini, Botswana, Malawi, Mozambique, Zambia, and Zimbabwe (Sigauke, 2014). Nigeria hosts a substantial number of sex workers from Cameroon, Liberia, and Ghana (Sakyi, 2013; Unah, 2015).

African sex workers' diverse modus operandi and social characteristics notwithstanding, they are united by a common experience of stigma, discrimination, social condemnation, violence and abuse by police officers, communities, neighborhoods, clients, and where they exist, pimps (Fick, 2006; Mgbako and Smith, 2009; Bonthuys, 2012; Shannon and Montaner, 2012; Scorgie et al., 2013; African Sex Worker Alliance, 2019). Police in Africa have a longstanding history of denying sex workers protection and ignoring their reports of attacks, mistreatment, and abuse by clients and the public (Richter and Massawe, 2009, 2010; Scorgie et al., 2011; Richter, 2012; Richter et.al., 2013). They also often collaborate with religious groups, neighborhoods, businesses, and communities to deter sex workers through arrests, harassment, and attacks (FIDA, 2008; Naidoo, 2009; Muldoon et al., 2017).

Few governments in the region actively seek to prevent the pervasive violence, stigma, and mistreatment against sex workers (Luiz and Roets, 2000; Fick, 2006; Poopola, 2013; Mgbako, 2016). In Senegal, the only African country where sex work is technically legal, registered sex workers are frequent targets of police harassment and report experiencing more stigma than clandestine sex workers (Foley, 2016). In Rwanda, where an estimated 12,278 sex workers operated in 2012 (DevInfo, 2016), government officials have often blamed sex work for diseases, moral decay, and backwardness in the country (Chrétien, 1991; Verwimp, 2006). Yet, sex workers in the country frequently suffer violence from clients, family members, and the community (Mutagoma et al., 2019). Between July and August 2012, about 18 women, mostly sex workers, were murdered in Kigali. One widely circulated story, which the Rwandan police quickly dismissed as mere rumor, was that carved on the body of one of the victims was the statement: "I will stop once I have killed 400 prostitutes" (quoted in Smith, 2012).

An overview of sex work and prostitution TSOs in Africa

A range of voluntary organizations, self-help and community interest groups, social enterprises, religious and professional societies, collectives, and cooperatives have emerged to address an array of issues related to sex work and sex workers in Africa. These organizations are independent of government and motivated by the hope of achieving what they regard as improvements to society and overall well-being, rather than the desire to make a profit. Most of these organizations have attained legal status as charities through registration with government agencies, are staffed by people with shared values and objectives, and maintain a not-for-personal-profit approach (Kempadoo, 2005, 2016).

Sex work and prostitution third sector organizations (TSOs) in Africa bloomed in the 1990s, a period marked by rapid NGO-ization of Africa's civil society, mounting pressures for electoral democracy, and immense Global North clamor for "grassroot participation" and voice in development action. The 1990s were also characterized by widespread transitions from military rule to electoral democracy in Africa and the collapse of several of the region's long-running dictatorships. Other critical developments during the period were rising poverty due to the impact of structural adjustment programs and the HIV/AIDS pandemic, which disproportionately devasted sex workers on the continent (Vuylsteke and Jana, 2011). Currently, the major source of funding for most of Africa's sex work and prostitution TSOs comes from abroad. While these funding sources differ based on the ideological positions of the TSOs, their modus operandi, and the nature of engagement with sex workers, they have huge implications on how these TSOs operate and on the values and frameworks on which they model their everyday work. Most African sex work and prostitution TSOs' aid dependency reduces their capacity to implement priorities that are responsive to their local contexts, clearly define their own agendas, and exert real influence on the global discourse related to sex work. More importantly, these relational dynamics and the conflicting loyalties and programs they inspire continue to stifle the development of a sustainable and collective agenda for transforming sex workers' lives in the region.

The TSOs discussed in this chapter have different levels of reach depending on how they engage sex workers, their relationship to government, and their capacity to raise funds. These TSOs in Africa are diverse, with wide-ranging work and interests. Some provide direct basic services and support, mobilize groups and communities to articulate solutions to issues related to sex work, or advocate for particular policies. Their organizational sizes, structures, and sources of support vary. Some are centrally organized or loosely affiliated through federating units with local, national, or regional operations (Jenkins, 2012). Some TSOs have several thousand sex worker members or claim to represent all sex workers, while others work with small numbers of venue-based sex workers or specific types of sex workers, and yet others engage with high-level political actors in their contexts of operation. As of 2005, Danaya So, a Malian sex worker-rights TSO was already 3,000-members strong. The African Sex Workers Alliance (ASWA) boasts a current membership of over 100,000 sex workers. On the other hand, South Africa's abolitionist TSO, Embrace Dignity prides itself on having supported hundreds of sex workers in South Africa to exit the trade. African TSOs work at municipal, national, and regional levels and with different types of sex workers, and all of them purport to advocate for sex workers at large (Open Society Foundations, undated).

These TSOs, even when they pursue similar objectives, may not define themselves similarly. As a result, while some anti-prostitution TSOs, such as the Committee for the Support of the Dignity of Woman (COSUDOW) and the Society Against Prostitution and Child Labour (SAP-CLN) (whose work is described in greater detail later in this chapter), support the prohibition and criminalization of all aspects of sex work on grounds that it is immoral, sacrilegious, and demeaning, others such as the Coalition for the Abolition of Prostitution in Africa (CAPA), South Africa's Embrace Dignity, and Malawi's People Serving Girls at Risk (PSGR) advance a neo-abolitionist stance that regards the sale of sex as a form of violence against women. Some of the region's TSOs advance a mix of regulationist, legalization, and decriminalization agendas that emphasize the regulation of entry into sex work and other practices related to it, or the penalization of certain aspects of sex work such as solicitation and pimping. In Uganda, the operations of the Women's Organization Network for Human Rights Advocacy (WONETHA), a sex worker-led pro-prostitution rights organization, indicate its regulationist stance in supporting sex work's legalization and regulation to ensure that only adults participate in it. On the other hand, HerStory, a Kenyan sex worker exit organization, touts a neo-abolitionist paradigm which acknowledges that only comprehensive social change, rather than criminalization, will stop the sale of sex.

African sex work and prostitution TSO leadership is also extremely diverse, including current and former sex workers, sex workers who identify as having been exploited in prostitution, ex- and current government functionaries, lawyers, religious leaders, physicians, politicians, researchers, social workers, and women's rights activists. Their stated visions or foci notwithstanding, these TSOs collaborate with national governments and international organizations and agencies. While anti-prostitution and prostitution-exit TSOs cooperate with governments to prevent entry into prostitution or to support exit from it, sex worker rights TSOs are often the preferred partner for government agencies seeking to address sex workers' public health needs. SAP-CLN in Nigeria, an anti-prostitution TSO, works with government agencies to rid the streets of suspected sex workers. Tiyane Vavasat, a Mozambican sex worker rights TSO, collaborates with government and international organizations to promote HIV prevention skills among sex workers. Yet, this TSO is also among the frontline organizations campaigning against the country's criminalization of sex work.

A common claim of sex work and prostitution TSOs is that they possess unique insights into the needs and answers to the challenges of the individuals they serve as a result of their close relationships with them. Sources of these supposed insights may derive from personal experiences, research, professional expertise, religion, and feminist ideology. These insights are often viewed as bestowing the organizations and their leaders with the unique abilities to successfully deliver innovative solutions and outcomes that the public sector cannot. While they hold different views on the perceived challenges facing people who sell sex, many sex work and prostitution TSOs claim to be feminist and egalitarian, to understand the sex work industry, and to do their work from a human rights perspective. They also engage with one another; sometimes in fierce ideological conflicts or competition for funding, and at other times, as programmatic and circumstantial allies. The focus of such TSOs could include one or a combination of the following activities: support to people who want to exit prostitution, rehabilitation of sex workers, lobbying for particular legal or policy approaches to regulation, health education, services, and counseling for sex workers, awareness campaigns about violence, skills-building, and provision of legal and other forms of support.

Sex work and prostitution TSOs in Africa agree on a number of key issues, namely that sex work is accompanied by critical social, health, and other risks, that sex workers are stigmatized and experience major rights abuses; that poverty is a key contributor to entry into sex work; and that these issues demand urgent attention. In their work, the TSOs largely constitute the sex worker or prostitute in Africa as a victim. However, they also imbue those who sell sex with agency in proposing different pathways for translating this agency into reality. Their key differences seem to lie largely in the solutions they proffer to sex workers' challenges, their ideas of what the state should do or not do with sex work and sex workers, the future they anticipate for sex work as a vocation, and whether they adopt a rehabilitative, tolerant, or facilitative approach in dealing with sex workers. They also differ on the focus of their interventions for sex workers and the amount of attention they pay to the social context of sex workers' lives. However, they all regularly claim success in their specific operations related to prostitution.

In what follows, we describe African TSOs working in the field of sex work and prostitution by analyzing their major forms, approaches, alliances, challenges, and impacts with careful attention to how they situate themselves within four primary approaches: anti-prostitution, sex worker rights, prostitution-exit support, and sex worker legal assistance. Our approach is not intended to provide incontrovertible typologies of these TSOs and we do not imply that these labels describe all the aspects these TSOs focus on. There are, as we show, fluidities and overlaps in the TSOs' foci and strategies, and it is not uncommon for a TSO to work on a number of issues concurrently. We will show that sex work and prostitution TSOs are, to a large extent, part of the landscape of a renewed form of dependency of the South on the North. These TSOs are local actors in the global weaponization of "charitable" funding by powerful interests in the global sex work debate. Through these financially dependent TSOs, states, interest groups, and donors from the Global North advance their influence and ideologies on key issues in Africa. Sex work and prostitution TSOs in Africa illuminate trans-local flows of ideas, knowledge, funding, and people, shedding light on how local issues are key sites where global political interests are performed and pursued. TSOs are thriving in the region not merely because they pursue locally relevant agendas and issues, but also because they have become indispensable to competing powerful interests and global networks seeking to cement, globalize, and advance their distinctive agendas and strategic goals.

Further, while some sex workers may be benefiting from the activities and services of these TSOs, their work is fragmenting the process of responding methodically to sex work and sex workers' issues in Africa. Contradictory foci on rescue, exit, rehabilitation, de-stigmatization, abolition, decriminalization, legal support, prevention of violence, stigma reduction, and access to health care promote irreconcilable models that hinder societal transformations that can yield sustained benefits for sex workers (Vanwesenbeeck, 2017). With no shared social and political agenda for equity for sex workers, TSOs in Africa are at best extensions of new "technical" solutions to development "problems"; solutions that merely promote provisional "survival strategies of sorts", offering little in the way of a decisive agenda for transforming sex workers' lives (Banks et al., 2015).

The following sections explore sociohistorical commonalities and discontinuities in, and conflicting work ideologies and strategies of sex work and prostitution TSOs in Africa, focusing on some of the ways they translate their values and approaches into practice and the kinds of subjects they produce in their work. We also explore some of their emerging challenges and the impacts of national contexts and global processes on the approaches and strategies employed by these organizations. We accordingly organize the examples featured in this chapter around the four primary approaches taken by sex work and prostitution TSOs— anti-prostitution, sex worker rights, prostitution exit support, and sex worker legal support—with a focus on the organizations' philosophy, funding source, achievements, and challenges.

Anti-prostitution TSOs

An anti-prostitution stance has historically enjoyed high-profile support in Africa that has only been recently boosted by rising global interest in human trafficking and commercial sexual exploitation (Horn, 1979; Opara, 2007; Emser and Francis, 2017; Ikeora, 2018). Anti-prostitution TSOs are thus the dominant, oldest, and most enduring voice about prostitution in contemporary Africa (Aderinto, 2012), and currently number over a hundred organizations in the continent. Despite the massive local and international support that anti-prostitution TSOs enjoy in Africa, it was not until 2020 that CAPA, a regional network of anti-prostitution organizations in Africa, was launched, with support from the Paris-based Coalition for the Abolition of Prostitution International. These TSOs reject the sale of sex as a respectable means of livelihood or economic survival and use the terms "sexually exploited persons", "prostitution survivors", and "prostituted persons" to describe the sale of sex and persons who do it. For anti-prostitution TSOs, prostitution is an immoral or depraved profession, a form (and the result) of violence against women and girls who are disproportionately impacted by poverty, trauma, coercion, patriarchal gender relations, and other manifestations of gender-based violence. They appeal to both local and foreign ideologies to advocate for the abolition and/or criminalization of prostitution. On the one hand, they argue that prostitution is "un-African", an affront to traditional "African" spirituality, morality, womanhood, sexuality, femininity, and family. On the other hand, they see the sale of sex as driven by patriarchy and poverty, inconsistent with modern and global feminist ethics of equality and human rights, and deprecated by received faiths in the region (Udeh, Uduka, and Mbah, 2019). In this regard, these TSOs define their work in terms of both protecting African cultural and moral decency and ensuring that the region's people are partakers in the contemporary global movement for universal dignity, rights, and well-being (Embrace Dignity, undated; COSUDOW, not dated). They consider prostitution to be one of the many forms of abuse and gender-based violence midwifed by colonialism to suppress people, particularly women in Africa, and keep them under men's control. Granting prostitution the status of proper work becomes an affront to both local and global values (Embrace Dignity, undated).

In using categories such as "prostituted persons" or "sexually exploited persons", anti-prostitution TSOs contest individuals' abilities to voluntarily consent to selling sex without being trafficked or forced by difficult economic circumstances (Vanderhurst, 2017; Vanyoro, 2019; Plambech, 2017). As popular allies of local and international conservative groups and the global anti-prostitution feminist movement, Africa's anti-prostitution TSOs earnestly began to conflate trafficking and sex work at the turn of the 21st century, which coincided with the neo-abolitionist shift to regarding the fight against trafficking in the sex industry as key to ending prostitution in the Global South (Ditmore and Allman, 2013; Kempadoo, 2005, 2016; Gould, 2014; Vanderhurst, 2017; Ohonba and Agbontaen-Eghafona, 2019). During this period, TSOs began to aggressively promote the argument that the legalization or decriminalization of commercial sex promotes human trafficking and related crimes. For them, the term "sex work" is merely a liberal plot to conceal the suffering and danger that face prostitutes and "prostituted" people in Africa (Embrace Dignity, undated). The agenda of anti-prostitution TSOs in Africa does not exclude persons who "prefer" to remain in prostitution, as such persons are considered victims of circumstances and false consciousness (Huschke, 2017) who require education and conscientization.

Variations exist in the solutions that Africa's anti-prostitution TSOs proffer for prostitution, with most of these variations driven by funders. When South Africa's Embrace Dignity was founded in 2010 by elitist public officials, it did not have a clear neo-abolitionist agenda. Rather, it focused on ensuring that sex work remains illegal in South Africa, and supporting economic skill-building and the provision of decent job alternatives for women in sex work. However, as Embrace Dignity began to receive funding from different Northern neo-abolitionist donors, Embrace also began to strengthen its advocacy for the decriminalization of the sale of sex and criminalization of the purchase of sex as the fountainhead of its work. Similarly, when COSUDOW, founded in 1999, began to receive funding from international anti-sex trafficking organizations, it began to clearly conflate sex work with sex trafficking and advocate for stronger laws against the sale and procurement of sex in Nigeria. Currently, the organization utilizes popular econo-religious narratives that explain prostitution in terms of a spiritual plunge from grace, limited awareness of the dangers of sex trafficking, poor implementation of existing prostitution laws, and poverty. COSUDOW claims that prostitution can be eradicated largely through moral campaigns, stronger implementation of laws that criminalize the sale and procurement of sex, spiritual restoration, and the provision of basic livelihood alternatives for prostitutes.

Conservative elite women and women who identify as having been exploited in the sex industry are visible in the leadership of contemporary anti-prostitution TSOs in Africa. Mickey Meji, a Black South African who leads Embrace Dignity's Advocacy portfolio, self-identifies as a survivor of prostitution. Her lived experience and grisly testimonies of being abused, exploited, trafficked, violated, and stigmatized add strong fervor to Embrace's campaigns against prostitution. The regular and often orchestrated invocation of these troubling testimonies of exploitation and abuse in local and global fora functions to rally allies, funding, and support for Embrace and similar TSOs (Meji, 2018). When South Africa's ruling party, the African National Congress (ANC), announced support for the decriminalization and recognition of sexual labor as legitimate work, Meji (2018) asserted that the party's disposition is a far-cry from her personal experience in prostitution observing, *inter alia*, that:

> Women in prostitution do not wake up one day and "choose" to be prostituted. Prostitution is chosen for them by [...] persistent inequalities, poverty,

past sexual and physical abuse, the pimps who take advantage of our vulnerabilities and the men who buy us in prostitution.

While they keep the voices of ex-prostitutes at the forefront of their work, many
of Africa's anti-prostitution TSOs are the brainchild of elite women. Nozizwe
Madlala-Routledge, a former South African Deputy Minister of Health and
Defense initiated Embrace Dignity. SAP-CLN in Nigeria was established by the
daughters of Nigeria's former Senate President, David Mark; and COSUDOW was
formed by elite women leaders of the Nigerian Conference of Religious Women
in Benin City, Nigeria. The Real Woman Foundation in Nigeria is an initiative of
Nike Adeyemi, an architect with postgraduate training in the Netherlands and at
Harvard Business School. Fatoumata Diakite, famous Malian activist and international consultant, founded the Association for the Progress and Defence of the
Rights of Malian Women (*Association pour le Progrès et la Défense des Droits
des Femmes*, APDF) and was onetime Africa regional executive director of the
Coalition Against Trafficking in Women (CATW). Both APDF and CATW view
prostitution as a violation of human rights and a form of violence and slavery
which should be criminalized (Mgbako and Smith, 2011). As critical actors in
social movements in Africa, conservative elite and middle-class women easily lay
claim to feminism, while also challenging it (Bouilly et al., 2016). While "dram-
atizing the global political contest between conservative and feminist women"
(Schreiber, 2002), these local elite women use their privileged positions to contest claims that there is nothing wrong with prostitution and that those who support the legalization or decriminalization of prostitution truly understand what
women in Africa want and can act in their best interest. One knock-on effect of
the active participation of elite women and ex-prostitutes in these TSOs has been
their increased capacity to attract funding (Foerster, 2009).

Africa's anti-prostitution TSOs make attractive partners to governments
and anti-sex work international agencies, funders, and bilateral organizations,
including the USAID (Arsovska and Begum 2014). When the United Nations
Interregional Crime and Justice Research Institute (UNICRI) and the Government
of Italy sought to strengthen the local response to international sex trafficking in
Edo state, Nigeria, they inaugurated and funded a loose consortium – the Edo State
Coalition Against Trafficking in Persons (ENCATIP) – in which COSUDOW was
central. The Coalition Against Prostitution (CAP) International currently funds
South Africa's Embrace Dignity and Malawi's PSGR to expand advocacy for the
criminalization of prostitution (Embrace, undated).

As relationships of dependency in the form of alliances with governments
and influential donors thrust anti-prostitution TSOs into the orbit of national and
global prostitution politics, these TSOs appear not as organizations empowered
to influence the real drivers of social change, but as implementors and purveyors
of agendas to which they may not have contributed. Consider for instance, the
recently launched Coalition for the Abolition of Prostitution in Africa's aim "to
abolish the system of prostitution through the enforcement of the Abolitionist

Equality Law in African countries as part of the global abolitionist movement" (Embrace Dignity, undated). Betraying the origins of CAPA's agenda in the Global North, Embrace Dignity, the current secretariat of CAPA, asserted that its goal is to build on the "principles and Nordic/ Equality model pioneered in Sweden, Norway, Canada, Northern Ireland, France, the Republic of Ireland, and Israel" to reduce prostitution and allow prostituted persons to exit.

The activities and services of anti-prostitution TSOs include campaigns to prevent persons from entering prostitution, "rescuing" and "rehabilitating" women involved in it, and high-level advocacy for prostitution's criminalization and recognition as a form of human exploitation (Iacono, 2014). In its work, COSUDOW (undated) asserts a focus on

> counseling and spiritual direction; (and to) provide security for young women and their families after they have opted out of prostitution; equip women with marketable skills and set up business ventures to help self-support [...] in collaboration with government and non-governmental agencies.

South Africa's Embrace Dignity (undated) describes its mission in terms of "empowering prostituted people and creating a legal and social environment that would support them and increase their options to exit sex work". The organization also actively pursues and supports "a law on prostitution in South Africa that recognizes that prostitution is violence against women, undermines gender equality and perpetuates patriarchy" (ibid.). As part of its legal reform efforts to decriminalize the sale of sex while simultaneously criminalizing its purchase, Embrace Dignity lobbies parliament through its public participation program, develops and distributes fact sheets on prostitution and trafficking, conducts research in partnership with universities, writes position papers, and shares information with the media to promote public support for prostitution law reforms.

Embrace Dignity supports the criminalization of sex purchasers and decriminalization of sellers because doing so, it argues, would: focus on demand by outlawing the purchase of sex, support those who have been "prostituted" by decriminalizing the sale of sex, increase skills and employment options for prostituted people, and criminalize third parties who exploit and benefit from prostitution-related income (Embrace Dignity, undated). Embrace Dignity anchors its work:

> on a vision to contribute to the emergence of a South African society that embraces the dignity of all people as enshrined in the South African Constitution and opposes commercial and sexual exploitation of those made powerless and vulnerable by poverty or the absence of choice.
>
> (Embrace Dignity, undated)

Support from and collaborations with government agencies have important implications for the work and public perceptions of anti-prostitution TSOs, as demonstrated by Nigeria's SAP-CLN. Contrary to its purported goal of rescuing and rehabilitating sex workers, SAP-CLN's partnership with the notorious Abuja

Environmental Protection Board (AEPB) is currently behind its reputation as an organization funded by organizations in the Global North and the Nigerian state to enforce laws against prostitution on behalf of the government. The AEPB is rather innocuously tasked by the state with "securing the quality of environment [...] and its natural resources for the benefit" of residents of Abuja, Nigeria's Federal Capital Territory [FCT], and to "minimize the impact of physical development on the ecosystems of the Territory" (FEPA Decree, 1997: 2). Yet, over time, the body has assumed the role of enforcing a prostitution-free Abuja by harassing women found on the street at night or near pubs and hotels. In an official statement in 2017, the FCT administration justified the harassment of suspected sex workers thus: "We are trying to discourage commercial sex workers in FCT, but they are smarter than us, they work as cartels" (Nigerian Vanguard Online, 2017). AEPB regularly boasts of its accomplishments in ridding Abuja of sex workers, noting in 2017 that it has arrested "over 789 prostitutes ... (and) repatriated them to their various states of origin within the last two years" (Jannah, 2017).

SAP-CLN works with AEPB and the Nigerian police to implement "search and dislodge" operations against sex workers in Abuja. In a country where stigma and discrimination impede sex workers' access to essential social and health services and heighten their risks for violence, the raid approach drives sex workers underground, disempowering them and frustrating efforts to reach them with programs and interventions (Isine and Akurega, 2014; Vanguard Online, 2017). The organization has run into legal troubles for its raid strategy; in 2014, Bimpo Ojo sued the organization and was awarded damages for "humiliation, pain and anguish of being falsely labeled as a prostitute". As she explained in court:

> Not only have I lost many job opportunities in Abuja after being charged to court on allegations of being a commercial sex worker, but I have also been cursed by my immediate family. I don't think I will ever overcome the stigma of this false and malicious accusation. My biggest headache is to clear my name because nobody who is aware of the allegation would want to marry me.
>
> (Isine and Akurega, 2014)

Sex worker rights TSOs

Like anti-prostitution TSOs, sex worker rights TSOs in Africa only became a headline story in the last three decades. While there is some evidence of sex worker rights activities in the early and mid-1970s in Africa, organized efforts for the recognition and protection of social and other rights of sex workers as a specific occupational category only emerged around the mid-1980s. Key developments that midwifed sex worker rights TSOs include: the realization that while HIV/AIDS disproportionately affected sex workers, they were also key to curbing its spread; the penetration of critical feminist perspectives in development discourses about Africa; and the global flow of development aid tied to gender mainstreaming, "grassroot participation", and the welfare of "key populations" (Wojcicki, 2003; FIDA, 2008; Naidoo, 2009; Vuylsteke and Jana, 2011). To a large extent, however, these TSOs articulate little that is independent of the Global North's liberal feminist thesis that people can choose to engage in sex work and that those who do are not victims (Gerassi, 2015).

The large number of these types of TSOs in the region is evidence that they are thriving. According to the NSWP (undated), over 70 sex worker rights TSOs currently operate in Africa. They are not only politically active but have, over the years, become increasingly bolder and more vocal. Many of them have identifiable physical addresses, strong online and social media presence, and elaborate formal organizational structures. The National Association of Nigerian Prostitutes (NANP), a sex worker-led organization with a publicly stated mission to challenge the country's prostitution laws, is headed by a president who is elected by the association's members every 12 months. The organization regularly encourages the members to join civil society protests and to vote against conservative politicians (Godwin, 2018). In 2019, when a Nigerian court ruled that sex work is not a criminal offense in a case involving 16 women who were arrested for prostitution, Amaka Enemo, national coordinator for the Nigeria Sex Workers Association, publicly welcomed the court ruling and granted interviews to the BBC (BBC Newsday, 2019). In Rwanda, the Feminist Action Development Alliance (FADA), a sex worker-led organization that seeks to promote sex worker-friendly sentiments in the country, was among civil society groups that submitted memos, gave testimonies, and resolutely lobbied lawmakers and policy actors to remove the prohibition of prostitution (except for forced prostitution) from Rwanda's 2018 Penal Code.

Often led by practicing or retired sex workers, sex worker rights TSOs reject the belief that sex work is, in itself, gender-based violence (Sanders and Campbell, 2007; Mgbako, 2016). They argue, instead, that sex work-related risks derive largely from stigma, criminalization, and limited support for sex workers. These TSOs oppose coercive programs, mandatory testing, raids, and forced rehabilitation, and challenge stigma and discrimination against sex workers, their families and partners, and others involved in sex work (Wojcicki, 2003; Naidoo, 2009; Mgbako, 2016; Mgbako and Smith, 2020). Further, rather than join debates on the ethical, religious, or personal attitudes toward sex work, sex worker rights TSOs in Africa focus on the legitimacy of sex work as a profession. They argue that voluntary adult sex work should be recognized as a legitimate means of livelihood in Africa, that people do not always go into sex work because of poverty, and that sex workers provide services to society (African Sex Workers Alliance, undated). If the enabling environment is created, these TSOs suggest, sex work can be a safe and respectable vocation (WONETHA, undated). For them, the problem is not with sex work per se, but the pervasive lack of enabling political and legal conditions for sex work and sex workers in the region. The notion of voluntary adult sex work is at the heart of these TSOs' rebuttal of the neo-abolitionist conflation of sex work with trafficking and child prostitution.

Opposition to criminalization and other forms of legal oppression, alongside advocacy and activism for sex worker rights and the legalization or decriminalization of sex work, are shared attributes of sex worker rights TSOs. While asserting that decriminalization, legalization, and sex workers' empowerment will improve social livelihood and health outcomes for those who sell sex, these TSOs are at the forefront of building sex workers' capacity to demand their rights, end violence and stigma, and mainstream sex workers' rights and voices within the larger agenda of African women's rights movement (Wojcicki, 2003; Mgbako, 2016; Naidoo, 2009; Mgbako and Smith, 2020). While acknowledging that sex workers are at an elevated risk for sexual, physical, and other forms of abuse from clients and others, sex worker rights TSOs locate the source of these challenges in stigma and punitive laws. The dishonor, powerlessness, shame, and stigma associated with sex work are viewed as products of widespread criminalization and lack of support for persons in the industry. Like their counterparts globally, African sex worker rights TSOs champion the recognition of sexual labor as work and promote the idea of respect for the rights (rather than rescue) of sex workers. To them, feminism is a global liberatory political movement, and to be against another adult persons' freedom to deploy their body and sexuality is to be an enemy of feminism.

Like other sex work-focused TSOs in Africa, sex worker rights TSOs tout how sex workers' own priorities, needs, and activities inform their work. They emphasize rights literacy training; health education and risk reduction; capacity building for sex worker movements; and national, regional, and global lobbying for law and policy reform. Rights not Rescue Trust Namibia, a sex worker rights TSO, articulates a mission to "promote access to health, rights, education and safety of sex worker industry in Namibia in a way that enables and affirms their occupational human rights and freedom" (Rights not Rescue Trust Namibia, 2021). Its vision is to decriminalize Namibia's sex work industry to create a rights-based work environment for all sex workers to have access to reproductive health rights as well as equitable legal services. The South Africa-based Asijiki Coalition for the Decriminalization of Sex Work claims to be at the frontlines of pressuring the government to reject criminalization. In Uganda, where HIV prevalence among sex workers is 50% and 10% among male clients, WONETHA envisions "a legal adult sex work industry in Uganda, to improve our living and working conditions and to fight for equal access to rights so that sex workers' human rights are defended and protected" (WONETHA, 2008). Homme Pour le Droit et La Sante Sexuelle (HODSAS), located in the Democratic Republic of Congo, and Association Femme Amazone (AFAZ), in Togo, share a mission to oppose criminalization, support recognition of sexual labor as work, and tackle violence against sex workers.

In most of Africa, sex worker rights TSOs face significant opposition and challenges (Iradukunda and Odoyo, 2015; EASHRI, 2015, 2016). Often accused of promoting immoral agendas from the Global North, misleading people by making prostitution look attractive, and promoting the abuse of women and children, these TSOs face vicious attacks from many quarters. For instance, the offices of the Human Rights Awareness and Promotion Forum (HRAPF), a Ugandan TSO that works to protect the rights of marginalized groups, including sex workers, were ransacked in 2019. The attackers broke into its office at night, stole and destroyed office equipment, and cut two guards with machetes, severely injuring them (Human Rights Watch, 2019). A recent survey of sex work organizing in East Africa shows that sex worker TSOs "find the process of registration difficult because in order to do so they are forced to censor the objectives contained in their constitutions and use the broader health-based terminology of key populations as an entry point" (EASHRI, 2015: 25). Explicit mention of advocacy for the rights of sex workers is often construed as "promotion of prostitution" and given as the reason for denial of registration.

The operations and strategies of African sex worker rights TSOs are shaped, to a large extent, by their local social contexts as well as global trends, including funding trends and priorities among liberal donors. In African countries where sex work is illegal, but where ample scope still exists for civil society organizing and activism, sex worker rights TSOs can formally register and pursue their mission with little or no state censorship. But in very unfriendly sociolegal contexts, they must devise dynamic ways to operate. South Africa's long history of coordinated civil society activism, experience with large-scale multi-stakeholder campaigns, and thriving democratic space has been particularly capitalized on by the country's sex worker rights TSOs to flourish and cooperatively design and implement initiatives to challenge particular aspects of sex workers' experiences. Sonke Gender Justice, Sex Workers Education and Advocacy Taskforce (SWEAT), Sisonke (National Sex Workers Movement in South Africa) and the Women's Legal Centre (WLC) – three South African sex worker rights organizations – collaboratively launched the Asijiki Coalition for the Decriminalization of Sex Work in 2015.

However, in Ethiopia, Tanzania, and Rwanda, where civil society organizations risk being denied registration if their missions do not clearly align with state politics, sex worker rights TSOs must navigate wearying bureaucratic hurdles that force them to temper their institutional missions to meet registration conditionalities in ways that only limit their potentials to operate, act, and openly challenge the marginalization of sex workers. NIKAT Charitable Association, founded in 2001, offers an example of how sex worker rights TSOs must innovate to overcome challenges associated with operating in illiberal political spaces. Established at a time of widespread repression and extensive state control in Ethiopia, NIKAT could not register as a human rights advocacy organization or receive external donor support as a civil society organization. It had to register as a charitable organization; yet it is a sex worker-led organization that openly disputes the value of coercive exit and rehabilitative sex work programs, asserting that the decision to exit sex work must be entirely left to individual sex workers. While its publicly enunciated mission is to improve the living condition of poor women and female sex workers in Ethiopia and address HIV/AIDS, NIKAT actively and closely works with Ethiopia's Justice, Women, and Youth Affairs ministries to protect sex workers' rights, implement health programs and conduct outreach to police, pimps, hotels, bars, and local drink houses, and other stakeholders who interact daily with sex workers. Yet, NIKAT has a stated long-term but often unspoken revolutionary political agenda "to work with the larger civil society to support sex workers to be politically active, run for political offices, and vote for those who will represent and amplify their voices" (NSWP, undated).

Africa's sex worker rights organizations compete feebly with rehabilitative and sexual and reproductive health-centered programs and large donor organizations and government agencies that take a neo-abolitionist stance in regarding prostitution and trafficking as synonymous. They contend with an overwhelming global "anti-trafficking industry" with its powerful anti-sex work, criminal justice, and border control agendas and rhetoric (Gesimov and Lepp, 2019). As in many countries globally, anti-trafficking rhetoric and interventions in Africa have targeted sex worker rights TSOs with highly detrimental impacts on their work and mission. Rwanda's FADA not only come under frequent denunciation and attack by conservative organizations and government agencies in the country, but also competes with multi-million-dollar anti-prostitution development initiatives such as the USAID, which implemented the *Roads to a Healthy Future (ROADS III) Program.* The program ran between 2013 and 2016 in Rwanda, reaching over 3,700 female sex workers and targeting them with support to exit prostitution (USAID, 2017).

The bulk of funding for sex worker right TSOs comes from liberal donors such as the Ford Foundation, Open Society Foundations, the Dutch Ministry of Foreign Affairs, Hivos, and other key multinational organizations including the UNFPA and WHO, which continue to call for an end to violence, stigma, and discrimination against sex workers alongside strengthening legal and health support systems for society's most marginalized populations. Many of these funders view giving voice to sex workers as key to addressing their multiple challenges and promoting their health, human rights, and self-determination. As a result, a lot of the investments in sex worker rights TSOs have focused on organizing them, facilitating activism and advocacy, and promoting "empowerment". Important as these efforts are, they tend to ignore the crippling circumstances of sex workers' lives in Africa and rarely invest in changing the structural contexts that surround sex work in the region. For instance, in Zimbabwe, Aidsfonds and the Dutch Ministry of Foreign Affairs work with Pow Wow (sex worker-led organization from Bulawayo), ZIMSWA (Zimbabwe Sex Worker Alliance), and the Sexual Rights Centre to promote a sex worker leadership and mentorship academy that builds the capacity of sex workers to advocate for their own rights. In Uganda, donors including the Open Society Foundations and the Urgent Action Fund support the Alliance of Women Advocating for Change (AWAC), a sex worker rights organization to strengthen the "sustainability" of rural sex workers organizations in Uganda.

One of the more important and recent trends in sex worker rights TSOs in contemporary Africa is the emergence of regional TSOs that work through national affiliates or branches to coordinate and provide support to community-based and local sex worker organizations. Often created with the support of donors from the Global North and sex worker alliances, these regional organizations focus on cross-country alliance building and campaign for sex workers' rights (NSWP, undated). One such transnational sex worker rights TSO is the African Sex Workers Alliance (ASWA), a pan-African conglomeration of sex worker-led organizations. Established in 2009, with support from the Edinburgh–based Network of Sex Work Projects (NSWP) to coordinate and support African sex workers, African sex worker-led organizations, and the African sex workers' movement to be the designers and agents of their own change, ASWA seeks to "respond to the ever-changing realities of Africa-based sex workers in general". For instance, the national arm of ASWA in Nigeria is the Nigeria Sex Worker Alliance (NASWA), in Kenya, Kenya Sex Worker Alliance (KESWA), in Tanzania the Tanzania Sex Worker Alliance (TASWA), and ZIMSWA in Zimbabwe. However, much of the work of ASWA is informed by agendas set by NSWP. For instance, the Global Network of Sex Work Projects (NSWP), in partnership with WHO, UNFPA, and UNAIDS, relying on funding from the Robert Carr Fund, developed tools for ASWA's use in HIV/STI prevention projects (WHO, 2013). While the guidelines, *the Sex Worker Implementation Tool (SWIT)*, drew on international "best" practices, they also served to diffuse notions of sex worker "empowerment" from the Global North through ASWA's platforms in over 30 African countries (NSWP, 2013).

ASWA's regional focus makes it one of the major continental actors in advocacy and activism for the recognition and protection of sexual labor as legitimate work in Africa, rendering it an attractive partner for liberal donors and organizations. One of the organization's key programs, the Sex Workers Academy Africa (SWAA) brings together national sex worker collectives from across Africa to strengthen their organizing skills, learn best practices, stimulate national sex workers' movements, and bolster regional networking. The Academy is facilitated by a select faculty of sex workers trained in a bespoke curriculum developed in collaboration with Ashodaya Academy and VAMP Institute (sex worker collectives) in India, the Asia Pacific Network of Sex Workers (APNSW), and the NSWP. Academy participants are nominated at the country level and receive certificates of competency upon completion. ASWA also regularly works with the police, law enforcement, and service providers to improve their interactions with sex workers. National wings replicate ASWA programs in their respective countries, coordinating the activities of in-country sex workers' movements and conducting large-scale advocacy activities.

ASWA's national arm in Kenya, KESWA, currently brings together over 15 sex worker-led organizations drawn from a wide range of constituencies: men who sell sex to men, bar hostesses, small-town sex workers, street-based sex workers, and women in escort services. One of KESWA's affiliates in Kenya is the Bar Hostess Empowerment & Support Programme (BHESP), a loosely structured sex worker-led organization that advocates for and promotes the rights and recognition of women who have sex with women, sex workers who use drugs, sex workers who work in saloons or pubs, and bar hostesses. KESWA affiliates such as the Coast Sex Workers Alliance (COSWA), Eldoret Sex Workers Alliance (ESWA), and Kisumu Sex Workers Alliance (KISWA) represent sex workers operating in some of Kenya's major cities. In contrast, HOYMAS (Health Options for Young Men on HIV/AIDS/STI), another affiliate of KESWA, is a male sex worker-led and focused organization. John Kwasi Anarfi (1995) argues that sex workers in African cities have historically organized themselves based on several factors, including ethnicity, nationality, and location of work. Each sex worker organization is often headed by a president, aided by several elected officers. These leaders are typically older sex workers who are deemed wiser, more practiced, and dependable in protecting the interest of members. By bringing together these different sex worker rights groups, KESWA, like other ASWA national sex worker rights affiliates, built a broad-based movement that permits diverse, but allied organizations to jointly contribute to a collective struggle for sociolegal change. Led by well-educated local sex workers who are conversant with both the national context of sex work and global trends and debates surrounding sex work, KESWA connects established, emerging, and fragile local sex workers' organizations to global movements, enabling them to assimilate inputs and tap into expertise, platforms, structures, and processes that would ordinarily not be accessible to them. Studies are still lacking on how effectively these giant parent regional and national TSOs represent the interests and perspectives of the disparate TSOs they subsume.

Open state support for the sex worker right TSOs may be rare in Africa, but it is not entirely lacking. During a well-attended 2007 international conference involving sex worker rights TSOs in Maputo, Mozambique's then-Deputy Minister of Women's Affairs and Social Welfare, Joao Kandiyane, urged Southern African governments to "establish a legal framework appropriate to its own reality, in order to respect the fundamental rights of prostitutes". These rights, she argued, must include "the right to health, to dignity, protection against violence and other forms of abuse, and respect for the women's choice of profession, regardless of their motives for becoming prostitutes" (Katerere, 2007). Where they exist, sex worker rights TSOs' partnerships with government agencies and international development agencies take a variety of forms, often primarily focusing on health and contingent on the legal status of sex work in the country. In Senegal, where sex work is permitted, the sex worker-led Association for Women at risk from AIDS (AWA) works with the government to ensure the registration of sex workers and their access to government facilities for regular health checks. But in Madagascar where sex work is neither legal nor proscribed, but procurement and solicitation of and for sex in public places are, sex worker rights organizations like Fikambanaina Vehivavy Miavotena Toamasina (FIVEMITO) work with government agencies to establish an identity card system to provide sex workers above the age of 18 with legal protection, among other services. In Kenya and Uganda, where sex work is outlawed, sex worker rights TSOs' partnerships with government revolve around bringing and retaining sex workers in STI testing and treatment, as demonstrated by KESWA's partnership with the National AIDS and STI Control Programme (NASCOP), and AWAC's collaboration with Uganda's Ministry of Health.

Prostitution-exit support TSOs

Positioned between anti-prostitution and sex worker rights TSOs in Africa are prostitution-exit support organizations, which claim to primarily focus on supporting sex workers to voluntarily end their involvement in the sale of sex. They share some of the arguments of both anti-prostitution and sex worker rights TSOs. Like the former, they argue that the sale of sex is demeaning and exposes those who do it to risks and severe violence. But like sex worker rights TSOs, they contend that the criminalization and other forms of legal oppression of sex workers are important sources of harm to them. In their use of language, prostitution-exit support TSOs oscillate between "sex work" and "prostitution" and are not particular in how they describe persons who sell sex for a living. They also neither advocate for the decriminalization of sex work nor for its criminalization, but often keenly challenge the conflation of trafficking and sex work. While recognizing that people join the sex industry for a variety of reasons, prostitution-exit support TSOs hold that prostitution can also be an agentive choice for persons facing poverty and limited opportunities. Their missions tend to revolve around expanding the "structural and relational supports and capacities for change through the identification and mobilization of available assets and resources" for sex workers (Glasgow Centre for Population Health, 2012).

For these TSOs, sex work may never be eliminated but should also not necessarily be promoted or overtly encouraged. They argue that while criminalization will not stop sex work, decriminalization will also not sufficiently empower sex workers (HerStory, undated). The work of prostitution-exit support TSOs hinges on the belief that poverty is the major driver of sex work, and that many sex workers want to quit it. The answer to the problem of sex work therefore lies in ensuring quality economic opportunities for everybody, particularly women, and supporting sex workers who want to exit to succeed. This can be achieved, among other things, by offering them viable economic opportunities. Once it dawns on a sex worker to exit, s/he can be supported to leave in a non-stigmatizing and respectful way through counseling, training, skills, and entrepreneurship. If prostitution exiters succeed in business, they can serve as a model to others. These TSOs emphasize the importance of individual willpower among sex workers if they must exit successfully. Such persons must focus on the critical advantages of exiting, including the promise of respectability, reduced risk for adverse health outcomes, long-term economic sufficiency, and societal acceptance.

Because these TSOs pose few major political challenges, place a lot of responsibility in the hands of individual sex workers, and espouse the "sex-work-is-un-African" narrative, they are attractive partners for conservative states and anti-prostitution TSOs. In most cases, exit TSOs do not engage in advocacy or activism related to sex work, but work directly with sex workers and other organizations by offering education, health information, and, most importantly, vocational training and empowerment support. They rarely participate in efforts to demand change in the social and legal conditions that circumscribe sex work in the region, do not often define their activities as rescue work, and are subtle in how they pressure sex workers to exit the industry. But the seemingly innocuous location of prostitution-exit organizations in the debates on sex work in Africa does not inoculate them against the broad exercise of domination in cultural relationships with donors from the Global North. As part of conditions associated with its "charitable" funding, the Scottish Catholic Aid Fund (SCIAF) pressured the Centre d'Encadrement des Jeunes pour le Développement (CEJEDER) in the Democratic Republic of Congo to rehabilitate sex workers and support them to exit sex work. Although this contradicted its mission and beliefs, CEJEDER took the grant and did the donor's bidding. An evaluation of the project program later showed that the initiative failed to deliver its anticipated impacts (NSWP, undated).

While many prostitution-exit support TSOs argue that their strategy is devoid of compulsion, they regularly apply pressure on sex workers to exit (Katongo, 2012). Visiting places where sex workers operate to recruit them amounts to pressure and can be stigmatizing to them. Prostitution-exit support TSOs also frequently recruit exiters through deception. Tasintha, which means "deeper transformation" in Chewa, a Zambian language, is a grassroots TSO that aims to eliminate commercial sex work in Zambia by supporting people who want to exit the profession. Tasintha promotes rehabilitation, recovery, and restoration of sex workers, as well as HIV prevention. Since 1992, Tasintha claims to have recruited and provided skills training to 7,000 female sex workers in Lusaka. Mwansa, one of the women supported by Tasintha to exit sex work, reported that she only began to think about exiting after Tasintha staff urged her to quit. When Mwansa joined Tasintha, she underwent psychological and spiritual counseling and learned various life skills, such as "hunger management", nutrition, and HIV prevention. She also received training in tailoring, poultry farming, and information and communication technology. Kunda Matipa, Tasintha's operations officer, noted,

> recruiting sex workers on the street to stop sex work and join Tasintha is a challenge [...] At times, during the process of recruitment, we ... pretend to be a sex worker, ... Or if you are a man, you have to pretend to be buying sex.
> (Katongo, 2012)

The variations that exist among prostitution-exit support TSOs is also evident in the example of Red Rain, a South Africa-based TSO that runs a program targeted specifically at sex workers who want to exit due to sickness. The organization asserts that "many sex workers are not prepared to deal with the reality that one day they will not be able to work due to illness, and hence the need to prepare them for exit situations that are beyond their control" (Red Rain, undated). Noting the critical role of individual situation and choice in exit decisions, Red Rain believes that sex workers will be forced, at some point, to retire due to matters beyond their control. The organization works to ensure that sex workers who are dealing with illness have both the support they need to exit as well as an alternative livelihood to support them after they quit. Red Rain considers exit to be a gradual and long-term process, requiring high levels of support. As the SAFE in Collingwood Project (undated) asserts that the sex trade "is not solely dependent on individual traits such as a deep desire to leave. There are many 'trappings' factors such as criminal records, the lack of resources for transition or the lack of available employment".

HerStory Centre, a prostitution-exit support TSO based in Kenya, was founded by the late Professor Elizabeth Ngugi in 1984 "to address the growing need for social support for sex trade workers" (HerStory Centre, 2014). The organization, which ran the Kenya Voluntary Women's Rehabilitation Centre (K-VOWRC), engages with sex workers through outreach at brothels, bars, lodgings, and on city streets to sex workers to identify, interview, and support those interested in exiting the career. HerStory holds that its "programs provide a foundation for sex workers to find their productive place in society" (HerStory Centre, 2014). The organization believes that "sex workers suffer from violence, abuse, intolerance, stigma and prejudice in their line of work and are sometimes sexually brutalized in their quest to earn money to support themselves and their families" (ibid.). HerStory promises to lead willing and ready sex workers out of abuse to empowerment, providing them health education and counseling on family planning and reproductive health, nutrition, parenting skills, STI/HIV/AIDS, and negotiating safer sex practices. The organization's prostitution-exit strategies include supporting sex workers to develop business plans, manage micro-loans, and benefit from peer group support. In 2014, HerStory claimed that 75% of the sex workers it worked with in developing an exit plan have successfully left the industry. The organization noted that these women:

> have started businesses of their choice and are financially stable, and as a result, earn more than they did as sex workers, have higher levels of self-esteem, are more successful at parenting, and are living a life without the constant fear and risk of HIV infection. Moreover, those living with HIV have a better quality of life and a more positive outlook on life.
>
> (Herstory, undated)

HerStory's "Working Together Centre" "enrolls sex workers in a variety of programs and opportunities to help them succeed in life – and become self-reliant, and independent to make her-story" (HerStory, 2014). Sex workers who join the program are put into groups of five and are supported to open bank accounts and start small enterprises. Within the groups, women provide peer counseling, home-based care for sick members, peer education outreach, and form lasting bonds on which they can rely through any difficulty. Businesses commonly established by sex workers in the program include small-scale beauty salons, tailoring, weaving, restaurants, and artwork retailing, among others. HerStory has received funding from a wide range of sources, including state agencies, secular philanthropies such as the Gates Foundation, faith-based organizations, and multilateral organizations.

HerStory reported that its program resulted in positive changes in "health status, drug use, social interaction, and economic status" (2014). However, one study showed that "though the program delivered on its intended social outcomes, its model was …financially unsustainable" (Moret, 2014: 15). In many Global South contexts, microbusinesses such as those touted by HerStory hardly keep women out of the sex industry because they have small profit margins and require a lot of fiscal discipline to grow. Cheryl Overs (2014) argues that many of the enterprises the sex workers undertake lack viability; do not provide sustainable, living wages; and may not thrive in communities already flooded by similar business. If they survive, such micro-enterprises may at best only provide additional sources of income for sex workers, reducing their desperation and consequently their involvement with high-risk clients (Odek et al., 2009). Reports show that many sex workers in Africa may earn far more in sex work than in microbusinesses (Baleta, 2015; Famuyiwa, 2019). The top-down and "one-size-fits-all" approach of prostitution-exit support TSOs is also concerning. To be sustainable, economic empowerment projects need to adopt a long-term vision, be alert to the multiple differences among sex workers, and involve sex worker-led organizations (INCLUDE, 2017).

Further, many prostitution-exit support TSOs require women to abandon sex work as a condition of benefiting from their programs (INCLUDE, 2017; NSWP, undated). Funding is hardly available at the start of these initiatives as sex workers undergo training and set up their small businesses. There is also very little training that can be provided indefinitely because costs become unaffordable. These factors, combined with the rehabilitation approach, create a situation where sex workers can find themselves worse off after exiting sex work, which allowed them to generate a relatively stable income, making them quickly become dependent on sex work again once their new business ventures are not as successful as they were told they would be. Moreover, the communities which sex workers are "reintegrated" into also frequently discriminate against and stigmatize sex workers. A study of an exit intervention implemented by Empowered at Dusk Women's Association (EADWA), a TSO in Uganda, showed that the participants ended up being more marginalized in their communities because the program did not properly consider how stigma and discrimination affected the other income-generating activities that sex workers undertook. The study concluded that:

> There was no demand for sex workers' products because of social discrimination, and culturally, the community believed that sex workers' products were bad omens. Moreover, members were not used to these somewhat outdated types of jobs and they were inexperienced. Sex workers had to work

long hours and they were subjected to sexual exploitation by the buyers: one member stated that "once they knew that we were sex workers, they wanted free sex in order to buy our goods".

(NSWP, undated: 28)

Sex worker legal support TSOs

A fourth category of sex work and prostitution TSO in Africa focuses primarily on providing legal support to sex workers. Unlike, sex worker rights TSOs, the bulk of sex worker legal support organizations do not undertake advocacy or direct action to change laws related to sex work. They also do not worry about the social and economic conditions that drive people into sex work. Rather, they seek to take advantage of regional and international laws and instruments or ambiguities in national penal codes to support sex workers who have been arrested, detained, abused, and mistreated. Their primary activity is actual legal representation for sex workers against clients, the police, or the state. Some of them conduct legal research on sex work and offer paralegal support in the form of evaluating and reviewing depositions, preparing and answering interrogatories, drafting procedural submissions and legal research on behalf of sex workers. Most of these organizations are run by lawyers and their legal services are usually *pro bono* to sex workers or their collectives. But they also receive support from many liberal donors to do their work. In many instances, the services of sex worker legal support organizations are often part of a suite of human rights and legal protection services which they offer to disadvantaged national groups, including widows, children, poor communities, landless rural women, LGBTQ+ persons, and young people.

Sex worker legal support TSOs agree that criminalization of sex work increases the vulnerability of sex workers to multiple human rights abuses by actors such as the state, police, public, and clients. In 2008, Namibia's Legal Assistance Centre, a Windhoek-based nonprofit human rights organization that supports sex worker rights stated that the decriminalization of prostitution would curb the country's high HIV/AIDS rate and advance the human rights of prostitutes (Tjaronda, 2009). The many legal organizations that support sex workers' causes and human rights issues in Africa also often belong to different national, regional, and international networks of human rights legal organizations. They focus on the laws of their countries and sometimes appeal to international and regional human rights standards to do their work. While most legal support TSOs avoid debates on whether sexual labor should be formally recognized as work, they tend to call for its decriminalization to address the problems facing sex workers in the region.

Legal support TSOs are also active in police sensitization work. Many of them, such as Sonke Gender Justice in South Africa, have developed detailed training curricula to support police to work with sex workers. They also sometimes work with sex worker rights TSOs to establish informal relationships with police officers, and/or high-level political allies to support them during difficulties. Some of them, such as AdvocAid in Sierra Leone, do not merely provide direct legal support but also conduct rights awareness and legal literacy for sex workers and other groups. AdvocAid (undated) observed that

> poverty and imprisonment frequently go together, both as the reason for women's offenses and because women can rarely afford legal services, fines or bail. Alongside this, poor education means too many women don't know or understand their legal rights, resulting in admission to crimes they did not commit and no knowledge of their rights when arrested.

AdvocAid works across Sierra Leone to ensure these women receive fair legal representation, are educated on their legal rights, and are offered rehabilitation support upon release. They also run advocacy and law reform projects focused on wider issues impacting women in the justice system, literacy classes, vocational training, and business skills training for women in detention.

The work of sex worker legal support TSOs has become important in many African contexts where marginality and poverty constrain the capacity of many vulnerable groups to access justice. A report by the Open Society Foundations (undated) indicates that sex worker legal support TSOs have helped sex workers challenge laws and practices that negatively impact them. They have initiated and won court cases that have expanded protections for sex workers or resulted in more progressive interpretations of laws related to sex work. In South Africa, sex worker legal support TSOs have won major labor protections for sex workers and helped block the police from repeatedly detaining and arresting sex workers without charging or taking them to court. In some instances, these legal support TSOs also collaborate with the police to respond to the abuse of sex workers by clients and the public. In 2014, nine Zimbabwean women were convicted of solicitation. However, according to the country's law, both the *conduct* of solicitation must be specified (i.e. evidence of proactive attempt to procure a client rather than based on the person's location and/or clothing) and the solicitee needs to be present in court. Noting the lack of these requirements in the convictions, the Zimbabwe Lawyers for Human Rights (ZLHR) and other sex worker legal support organizations took the case to the Constitutional Court, successfully arguing that the women's conviction was in violation of the country's 2013 Constitution. In 2015, a court order rescinding the sex workers' conviction was issued. The order was widely reported by Zimbabwe's media as suggesting that the police had no powers to arrest sex workers (Busza et al., 2017). In the same country, the Sexual Rights Centre (SRC), another legal support TSO which envisions a Zimbabwean society where sex workers are free from abuse and stigma, had also successfully challenged a police order that barred sex workers from organizing and marching on the street.

Similarly, in a case instituted by TSOs Southern Africa Litigation Centre (SALC) and the Centre for Human Rights Education, Advice and Assistance (CHREAA) in 2016, a Malawi court ruled that it was illegal to arrest, detain, and fine sex workers or violate their human rights. The Court found the country's

Penal Code does not criminalize sex work, but rather seeks to protect sex workers. The court ordered that the conviction be set aside, and the fines be refunded to the women. In 2017, Lawyers Alert, a Nigerian TSOs that works to decriminalize petty offenses in Nigeria and promote the socioeconomic development of women, the poor, and marginalized populations in Nigeria, filed a case on behalf of Constance Nkwocha and 15 others accused of prostitution. In the ruling, the court stated that sex work was not illegal in the country and that the arrest of commercial sex workers in the country was unlawful (Mukabana, 2019).

Noteworthy, however, is that many of the region's legal support TSOs do not make the decriminalization of sex work their core mission. Rather, they merely support sex workers who experience arrests, detention, and other abuses through *pro bono* legal defense and litigation services. As a result, concern continues to be expressed about the proactivity of sex worker legal support TSOs in Africa. Critics have noted that they tend to wait for sex workers or sex worker TSOs to be victimized before they act. They are also only able to address the cases that reach them, leaving a majority of sex worker victimization cases unremedied. The inability of this category of TSOs to seek or pursue fundamental changes to the judicial foundations of sex workers' rights matters leaves major gaps in their efforts to challenge the structural basis of sex workers' marginality in Africa.

Given the nature of their work, legal support TSOs work are often strong allies to sex worker rights TSOs. The Women's Legal Centre (WLC) in South Africa, a sex worker legal support TSO, works closely with both individual sex workers and their collectives. Founded in 1999 in Cape Town by a group of women lawyers as a non-profit independently funded legal center focusing exclusively on women's rights, WLC prides itself as having a solid

> reputation as a non-profit law center that seeks to achieve equality for women, particularly Black women through impact-based litigation, the provision of free legal advice, legal support to advocacy campaigns run by other organizations…and training that ensures people know and understand the impact of judgments of the courts on the subject.
>
> (WLC, undated)

The Centre's vision is that South Africa becomes violence-free and that women in the country are "empowered to ensure their own reproductive and health rights, free to own their own share of property, having a safe place to stay and empowered to work in a safe and equitable environment" (ibid.). One of the big wins of the WLC is the now famed Kylie case which effectively challenged the interpretation of an "employee" in the Labour Relations Act which prevented sex workers from obtaining the necessary labor protections in terms of the labor legislation and the Constitution. In South Africa, sex workers are routinely harassed and intimated by police. Police use municipal laws against loitering, solicitation, and drunken behavior to threaten, arrest, or detain sex workers for days at a time. WLC's outreach and workshops employ former and current sex workers to offer peer-based legal assistance to sex workers. The organization also partners with other established sex worker counseling and advocacy organizations such as SWEAT to "provide male, female, and transgender sex workers with legal information and advice, and assist with court hearings, bail applications, and filing complaints about police abuse" (WLC, undated).

The Kenya Legal and Ethical Issues Network on HIV and AIDS (KELIN), formed in 1994 and registered as TSO in 2001, also works closely with Kenya's sex worker rights TSOs in relation to violations of health-related rights of sex workers. Like the WLC, it seeks to protect and promote HIV/AIDS-related human rights and to advocate for a holistic and rights-based system of service delivery in health and for the full enjoyment of the right to health by all, including vulnerable, marginalized, and excluded populations. KELIN describes itself as a promoter of "justice in respect of violations of health-related human rights" and a stakeholder "in strategic partnerships at the national, sub-regional and regional and global levels for the strengthening of the rights-based approach to the delivery of health services" (KELIN, 2015). KELIN understands that the illegal status of prostitution in Kenya directly affects sex workers' ability to organize and demand their rights, noting that "criminalization of prostitution and thus criminalization of sex workers themselves leave these women without legal and health protection and further entrench the stigma and discrimination they face" (ibid.).

Conclusion

While organizations focused on preventing sex work, "rescuing" sex workers, and providing them with economic alternatives had operated in Africa since colonial times, local movements and organizations focused on supporting the rights of sex workers did not emerge in Africa until the last decades of the 20th century (Wojcicki, 2003; FIDA, 2008; Naidoo, 2009). But since the early 1980s, all of these types of TSOs have proliferated in Africa, driven largely by the rapid NGO-ization of Africa's civil society, rising poverty due to the impact of structural adjustment programs, and the devastating impact of HIV/AIDS on sex workers on the continent.

Africa's sex work and prostitution TSOs coexist, sometimes collaborating harmoniously, and at other times competing fiercely for resources, partnerships, support, and influence. Our analysis of these TSOs shows not only fluidities and overlaps in their foci, but also their increasingly important role in advancing competing powerful global narratives about sex work in Africa. Their activities are no doubt supporting some sex workers in the region to build alternative means of livelihoods; reduce their risk for poor health outcomes; be better treated by service providers, the public, and the police; and enjoy legal relief for their mistreatment. Through their wide-ranging efforts such as campaigning, mobilization, legal representation, advocacy, lobbying, agenda-setting, and negotiation, sex work and prostitution TSOs are therefore also creating possibilities for both sex workers and policy and programmatic options for governments and agencies to engage with sex work and sex workers (Jenkins, 2012).

These organizations are united by their dependency on funding from the Global North, which not only reduces their capacity to exert any real influence on the global discourse on sex work, but also transforms them into channels for the transmission of western values and ideologies of development. As dependents on charitable donations of very influential entities and governments, sex work and prostitution TSOs in Africa prioritize and focus deliverables that advance the interests of their donors, leaving little room for broadminded local research on, discovery of, and experimentation with alternatives and contrasting worldviews. Taken together, Africa's sex work and prostitution TSOS have generated multiple and conflicting agendas that furnish irreconcilable models of action and change, hindering the emergence and articulation of a robust social and political blueprint for equity and well-being for the sex worker in Africa.

References

Achebe, N. 2004. "The road to Italy: Nigerian sex workers at home and abroad." *Journal of Women's History* 15(4): 178–185.

Aderinto, S. 2010. "Sexualized nationalism: Lagos and the politics of illicit sexuality in Colonial Nigeria, 1918–1958." PhD thesis. Department of History, University of Texas at Austin.

——— 2012. "'The problem of Nigeria is slavery, not white slave traffic': Globalization and the politicization of prostitution in Southern Nigeria, 1921–1955." *Canadian Journal of African Studies/Revue Canadienne des Etudes Africaines* 46(1): 1–22.

——— 2015a. *When Sex Threatened the State: Illicit Sexuality, Nationalism, and Politics in Colonial Nigeria, 1900–1958.* Chicago, IL: University of Illinois Press.

——— 2015b. "Journey to work: Transnational prostitution in colonial British West Africa." *Journal of the History of Sexuality* 24(1): 99–124.

Advocaid 2018. "Access to justice." Accessed 6th May 2019. https://advocaidsl.org/ac cess-to-justice/.

African Sex Workers Alliance 2018. "Who we are." Accessed 4th January 2020. https://as waalliance.org/dict_services/business-povertys/.

African Sex Worker Alliance 2019. "Every sex worker has got a story to tell about violence." *Violence Against Sex Workers in Africa.* Nairobi: ASWA.

Akyeampong, E. 1997. "Sexuality and prostitution among the Akan of the Gold Coast c. 1650–1950." *Past and Present* 156(1): 144–173.

Albertyn, C. 2016. "Debate around sex work in South Africa tilts towards decriminalization." *The Conversation*, May 15, 2016.

Anarfi, J.K. 1990. "International migration of Ghanaian women to Abidjan, CBte dfIvoire: A demographic and socio-economic study." PhD thesis. Regional Institute for Population Studies (RIPS). University of Ghana, Legon.

Anarfi, J.K. 1995. "Female migration and prostitution in West Africa. The case of Ghanaian women in Côte d'Ivoire." Deutsche Gesellschaft fur Technische Zusammenarbeit (GTZ) Regional AIDS Programme for West and Central Africa: Studies in Sexual Health, No.I. Accra.

Arsovska, J., and P. Begum 2014. "From West Africa to the Balkans: Exploring women's roles in transnational organized crime." *Trends in Organized Crime* 17(1–2): 89–109.

Asongu, S.A., and J.C. Nwachukwu 2016. "Foreign aid and governance in Africa." *International Review of Applied Economics* 30(1): 69–88.

Baleta, A. 2015. "Lives on the line: Sex work in sub-Saharan Africa." *The Lancet* 385(9962): e1–e2.

Banks, N., D. Hulme, and M. Edwards 2015. "NGOs, states, and donors revisited: Still too close for comfort?" *World Development* 66: 707–718.

Bidemi, G.B. 2017. "Internet diffusion and government intervention: The parody of sustainable development in Africa." *Journal of Pan African Studies* 10: 6–12.

Bindman, J., and J. Doezema 1997. *Redefining Prostitution as Sex Work on the International Agenda*. London: Anti-Slavery International and the Network of Sex Work Projects.

Bonthuys, E. 2012. "The 2010 football world cup and the regulation of sex work in South Africa." *Journal of Southern African Studies* 38(1): 11–29.

Bouilly, E., O. Rillon, and H. Cross 2016. "African women's struggles in a gender perspective." *Review of African Political Economy* 43(149): 338–349.

Busza, J., S. Mtetwa, E. Fearon, D. Hofisi, T. Mundawarara, R. Yekeye, T. Magure, O. Mugurungi, and F. Cowan 2017. "Good news for sex workers in Zimbabwe: How a court order improved safety in the absence of decriminalization." *Journal of the International AIDS Society* 20(1): 21860.

Chandy, L. 2017. "No country left behind: The case for focusing greater attention on the world's poorest countries." In: *Global Economy and Development at Brookings*. Washington, DC: Brookings Institute.

Chrétien, J.P. 1991. "Presse libre et propagande raciste au Rwanda: Appel à la conscience des Bahutu." *Politique Africaine* 42(6): 109–120.

Committee for the Support of the Dignity of Woman (COSUDOW). n.d. "Organizational profile." http://www.ncwr.org.ng/committee-for-the-support-of-the-dignity-of-woman .html. Accessed June 12, 2019.

Connelly, M.T. 2018. *The Response to Prostitution in the Progressive era*. Chapel Hill, NC: UNC Press Books.

Currier, A., and T. McKay 2017. "Pursuing social justice through public health: Gender and sexual diversity activism in Malawi." *Critical African Studies* 9(1): 71–90.

Devinfo 2016. "Sex workers: Population size estimate – Number, 2016." *UNAIDS*. Accessed 3rd January 2020. www.aidsinfoonline.org.

Ditmore, M.H., ed. 2006. *Encyclopedia of Prostitution and Sex Work*. London: Greenwood Publishing Group.

Ditmore, M.H., and D. Allman 2013. "An analysis of the implementation of PEPFAR's anti-prostitution pledge and its implications for successful HIV prevention among organizations working with sex workers." *Journal of the International AIDS Society* 16(1): 17354.

Dlamini, S., and N.P. Nzama 2019. "A criminological exploration of cyber prostitution within the South African context: A systematic review." *American Journal of Humanities and Social Sciences Research* 3(1): 136–145.

EASHRI 2015. *The Other Tanzanians: A Landscape Analysis of the Human Rights of Sex Workers and LGBT Communities in Tanzania, 2015–2016*. Nairobi: UHAI EASHRI.

EASHRI 2016. *Turi Abande Where Do We Belong? A Landscape Analysis of the Human Rights of Sex Workers and LGBT Communities in Burundi*. Nairobi: UHAI EASHRI.

Elias, P. 2018. "African development initiatives." In: *The Development of Africa: Issues, Diagnoses, and Prognoses*, edited by Akanle and Olálékan Adésìnà, 357–374. Cham: Springer Nature.

Embrace Dignity. n.d. "What we do." Accessed 16th February 2020. http://embracedignit
y.org.za/about-us/#who.

Emser, M., and S. Francis 2017. "Counter-trafficking governance in South Africa: An analysis of the role of the KwaZulu-Natal human trafficking, prostitution, pornography and brothels task team." *Journal of Contemporary African Studies* 35(2): 190–211.

Famuyiwa, D. 2019. "Thriving businesses around Allen Avenue's commercial sex hub." *Nairametrics*. Accessed 13th May 2020. https://nairametrics.com/2019/04/15/thriving-businesses-around-allen-avenues-commercial-sex-hub/.

Farley, M., A. Cotton, J. Lynne, S. Zumbeck, F. Spiwak, M.E. Reyes, D. Alvarez, and U. Sezgin 2004. "Prostitution and trafficking in nine countries: An update on violence and posttraumatic stress disorder." *Journal of Trauma Practice* 2(3–4): 33–74.

Fayemi, A.K. 2009. "The challenges of prostitution and female trafficking in Africa: An African ethico-feminist perspective." *Journal of Pan African Studies* 3(1): 200–213.

Federal Environmental Protection Agency (FEPA) 1997. *FEPA Decree 10 of 1997*. Abuja: Federal Government of Nigeria.

Federation of Women Lawyers (FIDA) Kenya 2008. "Documenting human rights violations of sex workers in Kenya. Report." Accessed 4th May 2019. http://www.soro s.org/reports/documenting-human-rights-violations-sex-workers-kenya.

Fick, N. 2006. "Sex workers speak out: Policing and the sex industry." *South African Crime Quarterly* 15(15): 13–18.

Foerster, A. 2009. "Contested bodies: Sex trafficking NGOs and transnational politics." *International Feminist Journal of Politics* 11(2): 151–173.

Foley, E.E. 2017. "Regulating sex work: Subjectivity and stigma in Senegal." *Culture, Health & Sexuality* 19(1): 50–63.

—— 2019. "'The prostitution problem': Insights from Senegal." *Archives of Sexual Behavior* 48(7): 1937–1940.

Gerasimov, B., and B. Lepp 2019. "*Rights, rescues and resistance in the global movement for sex workers' rights.*" Accessed 2nd March 2020. https://www.opendemocracy .net/en/beyond-trafficking-and-slavery/rights-rescues-and-resistance-in-the-global-mo vement-for-sex-workers-rights-introducing-the-series/.

Gerassi, L. 2015. "A heated debate: Theoretical perspectives of sexual exploitation and sex work." *Journal of Sociology and Social Welfare* 42(4): 79–100.

Glasgow Centre for Population Health 2012. "Putting asset based approaches into practice: Identification, mobilisation and measurement of assets: Briefing paper 10." Accessed 6th January 2021. http://www.gcph.co.uk/assets/0000/3433/GCPHCS10for web_1_.pdf.

Godwin, A. 2018. "Nigerian prostitutes back Saraki, reveal why Buhari must go." *Daily Post*, August 31, 2018. Accessed 17th September 2019. https://dailypost.ng/2018/08/3 1/2019-nigerian-prostitutes-back-saraki-reveal-buhari-must-go/.

Gould, C. 2014. "Sex trafficking and prostitution in South Africa." *The Annals of the American Academy of Political and Social Science* 653(1): 183–201.

Hassan, T.L. 2015. "Prostitution in Uganda: A burden or a service?" *International Journal of Developing Societies* 4(2): 62–72.

HerStory 2014. "What we do." Accessed 12th June 2019. http://www.herstorycentre.org/.

Hodgskiss, B. 2004. "Lessons from serial murder in South Africa." *Journal of Investigative Psychology and Offender Profiling* 1(1): 67–94.

Hofmann, C. 1997. "SEX: From human intimacy to 'sexual labor' or is prostitution a human right? CATW." *Asia Pacific*. Accessed 9th March 2019. https://catwap.wordp

ress.com/resources/speeches-papers/sex-from-human-intimacy-to-sexual-labor-or-is
-prostitution-a-human-right/.

Homaifar, N. 2008. "The African prostitute: An everyday debrouillard in reality and
African fiction." *Journal of African Cultural Studies* 20(2): 173–182.

Horn, A. 1979. "Uganda's theatre—The exiled and the dead." *Index on Censorship* 8(5):
12–15.

Human Rights Watch 2016. "Uganda: Human rights group targeted in violent break-in."
https://www.hrw.org/news/2018/02/09/uganda-human-rights-group-targeted-violent-b
reak

KELIN 2015. "KELIN strategic plan 2015–2019." Accessed 2nd May 2019. https://www
.kelinkenya.org/kelin-strategic-plan-2015-2019/.

Huschke, S. 2017. "Victims without a choice? A critical view on the debate about sex work
in Northern Ireland." *Sexuality Research and Social Policy* 14(2): 192–205.

Iacono, E. 2014. "Victims, sex workers, and perpetrators: Gray areas in the trafficking of
Nigerian women." *Trends in Organized Crime* 17(1–2): 110–128.

Igbinovia, P.E. 1984. "Prostitution in Black Africa." *International Journal of Women's
Studies* 7: 430–449.

Ikeora, M. 2018. "Anti-trafficking in Nigeria: The context of a source country." In:
Bilateral Cooperation and Human Trafficking, edited by Ikeora, 137–167. Cham:
Palgrave Macmillan.

INCLUDE. 2017. "Strategic actors November 2017 final findings economic empowerment
and sex work." Accessed 10th April 2020. https://includeplatform.net/wp-content/u
ploads/2019/07/Nencel_finalfindings.pdf.

Iradukunda, I., and R. Odoyo 2015. *AGACIRO: A Landscape Analysis of Human Rights of
Sex Workers and LGBT Communities in Rwanda*. Nairobi: UHAI EASHRI.

Isine, I., and M. Akurega 2014. "How Abuja NGO, AEPB, arrest innocent women, label
them prostitutes." *Premium Times*, February 10, 2014. Accessed 16th May 2019. https
://www.premiumtimesng.com/news/154446-how-abuja-ngo-aepb-arrest-innocent-wo
men-label-them-prostitutes.html.

Izugbara, C.O. 2011. "Everyday negotiations of state regulation among female sex workers
in Nairobi, Kenya." In: *Policing Pleasure: Sex Work, Policy, and the State in Global
Perspective*, edited by Dewey and Kelly, 115–130. New York: NYU Press.

——— 2012. "Client retention and health among sex workers in Nairobi, Kenya." *Archives
of Sexual Behavior* 41(6): 1345–1352.

Jannah, C. 2017. "Minister sacks 789 prostitutes from Abuja." *Daily Post*, June 28, 2017.
Accessed 16th August 2019. https://dailypost.ng/2017/06/28/minister-sacks-789-pros
titutes-abuja/.

Jenkins, G. 2012. "Nongovernmental organizations and the forces against them: Lessons
from the anti-NGO movement." *Brooklyn Journal of International Law* 37(2): 459–526.

Joint United Nations Programme on HIV/AIDS (UNAIDS) 2014. "The gap report."
Accessed 5th January 2020. http://www.unaids.org/sites/default/files/media_asset/U
NAIDS_Gap_report_en.pdf.

Katerere, F. 2007. *Mozambique: Respecting Sex Work*. Maputo: Agencia de Informacao
de Mocambique.

Katongo, C. 2012. "Zambian sex workers offered 'transformation." *We News*. Accessed
15th January 2012. https://womensenews.

Kempadoo, K. 2005. "Sex workers' rights organizations and anti-trafficking campaigns."
In: *Trafficking and Prostitution Reconsidered: New Perspectives on Migration, Sex*

Work, and Human Rights, edited by Kempadoo, Sanghera, and Pattanaik, 149–155. Boulder, CO: Paradigm.

Kempadoo, K. 2016. "Sex workers' rights organizations and anti-trafficking campaigns." In: *Trafficking and Prostitution Reconsidered*, 2nd ed, edited by Kempadoo, 147–157. New York: Routledge.

Kenya Legal and Ethical Network on HIV & AIDS (KELIN) 2015. "Our strategic plan: 2015–2019." Accessed 5th September 2019. https://www.kelinkenya.org/about-us/.

Longe, O., O. Ngwa, F. Wada, V. Mbarika, and L. Kvasny 2009. "Criminal uses of information & communication technologies in sub-Saharan Africa: Trends, concerns and perspectives." *Journal of Information Technology Impact* 9(3): 155–172.

Longo, J.D., M.M. Simaléko, R. Ngbale, G. Grésenguet, G. Brücker, and L. Bélec 2017. "Spectrum of female commercial sex work in Bangui, Central African Republic." *SAHARA J: Journal of Social Aspects of HIV/AIDS Research Alliance* 14(1): 171–184.

Lonsdale, J. 2016. "State and peasantry in colonial Africa." In: *People's History and Socialist Theory*, edited by Samuel, 106–117. London: Routledge & Kegan Paul.

Luiz, J.M., and L. Roets 2000. "On prostitution, STDs and the law in South Africa: The state as pimp." *Journal of Contemporary African Studies* 18(1): 21–38.

Marwick, M. 1965. *Sorcery in the Social Setting: A Study of the Northern Rhodesian Chewa*. Manchester: Manchester University Press.

Meji, M. 2018. "ANC resolution to decriminalize prostitution fails black women." Accessed 8th June 2019. https://smonza.wordpress.com/2018/01/26/anc-54th-congre ss-resolution-to-fully-decriminalize-prostitution-and-recognize-it-as-work-fails-black -poor-and-disadvantaged/.

Mgbako, C.A. 2016. *To Live Freely in This World: Sex Worker Activism in Africa*. New York: NYU Press.

Mgbako, C.A., and L.A. Smith 2009. "Sex work and human rights in Africa." *Fordham International Law Journal* 33(4): 1178–1220.

Michalopoulos, S., and E. Papaioannou 2020. "Historical legacies and African development." *Journal of Economic Literature* 58(1): 53–128.

Moret, W. 2014. *Economic Strengthening for Female Sex Workers: A Review of the Literature*. Durham, NC: ASPIRES, FHI 360.

Muchomba, F.M. 2014. "Colonial policies and the rise of transactional sex in Kenya." *Journal of International Women's Studies* 15(2): 80–93.

Mukabana, S. 2019. "Nigerian court rules sex work isn't illegal." *Africa*, December 21, 2019.

Muldoon, K.A., M. Akello, G. Muzaaya, A. Simo, J. Shoveller, and K. Shannon 2017. "Policing the epidemic: High burden of workplace violence among female sex workers in conflict-affected northern Uganda." *Global Public Health* 12(1): 84–97.

Mutagoma, M., L. Nyirazinyoye, D. Sebuhoro, D.J. Riedel, and J. Ntaganira 2019. "Sexual and physical violence and associated factors among female sex workers in Rwanda: A cross-sectional survey." *International Journal of STD and AIDS* 30(3): 241–248.

Naanen, B.B. 1991. "'Itinerant gold mines': Prostitution in the cross river basin of Nigeria, 1930–1950." *African Studies Review* 34(2): 57–79.

Naidoo, N.P. 2009. *Report on the 1st African Sex Worker Conference: Building Solidarity and Strengthening Alliances*. Johannesburg, South Africa: Sex Worker Education & Advocacy Taskforce and Reproductive Health & HIV Research Unit.

Ndjio, B. 2009. "'Shanghai Beauties' and African desires: Migration, trade and Chinese prostitution in Cameroon." *The European Journal of Development Research* 21(4): 606–621.

Ndjio, B. 2017. "Sex and the transnational city: Chinese sex workers in the West African city of Douala." *Urban Studies* 54(4): 999–1015.

Network of Sex Workers Project. n.d. "Where we work." https://www.nswp.org/members /africa.

Network of Sex Workers' Projects (NSWP). n.d. "NIKAT Charitable Association." Accessed 14th October 2019. https://www.nswp.org/members/africa/nikat-charitable-association.

Newsday, B.B.C. 2019. "Nigerian Court rules that sex work is not a crime." Accessed 12th January 2019. https://www.bbc.co.uk/programmes/p07ygj8w.

Ngugi, E.N., E. Roth, T. Mastin, M.G. Nderitu, and S. Yasmin 2012. "Female sex workers in Africa: Epidemiology overview, data gaps, ways forward." *SAHARA J: Journal of Social Aspects of HIV/AIDS Research Alliance* 9(3): 148–153.

Nigerian Vanguard Online 2017. "*Men beg FCT minister to allow 789 prostitutes stay.*" https://www.vanguardngr.com/2017/06/men-beg-fct-minister-allow-789-prostitutes-stay/.

NSWP. n.d. "Economic empowerment programmes for sex worker." Edinburgh. https:// www.nswp.org/sites/nswp.org/files/SUSO%20Report%20Africa.%20final%20EN.pdf.

NSWP 2013. "Sex Worker Implementation Tool (SWIT)." https://www.nswp.org/reso urce/sex-worker-implementation-tool-swit.

Odek, W.O., J. Busza, C.N. Morris, J. Cleland, E.N. Ngugi, and A.G. Ferguson 2009. "Effects of micro-enterprise services on HIV risk behaviour among female sex workers in Kenya's urban slums." *AIDS and Behavior* 13(3): 449.

Ohonba, A., and K. Agbontaen-Eghafona 2019. "Transnational remittances from human trafficking and the changing socio-economic status of women in Benin City, Edo State Nigeria." *Women's Studies* 48(5): 531–549.

Opara, V.N. 2007. "Emerging issues in the trafficking of African women for prostitution." In: *The Human Cost of African Migrations*, edited by Afolabi and Falola, 165–220. New York: Routledge.

Open Society Foundations. n.d. *No Turning Back: Examining Sex Worker-Led Programs that Protect Health and Rights*. New York: Open Society Foundations.

Overall, C. 1992. "What's wrong with prostitution? Evaluating sex work." *Signs: Journal of Women in Culture and Society* 17(4): 705–724.

Overs, C. 2014. *Sex Workers, Empowerment and Poverty Alleviation in Ethiopia, IDS Evidence Report 80*. Brighton: IDS.

Pankhurst, R. 1974. "The history of prostitution in Ethiopia." *Journal of Ethiopian Studies* 12(2): 159–178.

Pickering, H., J. Todd, D. Dunn, J. Pepin, and A. Wilkins 1992. "Prostitutes and their clients: A Gambian survey." *Social Science and Medicine* 34(1): 75–88.

Pitpitan, E.V., S.C. Kalichman, L.A. Eaton, S.A. Strathdee, and T.L. Patterson 2013. "HIV/ STI risk among venue-based female sex workers across the globe: A look back and the way forward." *Current HIV/AIDS Reports* 10(1): 65–78.

Plambech, S. 2017. "Sex, deportation and rescue: Economies of migration among Nigerian sex workers." *Feminist Economics* 23(3): 134–159.

Popoola, B.I. 2013. "Occupational hazards and coping strategies of sex workers in southwestern Nigeria." *Health Care for Women International* 34(2): 139–149.

Raymond, J.G. 2004. "Ten reasons for not legalizing prostitution and a legal response to the demand for prostitution." *Journal of Trauma Practice* 2(3–4): 315–332.

Red Rain. n.d. "Executive summary." Accessed 6th January 2021. https://www.indiegogo.com/projects/exit-programme-for-hiv-and-aids-sex-workers#/

Richter, M. 2012. "Sex work as a test case for African feminism." *BUWA! A Journal on African Women's Experiences* 2(1): 62–69.

Richter, M., M. Chersich, M. Temmerman, and S. Luchters 2013. "Characteristics, sexual behaviour and risk factors of female, male and transgender sex workers in South Africa." *South African Medical Journal = Suid-Afrikaanse Tydskrif vir Geneeskunde* 103(4): 246–251.

Richter, M., and D. Massawe 2009. *A Report on the Consultation on HIV/AIDS, Sex Work and the 2010 Soccer World Cup—Human Rights, Public Health, Soccer and Beyond.* South African National AIDS Council and Sex Worker Education and Advocacy Taskforce.

——— 2010. "Did South Africa's soccer bonanza bring relief to sex workers in South Africa? The 2010 FIFA World Cup and the impact on sex work." *Agenda* 85: 21–30.

Rights not Rescue Trust Namibia. 2021. About us. Accessed 5th January 2021 from: https://rightsnotrescue.weebly.com/about.html

SAFE in Collingwood n.d. "Exiting SAFE in Collingwood sex work awareness for everyone: A demonstration project of living in community." http://safeincollingwood.ca/info-for-sex-workers/exiting/.

Sakyi, K. 2013. "Prostitution in Ghana—Causes, effects, remittances and solutions." Unpublished essay. Prostitution-in-Ghana-Kwesi-Sakyi.docx – Ghanaian Diaspora www.ghanaiandiaspora.com › uploads ›.

Sanders, T., and R. Campbell 2007. "Designing out vulnerability, building in respect: Violence, safety and sex work policy." *The British Journal of Sociology* 58(1): 1–19.

Schreiber, R. 2002. "Playing 'Femball': Conservative women's organizations and political representation in the United States." In: *Right-Wing Women: From Conservatives to Extremists Around the Globe,* edited by Bacchetta and Power, 211–224. New York: Routledge.

Scorgie, F., D. Nakato, E. Harper, M. Richter, S. Maseko, P. Nare, J. Smit, and M. Chersich 2013. "'We are despised in the hospitals': Sex workers' experiences of accessing health care in four African countries." *Culture, Health and Sexuality* 15(4): 450–465.

Scorgie, F., D. Nakato, D.O. Akoth, M. Netshivhambe, P. Chakuvinga, et al. 2011. *"I Expect to Be Abused and I Have Fear": Sex Workers' Experiences of Human Rights Violations and Barrers to Accessing Healthcare in Four African Countries.* Cape Town: African Sex Worker Alliance.

Shannon, K., and J.S. Montaner 2012. "The politics and policies of HIV prevention in sex work." *The Lancet Infectious Diseases* 12(7): 500–502.

Sigauke, S. 2014. "Zim women resorting to prostitution in South Africa." *Harare. Com,* January 6, 2014. Accessed 6th May 2019. https://iharare.com/zim-women-resorting-to-prostitution-in-south-africa/.

Smith, D. 2012. "Rwandans fear serial killer is at large after murder of 15 women." *The Guardian,* September 10, 2012. Accessed 17th May 2019. https://www.theguardian.com/world/2012/sep/10/rwanda-fears-serial-killer-women-murdered.

Teunis, N. 2001. "Same-sex sexuality in Africa: A case study from Senegal." *AIDS and Behavior* 5(2): 173–182.

Tjaronda, W. 2009. "Child law under revision, new era." Accessed 6th January 2021. http://www.lac.org.na/news/inthenews/archive/2009/news-20090420.html.

Udeh, P.C., U.K. Uduka, and S.C. Mbah 2019. "Socio-economic effect of commercial sex work in Abuja suburb: A survey of selected brothels in Mararaba, Nigeria." *Sociology and Criminology*: 200.

Unah, C. 2015. "Cameroon girls take over Calabar sex market." *Vanguard*, October 17. https://www.vanguardngr.com/2015/10/cameroon-girls-take-over-calabar-sex-market/.

USAID 2017. "From sex worker to community to leader in Western Rwanda: Training brings new options and livelihoods to women." Accessed 6th January 2021. https://2012-2017.usaid.gov/results-data/success-stories/sex-worker-community-leader-western-rwanda.

Van Heyningen, E.B. 1984. "The social evil in the Cape colony 1868–1902: Prostitution and the contagious diseases acts." *Journal of Southern African Studies* 10(2): 170–197.

Vanderhurst, S. 2017. "Governing with god: Religion, resistance, and the state in Nigeria's counter-trafficking programs." *PoLAR: Political and Legal Anthropology Review* 40(2): 194–209.

Vanguard Online 2017. "Men beg FCT minister to allow 789 prostitutes stay." Accessed 28th June 2019. https://www.vanguardngr.com/2017/06/men-beg-fct-minister-allow-789-prostitutes-stay/.

Vanwesenbeeck, I. 2017. "Sex work criminalization is barking up the wrong tree." *Archives of Sexual Behavior* 46(6): 1631–1640.

Vanyoro, K. 2019. "'Skeptics' and 'believers': Anti-trafficking, sex work, and migrant rights activism in South Africa." *Gender and Development* 27(1): 123–137.

Verwimp, P. 2006. *Peasant Ideology and Genocide in Rwanda under Habyarimana*. New Haven, CT: Yale University Press.

Vuylsteke, B., P.D. Ghys, G. Mah-bi, Y. Konan, M. Traoré, S.Z. Wiktor, and M. Laga 2001. "Where do sex workers go for health care? A community-based study in Abidjan, Cote d'Ivoire." *Sexually Transmitted Infections* 77(5): 351–352.

Vuylsteke, B., and S. Jana 2011. "Reducing HIV risk in sex workers, their clients and partners." In: *HIV/AIDS Prevention and Care in Resource-Constrained Settings; A Handbook for the Design and Management of Programs*, edited by Lamptey and Gayle, 187–210. Arlington: Family Health International (FHI).

Wallis, E. 2019. "Tricked, trafficked and sold: How criminal gangs are bringing Nigerian women to Italy." *Info Migrants*. Accessed 10th June 2019. https://www.infomigrants.net/en/post/14725/tricked-trafficked-and-sold-how-criminal-gangs-are-bringing-nigerian-women-to-italy.

White, L. 1984. "A history of prostitution in Nairobi, Kenya, c. 1900–1952." PhD thesis. University of Cambridge, Cambridge.

——— 1986. "Prostitution, identity, and class consciousness in Nairobi during World War II." *Signs: Journal of Women in Culture and Society* 11(2): 255–273.

——— 2009. *The Comforts of Home: Prostitution in Colonial Nairobi*. Chicago, IL: University of Chicago Press.

WHO 2013. *Implementing Comprehensive HIV/STI Programmes with Sex Workers: Practical Approaches from Collaborative Interventions*. World Health Organization,

Geneva, Switzerland, 24. Accessed 12th September 2019. http://apps.who.int/iris/bitst ream/10665/90000/1/9789241506182_eng.pdf?ua=1.

Wojcicki, J.M. 2003. "The movement to decriminalize sex work in Gauteng Province, South Africa, 1994–2002." *African Studies Review* 46(3): 83–109.

Women's Legal Center n.d. "About the women's legal center." Accessed 10 July 2019. https://wlce.co.za/about-us/.

Women's Organization Network for Human Rights Advocacy (WONETHA) 2008. "Organizational profile." Accessed 2nd December 2019. https://wonethauganda.org/.

Sex work and prostitution third sector organizations in the Americas

Susan Dewey

Introduction

The Americas comprise 46 countries spanning the two hemispheres between the North and South Poles: 12 in South America, 7 in Central America, 25 independent Caribbean states, Canada, and the United States. From the arctic tundra of Canada's Nunavut Province to the ice-bound steppe of Patagonia in Argentina and Chile, every part of the Americas shares the painful "New World" legacy of conquest, genocide, and settler colonialism initiated by wealthy Europeans' pursuit of mineral wealth and cash crops such as sugar, cotton, tobacco, and coffee (Wolf, 2010). This legacy continues to shape everyday socioeconomic realities in the Americas, such as the fact that the region is home to just four primary languages – English, Spanish, Portuguese, and French – with most Indigenous languages not widely spoken as a result of the cultural genocide intrinsic to settler colonialism (Saito, 2010).

The contemporary sex industry is likewise a product of gendered and classed forms of oppression with origins in plantation agriculture, extractive industries, and colonialism more generally (Kempadoo, 2001). People in the sex industry, like their peers globally, face extreme forms of marginalization that, when combined with discrimination as a result of their gender, race, drug use, or health status, increases their likelihood of experiencing arrest, assault, and other forms of violence (World Health Organization, 2013). For instance, in the United States, police arrest Black women at higher rates than white women, with prostitution arrest rates even higher for Black transgender women (Ritchie, 2017). Transgender women in Latin America and the Caribbean are violently victimized at far higher rates than their cisgender peers, and both cisgender and transgender women continue to struggle with pervasive sexualization, a significant gender wage gap, and violence from intimate partners as well as the threat of stranger violence (Lanham et al., 2019).

Such interpersonal violence is compounded by structural inequalities that more readily enable North American activists to grip the bullhorn of advocacy than their peers in Latin America and the Caribbean. Nearly half of the 150 third sector organizations (TSOs) that our research identified as engaged with people in the

sex industry are located in the United States, reflecting that country's politico-economic dominance and cultural values that regard volunteerism as an essential ele-
ment of civil society. Our research also located sex work and prostitution TSOs in
Antigua and Barbuda, Argentina, Bolivia, Brazil, Canada, Chile, Colombia, Costa
Rica, Curaçao, Ecuador, El Salvador, Guatemala, Guyana, Jamaica, Mexico,
Nicaragua, Paraguay, Peru, Trinidad and Tobago, and Uruguay, and surely there
are others that exist and unfortunately were not identified in our research.

Four particularly unique aspects emerged in this analysis of sex work and
prostitution TSOs in the Americas: the scope of the neoliberal nonprofit industrial complex; cultural values of individualism, self-help, and self-actualization;
criminalization and militarization; and outlaw politics. This chapter uses these
unique aspects as a typological framework to interpret how regional cultures
and prevalent sociopolitical forces in the Americas variously structure, govern,
or exclude sex work and prostitution TSOs. Following a review of prostitution
legislation and the contexts in which sex work and prostitution TSOs operate in
the Americas, it discusses how funders manage activism through alignment with
professionally structured TSOs in conjunction with state devolution of essential
services for people facing social vulnerabilities to TSOs. It then uses the examples of peer-to-peer mutual support, microenterprise, and arts-based organizing
to illustrate how TSOs politically mobilize shared cultural values of individualism, self-help, and self-actualization. Next, it examines the ways that TSOs lobby
for legislative reform, provide legal and peer-to-peer support for those criminally
charged, and lead training for and/or cooperate with police. Finally, it explores
how outlaw politics, defined as political mobilization around a shared outsider
identity righteous in its opposition to dominant cultural norms, shape solidarity-
building and revolutionary tactics designed to achieve TSOs' respective visions
of freedom from oppression.

Prostitution legislation in the Americas

Sex work and prostitution TSOs in the Americas have followed a historical tra-
jectory in tandem with their peers in activism and research. As an introduction
to the typological framework used in this chapter to analyze TSOs' work, this
section provides a concise overview of the major debates and forces surrounding
sex work and prostitution in the Americas from the nineteenth century to the present. It explores the sex trade's nineteenth-century colonial roots, the emergence
of anti-prostitution activism in the late nineteenth and early twentieth-century
Progressive Era, and how the mid-to-late twentieth-century shift to neocolonialism impacted sexual labor practices in Latin America and the Caribbean. Next, it
examines how the burgeoning feminist movement catalyzed the sex worker rights
movement, followed by activist efforts to combat the HIV/AIDS pandemic, and
increased attention, in the 1980s and 1990s, to LGBTQ+ communities in response
to such activism. Finally, it concludes with a brief discussion of the emergence
of trafficking as the central lens through which state agents and neo-abolitionist

activists began to see prostitution in ways that preoccupied much of the first decade of the twenty-first century.

As is the case globally, prostitution-related regulatory and enforcement measures vary both within and across the countries of the Americas. The United States, which leads the world in incarceration rates, also leads the region in terms of the number of arrests, prosecutions, and sentences issued to women who sell sex. Yet, as is the case with most US legislation, regulation and enforcement fall to the 50 states and the municipalities that comprise them, which is why it is illegal to buy and sell sex in Las Vegas but not in some of the rural neighboring counties in Nevada that have authorized brothel prostitution under highly regulated circumstances (Brents, Jackson, and Hausbeck, 2010). Mexico takes a regulatory stance similar to that of the United States in that municipalities and towns may regulate the sale and purchase of sex, with 13 states in Mexico regulating sex work through the existence of tolerance zones that require women to register for a work permit in order to sell sex legally (NWSP, 2019). Canada, which generally looks to Western Europe in matters of public health and policy, adopted the Nordic Model by criminalizing the purchase and third-party facilitation, but not the sale, of sex (Government of Canada, 2014).

In Central America, prostitution tends to be legal although laws remain in place that prohibit soliciting, loitering, and operating a business for the purposes of selling sex, as is the case in Belize (US Department of State, 2003). Prostitution is legal in Guatemala but, as in Mexico, requires sex workers to register with local authorities and undergo mandatory health checks (Schlechter, 2019). Honduras and Nicaragua both legally permit the sale of sex by women operating independently of a third party (Silva, 2015; RedTraSex, 2017). El Salvador neither criminalizes nor legally recognizes sex work, although laws prohibiting third-party regulation of prostitution remain in place (RedTraSex, 2018). Prostitution is legal in both Costa Rica and Panama, although laws prohibit third-party involvement in prostitution as well as the promotion of sex tourism (Kone, 2016; Institute of Development Studies, 2020).

Almost every Caribbean country criminalizes prostitution (Kempadoo, 2016), although such criminalization often takes the form of restrictions on the conditions necessary for prostitution to take place. So, while prostitution may be decriminalized in many Caribbean countries, those who sell sex may face arrest for loitering, working with other sex workers, and related offenses. For example, Antigua and Barbuda, the Bahamas, Barbados, Curaçao, Jamaica, and Trinidad and Tobago all criminalize living on earnings from prostitution, operating a brothel, and persistent solicitation (Institute of Development Studies, 2020). Prostitution is fully criminalized only in Dominica, while Curaçao permits prostitution only for women who are not citizens of Curaçao, who have received a time-limited permit to legally sell sex in the country, and who undergo weekly medical examinations (Institute of Development Studies, 2020). Additionally, colonial laws against sex between people of the same gender remain in place in the Caribbean countries of Antigua and Barbuda as well as Dominica (Institute of Development Studies, 2020).

In South America, Argentina decriminalizes the sale and purchase of sex, although third-party management, living off the avails of prostitution, and soliciting near a school, church, or residence are all illegal (Institute of Development Studies, 2020). Bolivia, Colombia, Ecuador, Peru, and Venezuela all permit the sale of sex by licensed sex workers employed in legal brothels, while in Brazil and Uruguay, sex work is federally recognized as an occupation, although state and municipal governments in both countries variously implement their own laws and policies with respect to prostitution (Institute of Development Studies, 2020). Brothel-keeping and third-party management of prostitution are illegal in Chile although the purchase of sex is not illegal, as is also the case in Guyana (Institute of Development Studies, 2020).

Sex work and prostitution TSOs in context

As described in Chapter 2, sex work and prostitution in the Americas first emerged in conjunction with, and as a response to, nineteenth-century colonialism and its associated hierarchies of race, class, and gender. Sociologist Kamala Kempadoo observes how the emergence of racialized social constructions of gender and sexuality throughout the Americas date to the colonial encounter, with European colonists constructing Caribbean sexuality as "not normal, but excessive, at times pathological and at others unruly" (Kempadoo, 2004: 7). She argues that since the advent of colonialism, economically disadvantaged Caribbean women have historically endeavored to access their limited menu of opportunities in ways that problematize binary distinctions between agency and coercion and which sometimes include the exchange of sex for money (Kempadoo, 2004).

As settler colonialism expanded throughout the Americas, larger numbers of women began to migrate from Europe in search of a better life. Yet, unlike their male counterparts, who easily found resource extraction or agricultural work, women's opportunities were largely restricted to the same low status, exhausting jobs of laundering and childcare available to poor and working-class women in Europe (Goldman, 1987). A majority of sex workers in the American West were migrant women, and in regions dominated by mining and other extractive industries, such as the silver-ore-rich Comstock Lode of nineteenth-century northwestern Nevada, prostitution was "the single largest occupational category for women" (Goldman, 1981: 159). Women sold sex in brothels located in mining camps, small towns, and cities in the Western American states of Arizona, Idaho, Montana, New Mexico, Utah, and Wyoming from the nineteenth through the early twentieth century, often doing so as a means of escaping fraught families, poverty, and the otherwise extremely constrained economic opportunities available to women (MacKell, 2009).

Yet, even in these frontier societies far from European centers of power, nineteenth-century debates about prostitution hinged on contradictory popular depictions of women who sold sex as both subjects in need of regulation and active agents who were a critical part of frontier life. As historian Anne Butler notes, "the experiences of frontier prostitutes with a fledgling legal structure indicated that the rise of powerful institutions in part hinged upon the ability of society to build upon the rights and lives of the politically weak" (Butler, 1987). Similarly, historian Jeffrey Nichols' study of struggles over sexual morality in the nineteenth-century frontier state of Utah examines debates over prostitution and polygynous marriage practices among some Mormon communities. Nichols argues that public debates over these two varieties of sexual behaviors were part of a battle for political dominance between Mormons and non-Mormons, which took place as a result of broader cultural anxieties surrounding changing gender roles, religious and moral codes, and relationships between individuals and the state (Nichols, 2008).

Due to the lack of established state apparatuses in the so-called New World that was under construction by early- to mid-nineteenth-century settler colonialists, TSOs did not emerge in the Americas until the advent of the Progressive Era in the late nineteenth century. Popular and political attention to the sex industry has tended to coincide with rapid social changes to urbanization, migration, and/or gender roles in the Americas. Historian Robert Allen analyzes this phenomenon in his study of burlesque, which first emerged as a North American performance style in the 1890s and experienced continued popularity until the end of World War II. This time period is particularly significant in the North American context because it corresponds to the postindustrial emergence of leisure time and an increase in the number of young unmarried women migrating to cities. Allen contends that burlesque emerged when the question "what does it mean to be a woman?" was "constantly being asked in a wide range of forums" (Allen, 1991: 27). Yet despite its popularity, burlesque depended on the denigration of its performers because "the burlesque performer gave up any claim to consideration as a 'respectable' bourgeois woman. She became the low female whom the bourgeois male could safely gaze upon without immediately seeing his wife or her sister in her place" (Allen, 1991: 151).

Progressive Era debates about prostitution, as well as TSO responses to it, largely regarded the sex trade as "a moral problem that symbolized the shaky state of the nation's soul" (Rosen, 1983: 210). Many North American Progressive Era reform efforts among TSOs drew their theoretical force from a moral panic regarding what was then characterized as "white slavery", which sparked a social movement that ostensibly concerned itself with protecting white women from sexual exploitation by racialized migrant men (Donovan, 2006; Valverde, 2008). The result, predictably, included increased surveillance over young women's sexuality alongside xenophobic policing practices (Odem, 1995) at a time when emerging courtship practices and gendered differences in earning power sparked popular cultural concerns about changes to gender norms among young people. As historian Elizabeth Clement notes, "while working-class parents might tolerate sexual intercourse in courtship, they could not imagine it without the long shadow cast by the specter of prostitution" (Clement, 2006: 14). Historian Cathy Peiss likewise observes that, due to gendered economic inequalities that shaped young urban working women's lives, "a thin line divided these women from 'occasional prostitutes' who slipped in and out of prostitution when unemployed or in need of extra income" (Peiss, 1986: 110).

Moral panics about "white slavery" extended across the late nineteenth- and early twentieth-century Americas, as did TSO efforts to address prostitution and trafficking as social issues of concern on a broader scale. Historian Donna Guy's work on Buenos Aires demonstrates how feminized migration from Western Europe to Argentina resulted in widespread concerns in both the Americas and Europe that young women migrants might be forced into prostitution, which resulted in parallel developments among TSOs in both Europe and the Americas that sought to eradicate prostitution. Guy contends that Argentinean and European responses to such public anxieties reflect a strong public desire to regulate and restrain women's sexuality, particularly in migrant communities that faced considerable xenophobia (Guy, 1991).

Such anxieties were also evidenced in early twentieth-century Mexico City during a time of revolution and rapid urbanization during which historian Katherine Bliss observed "a predictable yet intriguing revolutionary politicization of leisure, family, and sexual behavior" (Bliss, 2002: 13). Mexico City leaders, including TSOs concerned with prostitution, relied on discourses of public health and morality that ultimately held women responsible for men's sexual behavior in ways that made prostitution "a necessary evil ... in preventing sexually adventuresome men from creating greater threats to the social order by engaging in such activities as rape" (Bliss, 2002: 29).

Class stratification continued to shape the sex industry throughout the mid-twentieth century in ways that impacted both women and men, although TSO energies remained focused on the former rather than the latter. In her study of the sex industry that arose in conjunction with the mid-twentieth-century Canadian port city of Vancouver's timber export industry, sociologist Becki Ross analyzes how first- and second-generation male migrants came to dominate the ownership and management of adult businesses. These migrant men, as relatively new arrivals to Canada, faced exclusion from membership in economic networks among "the port city's well-established Anglo-elite" who had arrived in Canada as part of earlier waves of settler colonialism (Ross, 2009: 29).

The concentration of the marginalized in the sex industry has historically spanned the Americas, although sex work and prostitution TSOs did not emerge in the Caribbean or Central and South America until well into the 1980s. This late emergence relative to the United States and Canada is itself reflective of the colonialism and subsequent neocolonialism that shaped this region. Independence from colonialism varied for islands of the Caribbean, with Haiti successfully overthrowing French rule in 1804, Cuba obtaining independence from Spain in 1902, and the majority of British colonies becoming independent in the 1960s and 1970s. Yet political independence did not automatically translate to economic independence in former colonies whose only infrastructure revolved around the production of sugar and coffee. "King Sugar" was quickly replaced by "King

Tourism" on many Caribbean islands, prompting anthropologist Mark Padilla "to consider the deep historical parallels between colonial structures and the shape of contemporary sexuality, as well as the influences of more recent formations, such as the growth of the global tourism industry, on expressions of sexuality and sexual-economic exchange" (Padilla, 2007: 3). Padilla observes how the paid sexual exchanges between Black men in the Dominican Republic and the predominantly white North American and Western European men who pay them for sex are redolent with the neocolonial weight of historical forms of exploitation that took place under colonialism.

Ethnic studies scholar Amalia Cabezas' study of Cuba and the Dominican Republic further complicates the relationship between neocolonialism, tourism, and sex work by examining "the ways in which third-world women negotiate new economies and navigate the contact zones between first and third world by using tactical sex with foreign visitors" (Cabezas, 2009: 4). Noting that "it is often difficult to distinguish those who participate in the sex economy from those who do not", Cabezas explores the global economic realities that make it possible for some Cuban and Dominican women to achieve social mobility through relationships with North American and Western European tourists (Cabezas, 2009: 10). Defining tactical sex "as part of a complex circulation of sex and affect to cultivate social relations with foreigners" (Cabezas, 2009: 120), Cabezas documents how such interactions can also allow individuals to participate in international systems of exchange, albeit rarely on terms that they are able to define for themselves. Such inequalities are likewise apparent in what anthropologist Denise Brennan terms "the opportunity myth", whereby Caribbean women become sex workers with the hope of attaining upward mobility but end up living in increased poverty after leaving the sex industry (Brennan, 2004). As was the case with colonial resource extraction, neocolonial tourism industries very much set the terms of the exchange in favor of the privileged.

In North America, sex work and prostitution TSOs began their efflorescence in the 1970s in tandem with numerous other rights-based movements that centered on identity. Sex worker and activist Carol Leigh coined the term "sex work" in response to a late-1970s political environment that universally labeled all sex industry forms anti-feminist (Leigh, 2010). She did so in the context of a burgeoning US sex worker rights movement founded in the early 1970s as part of an organization called Whores, Housewives, and Others, which later transformed into COYOTE, an acronym for Call Off Your Old Tired Ethics (Pheterson, 1989). Sex workers' political and labor organizing arose in response to their sense of isolation from the burgeoning feminist movement and, for some, the wide-ranging harms generated by criminalization. Simultaneously, sex workers in legal venues such as strip clubs faced increased pressure from owners, management, and clients to engage in higher degrees of physical contact for less money. This development arose in conjunction with "the production and promotion of ever-more graphic depictions of female sexuality in North America" (Ross, 2009: 178–179).

Sex worker rights TSOs sought to address these injustices confronting sex workers both in society and through exploitative workplace practices.

Sex work and prostitution TSOs throughout the Americas further expanded in the 1980s and 1990s in response to the HIV/AIDS pandemic and alongside a vast body of literature that emerged from studies of HIV/AIDS and included a more inclusive focus on men and transgender people who sell sex. This efflorescence was due to both the seriousness of the virus and the increased funding available to address it, resulting in both the growth of sex work and prostitution TSOs and academic research that primarily utilized quantitative methods to explore connections between illicit drug use and street-based sex trading due to the increased likelihood of HIV transmission among those engaged in such activities. These studies tended to frame both prostitution and illicit drug use as "risk factors" in ways that did not account for the diversity of individual motivations for engaging in these behaviors, nor did they always capture the nuances of how individuals contend with the structural inequalities that inform their everyday decision-making.

Yet studies also emerged during this time period that sought to fill these gaps through immersive qualitative methods designed to understand individuals' lived experiences of the sex industry on their own terms, just as sex worker rights and allied harm reduction TSOs sought to do. For example, social worker Michel Dorais, in his study of young male sex trade workers in Montreal, documented these young men's wide range of life experiences, with some regarding the sale of sex as a form of liberation from the constraints of life in a heteronormative society (Dorais, 2005). While this focus on men and transgender people who sell sex may have emerged from the activist organizing and related research that stemmed from the HIV/AIDS pandemic, by the 1990s it had made significant inroads into influencing the otherwise intractable debates surrounding heterosexual people's sale and purchase of sex by heightening attention to questions of how agency and constraint operate among marginalized people whose lives are shaped by structural inequalities and identity-based forms of oppression.

Activists and researchers alike accordingly began to document how the sale of sex can simultaneously be the product of marginalization and an impetus for community-building. For example, sociologist Annick Prieur's ethnographic work in a Mexico City house demonstrated how an AIDS educator created a shared space for poor and working-class gay men and transgender women who sell sex and are "poorly integrated into working life" to be themselves in a society with rigid gender norms (Prieur, 1998: 42). Criminologist Leon Pettiway likewise foregrounded the experiences of transgender women of color who sell sex through first-person narratives, thereby contesting the dominant cultural pathologization of street sex workers as completely lacking in agency (Pettiway, 1996).

Simultaneously, second-wave feminists and religious conservatives aligned in their opposition to the sex industry by promoting normative discourses on sexuality that, while unique to each group, regarded the sale of sex as fundamentally harmful to society. For second-wave feminists, women in prostitution were victims of false consciousness, whereas religious conservatives regarded prostitution as antithetical to the heterosexual nuclear family (Bell, Sloan, and Strickling, 1998). The neo-abolitionist TSOs that arose in response to such views of prostitution supported the emergence of neoliberal economic and urban policing strategies that displaced sex workers from outdoor public spaces where they formerly sold sex. As sociologist Deborah Brock notes, the confluence of these new developments in Canada resulted in "a battle of 'deviance' and social control, [in which] there have been no winners", and which scapegoated sex workers as vectors of disease, threats to public morality, and public enemies who lowered property values in neighborhoods where they congregated (Brock, 1998: 147). Brock further argues that debates about prostitution constituted a national backlash to movements for social and sexual liberation that emerged in the 1970s (Brock, 1998).

Sex wars-inspired debates about agency versus constraint combined with the public health focus on sexually transmitted infections, particularly HIV, continued to inform research throughout the first decade of the twenty-first century. Anthropologist Yasmina Katsulis, for instance, documents the complex terrain negotiated by sex workers in Tijuana, a Mexican border city where sex work is legal for those who obtain licenses from and register with local government officials but illegal for those who do not. Katsulis argues that legal regulation of sex work does not sufficiently reduce sex workers' risk of violent victimization or contracting infection (Katsulis, 2009).

The passage of the 2000 Victims of Trafficking and Violence Prevention Act (TVPA), itself a product of much lobbying and debates among TSOs and researchers throughout the 1990s, sparked a flurry of activist and research work that largely reflected polarized positions between those who regarded sex work as labor and those who envisioned prostitution as a form of violence against women. In many ways, this work continues today in the form of critiques of anti-trafficking law and policy as little more than xenophobic bolstering of morality-based policing based on the selective mobilization of evidence. Such work encourages activists and academics to consider the ways in which much of what is called trafficking is a response to deeply rooted structural inequalities, including the need to migrate in order to find work that pays a living wage. As the following sections' engagement with the fourfold analytical framework undergirding this chapter will demonstrate, a fraught set of structural, sociolegal, and economic dynamics inform the work that TSOs carry out on a daily basis.

The far-reaching scope of the neoliberal nonprofit industrial complex

Neoliberalism's efforts to privatize and otherwise prohibit the redistribution of wealth for the benefit of society have created what is referred to as the nonprofit industrial complex, a set of practices by which the state or other powerful interests utilize TSOs to manage and control activism through funding mechanisms that endorse particular ideologies or ways of promoting social change (Rodriguez,

2007). This section accordingly discusses how the far-reaching scope of the neo-liberal nonprofit industrial complex results in funders' disproportionate support of TSOs with professional, credentialed staff who work in offices and may accordingly be out of touch with the realities and lived experiences of those in the sex industry. As this section will illustrate, funders' disproportionate support for professionalized TSOs that focus on specific issues, such as sexual exploitation or HIV/AIDS, has restricted many TSOs to providing essential services, such as transitional housing and substance use disorder treatment, that fill gaps left by neoliberal states' retreat or absence. Nonetheless, sex worker-led TSOs have been successful in building cross-professional alliances that address a wider range of issues.

A majority of funders take a neo-abolitionist stance that regards prostitution and trafficking as synonymous and prioritizes conservative criminal justice approaches that rely on rescue, arrest, and prosecution to eradicate an inherently violent and abusive sex industry (Bernstein, 2012). Extraordinary ideological alignment exists between neo-abolitionist and US government approaches that have been globally exported since the passage of the 2000 Victims of Trafficking and Violence Prevention Act, which authorizes significant financial resources for TSOs that oppose prostitution and threatens sanctions to countries that do not comply (Dewey, 2008). Recipients of such US federal funding include Shared Hope International, a US-based TSO founded by US Congressperson Linda Smith after she visited Mumbai's red-light district, where she had a transformative religious experience described in her book, *From Congress to the Brothel: A Journey of Hope, Healing, and Restoration*:

> A 13-year-old girl crouched in a dark corner on the dusty floor, her hair dirty and tangled, her eyes hollow and lifeless. Raw sewage flowed through an uncovered ditch on the other side of the thin brothel wall. The scent of a hundred men clung to her small frame. Her expression revealed total desperation. This was not a look that said, "Please help me". This was a look that said, "I am doomed forever, beyond help, beyond hope". It was as if God Himself whispered in my ear, "Touch her for Me".... Would the filth make me vomit? Would I contract a deadly disease just by breathing the air? ... At my soft touch, the desperate little girl fell into my arms with gratitude. The simple gesture overwhelmed her because she was so utterly unloved in the world.
>
> (Smith, 2015: 1)

Ideological alignment between the Evangelical Christian standpoint Smith exemplifies and the official US government stance is such that, from 2003 through 2013, US government funding agencies prohibited grant recipients from collaborating with sex worker rights TSOs until the US Supreme Court ruled this practice a violation of Constitutional free speech protections (Ditmore and Allman, 2013). These prohibitions proved unacceptable for some, as in the 2005 case of Brazilian President Luiz Inacio Lula da Silva's rejection of 48 million dollars in

US aid on the grounds that, as noted by Brazil's former public health coordinator, "you can't control AIDS based on principles that are Manichean, theological, radical, and fundamentalist" (Amar, 2009: 534). Such rejections, however, are the exception rather than the rule given that many funders require ideological alignment at the proposal stage, which automatically excludes most sex worker rights TSOs. Brazil, like many countries in the Americas, has a vibrant movement of neo-abolitionist "moral entrepreneurs" whose research depicts sex trafficking as a dire problem to which funding should be immediately directed (Blanchette and da Silva, 2012). Such moral entrepreneurs gained political momentum following a rightward shift after the 2019 election of President Jair Bolsonaro.

Globally, sex worker rights TSOs are marginalized and face difficulties cultivating support from a general public that regards their cause as morally suspect, making funding almost exclusively available through international HIV/AIDS prevention and related initiatives in ways that do not necessarily reflect what TSOs regard as their main concerns. Exceptions, however, do exist. The St. James Infirmary, the only medical clinic in the world that exclusively serves people who sell sex, is made possible through a partnership between the San Francisco Department of Public Health and sex worker rights organizations (Lutnick, 2006). Davida, one of the most well-respected sex worker rights groups in Brazil, received pre-Bolsonaro government funding to produce and distribute a magazine and an online version of the same to sex worker rights TSOs in all 18 Brazilian states (Fundo Brasil, undated). Yet sex worker rights TSOs generally suffer from a totality of problems summarized in a post from the Trinidad and Tobago TSO RED Initiatives:

[Our major problems include] structural discrimination in funding as there is stigma directed towards sex workers and sex worker programming ... locally as sex work is considered illegal, immoral, and illicit. Sex workers are stratified and very little networking is done formally – there is no solidarity and certain groups create networks but it is not done in the interest of sex workers it is only used for political and financial gain by the organization.

(NWSP, 2019, RED Initiatives)

This bleak assessment concisely captures the problems TSOs confront as they navigate the nonprofit industrial complex in the course of their everyday operations and attempt to strategically plan for the future.

Part of the disillusionment among Latin American and Caribbean TSOs stems from the need to master multiple discourses related to migration, xenophobia, and dependency on donor aid from foundations based in the Global North. For example, the Dominican Republic's Women United Movement (MODEMU) was unable to establish a branch of their TSO to assist Dominican migrant women selling sex in the US territory of Puerto Rico because the state and dominant culture classified such women as racialized "illegal aliens" who voluntarily sold sex; had MODEMU described the women as victims of trafficking in need of state-endorsed support, the TSO may have been more successful in its efforts (Cabezas and Campos, 2016). Indeed, few TSOs exist for migrants who sell sex across the Americas, with some notable exceptions, such as the legal, health, safety, and English as a Second Language (ESL) information provided by the Canadian TSOs SWAN Vancouver, Butterfly (Toronto), and the Migrant Sex Workers Project (Toronto) (Timoshkina and McDonald, 2009), and peer-to-peer support provided in Nicaragua by Las Golondrinas [The Swallows], and in Mexico by the Sex Workers Movement of Mexico and the Chihuahua Transwomen Union.

In the wake of the neoliberal state's retreat or absence, some sex work and prostitution TSOs fill gaps with respect to the provision of services for people facing social vulnerabilities such as homelessness, substance use disorder, and poverty more generally. Homelessness is a primary concern for Lxs Callejerx [People of the Street] (Bogotá, Colombia), Projet Libres, Unies, Nuancées, Ensemble/Free, United, Nuanced, Together Project (LUNE, Quebec City), Stroll (Portland, Oregon), and Aspire Home (New York City). Many TSOs that serve street-based populations use a harm reduction approach to substance use and homelessness, such as Helping Individual Prostitutes Survive (HIPS) in Washington, D.C. In addition to a drop-in center with showers, laundry, and meals, HIPS offers syringe access and disposal, safer sex materials, HIV and Hepatitis testing and treatment, case management, medication-assisted drug treatment, a crisis line, PrEP access, overdose education, peer support, and assistance finding housing (HIPS, 2019). These TSOs emphasize the mutual respect and social justice approach fostered by harm reduction, as noted by the Newfoundland, Canada-based TSO Safe Harbor Outreach Project (SHOP), which provides safer sex and drug use supplies, street outreach, referrals, a "bad date" line to report violent sex buyers, and a "Words Count" public awareness campaign to challenge stereotypes and stigma as part of its belief "in the value of sex workers and their self-determination, the power of harm reduction, and the pursuit of social justice" (SHOP, 2019).

Neo-abolitionist TSOs also provide essential services in the form of transitional housing to women leaving the sex industry. Some of the most prominent TSOs in this area, such as Hookers for Jesus' Destiny House in Las Vegas, were founded and are led by women who previously sold sex. These TSOs regard Christianity as essential for women to heal from the traumas of prostitution, as do their Christian TSO peers who also provide transitional housing.[1] Some secular TSOs providing transitional housing are led by women who self-identify as having been harmed by their sex industry experiences, such as Girls Educational and Mentoring Services (GEMS, New York City), and Breaking Free (St. Paul, Minnesota). GEMS, which serves girls and young women aged 16–24, hires survivors of prostitution and trafficking to assist their clients (known as "members") with obtaining education, housing, and alternatives to incarceration through the family court system (GEMS, 2019). Breaking Free provides permanent housing at its 54-unit apartment complex and a recovery support group in which participants discuss prostitution as slavery and its connections to trauma and addictions, alongside a separate "Men Breaking Free" support group to educate men about the harms of purchasing sex (Breaking Free, 2019).

The relative lack of funding available to sex worker rights TSOs with a mission to promote widespread sociolegal reform has prompted the emergence of sex worker-led consortiums and networks to exert influence on international organizations as well as state and local governments. Yet language barriers between the predominantly English-speaking countries of North America and the Caribbean and the primarily Spanish- and Portuguese-speaking countries of Latin America nonetheless pose challenges to regional collaborations. Many websites, promotional materials, conferences, and publications remain inaccessible to monolingual English, Spanish, or Portuguese speakers if they are unavailable in a language they can understand. Regional networks accordingly tend to comprise either English-speaking North America, such as SWOP, or Spanish-speaking Latin America, such as RedTraSex and PLAPERTS, with Portuguese-speaking Brazil home to its own country-specific networks.

Two Latin American examples of such consortiums are the Network of Latin American and Caribbean Sex Workers (RedTraSex) and the Latin American Platform for People in Sex Work (PLAPERTS). Both fulfill essential functions as regional networks advocating for sex worker rights across Latin America, decriminalization, the right to be free from violence and stigma, and the freedom to migrate. RedTraSex emerged from a mid-1990s regional conference for sex workers hosted in Costa Rica and currently includes TSOs from almost all Latin American and some Caribbean countries (RedTraSex, 2019a). RedTraSex includes sex workers in political decision-making at the national, regional, and international levels by partnering with the UNAIDS Consultative Group on HIV and Sex Work, the Women's Meeting of Regional Networks in Latin America and the Caribbean, and hosting meetings with HIV/AIDS program leaders throughout the region (RedTraSex, 2019b). RedTraSex also issues a bimonthly newsletter, published a book, *A High Heels Movement* (RedTraSex, 2007), and conducted a Global Fund-sponsored study that created a regional strategy to reduce HIV/AIDS vulnerability among women who sell sex (RedTraSex, 2019b).

The Ecuador-based TSO PLAPERTS was created in 2014 as part of the Sex Worker Networks Consortium project sponsored by the Robert Carr Fund, which also supported the creation of regional networks in Asia, Africa, the Caribbean, and Central/Eastern Europe and Central Asia as part of the Global Network of Sex Work Projects (Robert Carr Fund, 2019). PLAPERTS also includes TSOs working in Peru, Brazil, Mexico, and El Salvador, and is almost entirely sex worker-led; it aims to "confront a political and social context that still stigmatizes, discriminates and criminalizes people who perform sex work, and a legal framework that focuses on control and regulation" (PLAPERTS, 2019).

The neoliberal nonprofit industrial complex's far-reaching scope has also prompted sex worker-led TSOs to build alliances, as is the case in the Sex Workers Outreach Project (SWOP) Chicago's collaborations with social services agencies in creating a TSO network that provides services to sex workers, partners with a legal clinic, provides training to social services professionals, and leads peer-based social services (Anasti, 2017). TSOs led jointly by people with sex industry experience and credentialed professionals such as social workers, health care providers, and lawyers ideally feature a combination of perspectives and qualifications that allow them to provide services that focus on sex workers' human rights. These services can include counseling, outreach, harm reduction, peer education, criminal record expungement or court support, health testing, and assistance with basic needs for sex workers struggling with addictions and poverty.

Some of these TSOs also provide political education from a human rights, anti-oppression, feminist, and anti-racist perspective that addresses intersectional harms targeting sex workers. Canadian TSOs have been particularly successful in creating board and other decision-making committees that include people with sex industry experience and credentialed professionals who support sex worker rights, who are often referred to as "allies". FIRST in Vancouver, Maggie's: The Toronto Sex Workers Action Project, Butterfly: Asian and Migrant Sex Workers Network (Toronto), Migrant Sex Workers Project (Toronto), and Stepping Stone (Halifax, Nova Scotia), all take this approach. In Latin America, the TSO Guiding Star (Florianopolis, Brazil) takes a jointly led approach with the goal of mobilizing community members in support for sex worker rights, such as by designing interactive workshops for healthcare workers to reduce disparities for those who sell sex (Fundo Posithivo, 2018).

Individualism, self-help, and self-actualization

From the importance of confession and *testimonio* in the predominantly Catholic countries of Latin America and the Caribbean to the self-help movement that pervades North America, the notion that liberation can accompany verbalization of one's innermost state prevails in the region. Self-help culture, and the associated power of positive thinking, holds that individuals can exercise significant control in their lives through perspectival shifts as part of the belief that a person's actions and sense of the world around them reflect their attitudes and thought processes rather than the world as they actually experience it. This section accordingly analyzes how TSOs across the ideological spectrum politically mobilize shared cultural values of individualism, self-help, and self-actualization as interpretive tools that help to justify the value and importance of their work. It also examines how these three shared cultural values manifest in examples of how TSOs implement peer-to-peer mutual support, microenterprise, and arts-based organizing.

The cultural value of individualism is readily apparent in how many TSOs mobilize around constituencies with a shared set of characteristics, experiences, or social vulnerabilities. These typically include, among others, experience working in a certain type of sex industry venue, residence in a particular neighborhood or region, a desire to leave prostitution, identification with a specific sexual or gender identity, or migrant status. Many TSOs' mission statements or other promotional materials note that the organization engages with people across a range of sex industry experiences but specializes in serving people in a particular venue or neighborhood due to the significant socioeconomic differences that often exist between people who sell sex. For example, some TSOs work exclusively with indoor sex workers, as does the Autonomous Women's Association of 22 June in Ecuador (Abad et al., 1998), while others work with people who sell sex on the street or in particular neighborhoods, such as AMMAR in Argentina (Hardy and Cruz, 2019). These site-specific forms of engagement may emerge from founders' and/or leaders' familiarity with a particular venue or neighborhood or from a TSO's belief that particular sites face specific challenges.

Pragmatic reasons also inform these choices, as all TSOs must clearly define – and hence limit – the types of constituents they serve in order to remain focused and convincingly advocate for those they hope to assist. TSOs, despite their altruistic motivations and practices, have to carefully consider how their peer TSOs provide services and target constituencies to avoid duplicating services and remain well-positioned for grant funds in what is ultimately a highly crowded, competitive field. Regional and national consortiums can likewise be difficult to maintain due to the inherent difficulties of limited funding, alongside geographic distance and the associated inability to meet in person on a regular basis, making TSOs that operate at the local level operations somewhat easier to sustain. Such localization does not, however, mean that TSOs do not have a significant impact. One example is the Coalition of Experiential Communities in Vancouver, which unites sex workers across the Canadian province of British Columbia to offer peer-driven rights-based organizing for legislative and policy change (BC Coalition of Experiential Communities, 2007). The Coalition has created province-specific community research guidelines, tips for individuals participating in community-based research, and reports on the Coalition's own research studies on how to reduce violence against sex workers (BC Coalition of Experiential Communities, 2019).

The operationalization of the cultural values of individualism, self-help, and self-actualization across the ideological spectrum is also notable in the examples of how TSOs depict trauma and the role of outreach in their work. With remarkable frequency that transcends ideological differences, TSOs across the Americas describe themselves by using terms such as trauma-informed, survivor-led, and strengths-based alongside the "meeting people where they are at" language of harm reduction. These concepts are almost always operationalized in practice through the lens of highly individualized self-help culture that regards individuals as the central units of society and places a high value on the perceived locus of control thought to exist within each individual, albeit in ways that can recast structural inequalities as medicalized individual problems that require psychological treatment (Conrad, 2007).

Neo-abolitionists regard prostitution as inducing traumatic psychological harms that require individual women survivors to recognize and overcome their victimization through expert assistance. As a Costa Rican Christian TSO leader explains of her program housing women leaving prostitution: "here they start to see themselves as victims. They are not the bad ones, and that's a very different focus. When they see themselves as victims, then they feel the love of God in their lives" (Rivers-Moore, 2018). Secular TSOs that provide services to women who sell sex likewise utilize individual trauma as an explanatory framework to understand and interpret their clients' lives; as a US counselor stated, prostitution is a byproduct of "some level of coercion, or experience of trauma, or something that makes them vulnerable to that" (Anasti, 2018: 465).

Now consider the ways in which two otherwise ideologically polarized TSOs describe outreach, with the first example from the Christian neo-abolitionist US TSO Created Women and the second from the Ecuador sex worker rights TSO Milagro Sexual Diversity Association (DISEMI):

> We go into the strip clubs, on the streets, and in the jails with the goal of befriending vulnerable women and sharing God's love for them. ... The goal of outreach is to love women where they're at ... our approach is unconditional love. We go into the dark places with gifts for the women, in hopes that we can redeem their past, broken experiences with The Church.
>
> (Created Women, 2019)

> We facilitate training and workshops on empowerment and leadership. We self-finance workshops to empower new leaders to make sure to consistently train brave and courageous people to act as spokespersons so they can stop the violation of our rights. These spokespersons help us to be more visible and, at the same time, to disseminate accurate evidence that reduces stigma and informs society in general. We also conduct workshops to promote dialogue on HIV/AIDS, safe sex, and human rights.
>
> (DISEMI, 2018)

Outreach has completely different connotations for these two TSOs, with the first regarding sex industry workers as "vulnerable women" and the second envisioning them as "new leaders". For Created Woman, outreach involves distributing bags of beauty products to women as part of their goal to "love women where they're at", which closely resembles harm reduction's mandate to "meet people where they are at" as a means to provide nonjudgmental services (Harm Reduction Coalition, 2015). Yet for DISEMI, outreach must actively involve sex workers as leaders following the sex worker rights maxim of "nothing about us without us", which mandates sex workers' leadership as peer educators who offer harm reduction-centered health, safety, and other advice based on their lived experiences (St. James Infirmary, 2010).

The goal of peer-to-peer mutual support is generally to help individuals self-actualize through identification with a shared set of experiences as a form of mutual support that regards individual lived experience as the most valuable form of knowledge. Peer-based TSOs regard people in the sex industry as authorities on their own lives and accordingly in the best position to share knowledge derived from experience. Peer education and support is a cornerstone of ensuring that people with sex industry experience have a meaningful role in designing and providing services, interventions, and nonjudgmental treatment in a supportive atmosphere. Peer education and support is a common component of TSOs with a rights-based and/or harm reduction approach to sex for sale.[2] For example, the Antiguan Resilience Collective, which works primarily with migrant sex workers in English-speaking Antigua and Barbuda, trains Spanish-speaking sex workers to counsel and support their peers on sexually transmitted infections, safer sex, and violence, with the goal of creating a network of sex worker advocates well-informed on human rights issues (Caribbean Vulnerable Communities, 2019). Similarly, the San Francisco-based Standing Against Global Exploitation (SAGE) Project is led by survivors of prostitution who provide peer-based support with job training and placement, and therapeutic treatment (Hotaling et al., 2004).

Many sex worker-led TSOs engage in peer-based organizing to support individuals who work in specific sex industry venues, which are often characterized by high levels of competition, stigma, and social isolation among those who sell sex. For example, the Women Prostitutes Association of Argentina (AMMAR) engages in "affective organizing" designed to create a collective consciousness among individual street sex workers through shared social events, caregiving, and other forms of positive community-building (Hardy and Cruz, 2019). The US national We Are Dancers supports exotic dancers by sharing information on rights and solidarity online in a practical question-and-answer format that addresses how to deal with labor violations, harassment, and police raids (We Are Dancers, 2018).

The perspective that individual lived experience is the most valuable form of knowledge exists among TSOs across the ideological spectrum. Among sex worker rights TSOs, this belief may prohibit those who are not sex workers from decision-making or involve non-sex workers solely in an advisory capacity to prioritize sex worker leadership. For example, the bylaws of the Canadian Prostitutes of Ottawa, Gatineau, Work, Educate and Resist Community Network (POWER) dictate that "the Board of Directors shall at all times be comprised of a majority of persons who identity as current or former sex workers" (POWER, 2019: 4). Among neo-abolitionists, individual lived experience is likewise important, as is evident in how Florida-based Beauty from Ashes Ministry founder Julie Shematz uses her personal experiences to encourage other women to leave the sex industry:

> I have walked and worked in your shoes ... trapped and enduring each week to make ends meet. ... I know what it is like to have to get as high as you can to go to work ... customers that make you feel like you are nothing but a piece of meat and less than human. My friend, there is only one way out of this captivity, and it is through the power of the God of the universe and His son, Jesus Christ. He loves you with a love that you desire and long for that no one and nothing else has or can fill you with. He wants you to be free from this destructive lifestyle.
>
> (Shematz, 2019)

Many neo-abolitionists also regard microenterprise as a valuable pathway out of prostitution by preparing women for work in the service sector. Originally developed for women leaving the sex industry in Nashville, Tennessee by the now international TSO Thistle Farms, microenterprise sex work and prostitution TSOs typically focus on making bath and home products to sell to women and self-identify as Christian although exceptions, such as Eden House (New Orleans) do exist. Examples of Christian social enterprise TSOs that feature microenterprise include Bravely (St. Louis, Missouri), Magdalene House (Charleston, South Carolina), and Fields of Hope (Dayton, Ohio). Wellspring Living's locations in New York City and Atlanta train residents in customer service through work in the TSO's thrift stores and restaurants, and Not for Sale (San Francisco), which is part of a larger national network, does the same in restaurants but does not offer housing.

Microenterprise, long a staple of aid projects throughout the world, has been implemented by national and international TSOs as part of the belief that individual women can empower themselves to leave prostitution if provided with the right resources. The Ti Kredit [Small Credit] microfinance program managed by the National Association for the Protection of Haitian Women and Children (ANAPFEH) provides women with loans to pursue market trading and other small business opportunities that otherwise would be off-limits to them without a credit history or collateral to guarantee a loan (ANAPFEH et al., 2014). The US-based Shared Hope International offers a Women's Investment Network in India, Jamaica, Nepal, and the United States, where women leave prostitution to receive job skills training in tailoring, jewelry making, baking, and cosmetology. Thistle Farms likewise has 30 social enterprise partners from 20 countries across 5 continents.

Individualism, self-help, and self-actualization are also evident in sex worker-led TSOs' arts-based initiatives to promote sex workers' representations of their own experiences. For example, the Trans Community Network in Bogotá, Colombia's Santa Fe tolerance zone, creates art with incarcerated sex workers as part of its community-building efforts. Operation Snatch (Toronto), Stella (Montreal), the Red Umbrella Project (New York City), and Stroll (Portland, Oregon) have all organized arts-based exhibits. Stroll hosted its fifth annual sex workers' art show in collaboration with the Portland Institute of Contemporary Art and encouraged entrants to create work that responded to questions regarding what it means to do sex work under capitalism, how race impacts sex workers' experiences, and navigating the glamorization of sex work alongside the prevalence of anti-sex worker politics (Stroll, 2019).

Criminalization and militarization

The scale, variety, and systemic brutality of criminal justice responses to prostitution in the Americas are truly striking given that none of the countries in the region are currently embroiled in civil war or cross-border conflict. Most TSOs acknowledge structural and interpersonal violence against people in the sex industry by sex buyers, police, and widespread stigma as a major problem for people who sell sex. This section discusses how TSOs respond to the impact of criminalization and militarization on people who sell sex through examples of TSOs lobbying for legislative reform, providing legal and peer-to-peer support for people criminally charged with prostitution-related offenses, and working with police.

The totalizing nature of criminalization and militarization in the Americas is such that sex worker rights TSOs in particular face significant risks in their work. For example, El Salvador's Liquidambar Association of Female Sex Workers, which operates in the context of widespread political turmoil and some of the highest incidences of violence against women in the world, regards the murders of women who sell sex, including the unsolved murder of the TSO's founder, Angelica Quintanilla, as femicides because they stem from dominant cultural norms that dehumanize and legitimize violence against women sex workers. As sex worker and Liquidambar coordinator Rosa Alma Ramos told a journalist for the global feminist Association for Women's Rights in Development (AWID):

> The threat is so real, we feel it every day. It comes from the gangs, but also from the state and others who think they own the sex work districts. The majority of our colleagues come from situations of extreme poverty. Those working in the street encounter threats and demands for "fees" by the gangs just to have the right to work in certain areas, and sometimes the situation leads to a lack of clients.
>
> (De Cicco, 2018)

Sex worker rights TSOs in the United States face similar challenges when providing services to people who sell sex on the street, where time and ways of earning money are organized around avoiding the near-inevitability of arrest. At over 2 million, the number of people incarcerated in US jails and prisons exceeds the total population of many Caribbean nations. Yet criminalization impacts all people who sell sex, as was evident when the US sex worker rights TSO Desiree Alliance chose to cancel its annual conference, which routinely has as many as 500 attendees, after fears that federal legislation passed by the Trump administration could be used to arrest its members. Director Cris Sardina noted on the TSO's website that the 2019 conference, titled "Transcending Borders: Immigration, Migration, and Sex Work", would be cancelled because "we cannot put our organization and our attendees at risk. We hope you understand our grave concerns and continue to resist every law that exists to harm sex workers! Keep fighting!" (Sardina, 2019).

These very real challenges lead many TSOs to engage in lobbying for legislative reform across the ideological spectrum. For example, US neo-abolitionist TSOs such as Breaking Free and Exodus Cry actively lobby to increase criminal penalties for men who buy sex as part of the "end demand" approach to eradicating the sex industry by punishing sex buyers. Likewise, GEMS was an enthusiastic proponent of early proposals for Safe Harbor legislation that protects New York City victims of trafficking, including all minors who sell sex, from criminal prosecution for prostitution-related offenses.

Sex worker rights TSOs throughout the Americas have actively combated hostility against their work both in the courts and by issuing statements in support of legislative reform. The Sex Professionals of Canada, in conjunction with a number of Canadian sex worker rights TSOs, challenged the constitutionality of criminalizing prostitution in federal court and temporarily succeeded in decriminalizing the sale, but not the purchase, of sex. Women with a Vision (New Orleans), which targets drug policy reform, partnered with attorneys to convince the Louisiana State Legislature to eradicate an 1805 law, Crime Against Nature by Solicitation, that New Orleans police used to disproportionately arrest and issue felony charges against transgender sex workers of color (McTighe and Haywood, 2017). Activists organized by the sex worker rights TSO Desiree Alliance collaborated with the Los Angeles branch of the American Civil Liberties Union, the chief US civil rights organization, to develop National Sex Worker Anti-Criminalization Principles which reiterate the rights of people in the sex industry to bodily autonomy, respect, and freedom from discrimination (National Sex Worker Anti-Criminalization Principles, 2018).

Some sex worker rights TSOs form specifically in response to the widespread impacts of criminalization on people who sell sex. For example, Coyote Rhode Island formed in 2009 in response to the recriminalization of indoor prostitution for the first time since 1979, when sex worker rights activist Margo St. James' class action lawsuit resulted in decriminalization (Coyote Rhode Island, 2019). Similarly, and in response to the widespread impacts of criminalization and militarization in El Salvador, Liquidambar provides sex workers with trainings on human rights, political lobbying, and self-care to overcome the psycho-social impacts of widespread violence against women (Mama Cash, 2017).

The US Sex Workers Outreach Project, founded in 2003, is a consortium that advocates for sociolegal changes at the national level through media outreach, public education, and local political organizing in 14 cities with members who "imagine a world where sex workers are not harmed by systemic and interpersonal violence" (SWOP-USA, 2016). With this central goal in mind, SWOP-USA's Board of Directors developed an advocacy agenda for 2016–2018 in conjunction with its local chapters to determine that the most important advocacy issues for people in the sex industry are ending violence, supporting decriminalization, reducing stigma-related discrimination, and responding to the anti-trafficking movement (SWOP-USA, 2016). As part of this advocacy agenda, SWOP-USA identified the need to create an inclusive environment for sex workers of all identities, research ongoing decriminalization efforts, create a national working group to develop a plan for widespread decriminalization, and foster research and media collaboration to reduce stigma.

In the US state of Alaska, Community United for Safety and Protection politically organizes people who have worked in the sex industry to demand their rights to equal protection under the law, negotiate their own labor conditions, communicate with one another without fear of being charged with sex trafficking, end police abuse, and eliminate discrimination in housing, work, child custody, and social services (CUSP, 2019). Latin American sex worker rights TSOs have been particularly successful in their political efforts, with the Association of Professional Prostitutes in Uruguay able to obtain pension benefits for retired sex workers (Cabezas, 2019). In Colombia, where a majority of trans people reportedly sell sex, transwoman Tatiana Pineros was a member of the Bogotá mayor's cabinet and ran on a sex worker and transgender rights platform for a seat in the Colombian Senate, although she did not win (Sobel, 2018).

Sex work and prostitution TSOs also provide legal and peer-to-peer support to people charged with prostitution-related offenses. The neo-abolitionist TSO Hookers for Jesus conducts outreach to people incarcerated for prostitution, with such visits akin to the work of attorneys and social workers who routinely visit correctional facilities in a professional capacity. The Orlando, Florida TSO SWOP Behind Bars provides monthly newsletters, books, study materials, and sex worker pen pals to women incarcerated on prostitution charges as well as basic needs support on release from jail or prison (SWOP Behind Bars, 2019). Peer-to-peer support is also evident in sex worker TSOs publicly sharing reports of police abuse, as occurred when the Canadian migrant rights TSO Butterfly used its members' experiences to denounce police officers' racial profiling and discriminatory treatment of Asian sex workers (Lam and Lepp, 2019).

Legal support for criminal record expungement and assistance with active court cases is not as prevalent as many sex workers would like it to be given criminalization's pervasiveness. The Women's Prostitutes' Association of Argentina (AMMAR) has a legal clinic for sex workers and in Bogotá, Colombia, Lxs Callejerxs [People of the Street] relays legal complaints from sex workers to the relevant authorities (AMMAR, 2019). The Migrant Sex Workers Project in Toronto offers legal training on immigration-related issues, and many TSOs offer rights-based legal training, including Stroll (Portland) and the Sex Professionals of Canada (Toronto), alongside legislative reform efforts that acknowledge sexual labor as work and decry the harms associated with criminalization and anti-trafficking legislation that neatly bifurcates those who sell sex into "innocent victims" and "criminal deviants" (Migrant Sex Workers Projects, 2019). Legal representation is a rare but important service offered by the Sex Workers Project at the Urban Justice Center in New York City, which has also written human rights reports designed to influence law and policy on police use of condoms as evidence (PROS Network and Sex Workers Project, 2012), indoor sex work (Sex Workers Project, 2005), and law enforcement raids targeting trafficking in persons (Sex Workers Project, 2009).

TSOs also lead trainings and engage in other forms of cooperation with police. Neo-abolitionist TSOs envision police as allies in their efforts to eradicate prostitution. In many cases throughout the United States, people arrested and detained on prostitution charges have just two equally difficult choices: incarceration in jail or detention in a transitional housing facility ostensibly designed to help them overcome the traumatic life circumstances that led them to prostitution. US TSOs that provide transitional housing rely heavily on criminal justice professionals to refer women who have been arrested, incarcerated, and may be interested in a TSO's services. Some of these TSOs are alternatives to incarceration – known as diversion programs because they redirect women from the criminal justice system to social services – such as Generate Hope, Selah Freedom, and Purchased: Not for Sale. Thistle Farms and the multi-city network of Magdalene Houses have criminal justice professionals on their respective Boards of Directors, indicating that they regard them as active partners in their work. Sensitization workshops in conjunction with law enforcement may also generate income for TSOs, as is the case for the Kansas City-based Veronica's Voice, which leads a John School that men arrested on charges of soliciting sex can attend for a fee in order to avoid a criminal conviction.

Some sex worker rights TSOs attempt to sensitize police about the issues facing people who sell sex, as does the Guyana Sex Work Coalition, Blue Angel Civil Association (Peru), Coyote Rhode Island, and Beauty from Ashes Ministries (Florida). In Peru, the Change and Action Association convinced Lima police to schedule solicitation hours at mutually agreed-upon time to minimize police harassment. In Ecuador, the Quito Trans Sex Workers Association trains police to challenge negative perceptions of people who sell sex and additionally provides conflict mediation (Mama Cash, 2017). El Salvador's Liquidambar trains police while simultaneously viewing such training as "opportunities to expose those in the force who are violent toward us" (De Cicco, 2018). In a remarkable instance of sex worker engagement with a national justice system, Nicaragua became the first country in the world to utilize sex worker judicial mediators when sex workers received conflict resolution training accredited by the National Supreme Court of Justice (Cabezas, 2019).

Outlaw politics

In her masterful history of Spanish and French New Orleans, Shannon Dawdy (2009) describes how this middle point of the Americas – located both geographically and culturally somewhere between Northern Latin America and the Southernmost regions of North America – is emblematic of what she terms "rogue colonialism". Vividly depicting a world in which pirates, politicians, and outlaws must work together to make a living, she captures how forging the "New World" of the Americas relied on a cobbled-together system of uneasy alliances. The rogue colonialism Dawdy identified, and the outlaw politics that enable and endorse it through the celebration of pirates and other folk heroes who defy the established social order, are evident in the creativity that TSOs exercise in their ongoing struggles to realize a world free from oppression.

Outlaw politics, defined as political mobilization around a shared outsider identity righteous in its opposition to dominant cultural norms, enable sex worker rights TSOs to fight against multiple sociolegal forms of oppression to uphold their human rights. They also enable neo-abolitionists to resist a dominant culture that sexually objectifies women in ways that cause widespread harm to society's moral fabric. Both sides of this ideological spectrum envision themselves as fighting an equally righteous battle in opposition to the status quo. In Latin America specifically, outlaw politics also has roots in liberation theology, which emerged in the mid-twentieth century as a revolutionary means to theorize the poor as primary agents of social change and socialist solidarity as the only feasible means by which to overcome capitalist exploitation (Petrella, 2016). Feminist and queer scholars of liberation theology have critiqued its focus on the poor as a moral category and associated exclusion of poor women who do not fit gender stereotypes endorsed by the Catholic Church (Althaus-Reid, 2000). Nevertheless, the approaches evident among sex work and prostitution TSOs throughout Latin America are markedly more radical than their counterparts in North America, where TSOs rarely reject capitalism even in the most strident arguments for sex workers' labor rights.

Approaches grounded in religious movements are hardly unique to Latin American Catholic traditions. Neo-abolitionist Christian TSOs regard their efforts to eradicate prostitution as synonymous with the work of the original nineteenth-century abolitionists who fought to end the trans-Atlantic slave trade (Bernstein, 2019). Consider, for example, the following excerpt shared by the neo-abolitionist TSO Exodus Cry:

> Slavery was seen as a benefit not just to society and trade, but even to the slaves themselves. The horrors of slavery were hidden beneath carefully constructed false cover narratives that made the lives of slaves seem good. This cover narrative was propagated and funded by those who benefited most from keeping the system of slavery in place. Those who promote the prostitution cover narrative want us to believe that women choose prostitution freely and that prostitution elevates their life. They want us to believe that prostituted women have no life without prostitution. They want us to believe that prostitution is a cross between freedom and social welfare.
>
> (Baraka, 2020)

Likening the work of sex worker rights TSOs to a "cover narrative" that conceals the real harms associated with prostitution, discourse featured here positions sympathetic readers as able to make a real and momentous difference in the lives of oppressed people. It also implies that powerful, albeit unspecified, forces have a stake in maintaining a status quo in which the kind of sexual objectification evident in prostitution is widespread and profitable. Yet sex worker rights TSOs also acknowledge the dominant cultural forces that endorse continued criminalization and stigmatization. Consider, for instance, the following description offered by the sex worker rights TSO Coyote Rhode Island:

> While we oppose society's Moral Witch Hunt against us and laws that criminalize us, we are aware that sex workers must live in the real world. At its best, that world disrespects and ostracizes us; at its worst, it seeks to exploit

and even harm us. [We are] here to offer a safe harbor from that world. We believe adult providers can make the best choices for themselves without interference from law enforcement on the one hand nor do-gooders who want to "help" us against our will on the other hand.

(Coyote Rhode Island, 2019)

Coyote Rhode Island depicts a dominant cultural order that targets sex workers as part of a "Moral Witch Hunt" that routinely disrespects and harms sex workers. Just as is the case in the excerpt from the neo-abolitionist TSO Exodus Cry, the sense of doing battle against oppression is palpable in this excerpt.

Given neo-abolitionist legal and political dominance throughout the Americas, some sex worker rights TSOs have led innovative partnerships designed to expose particular instances of oppression. Davida, one of Brazil's oldest sex work and prostitution TSOs, uses a model of solidarity in uniting researchers, sex workers, and TSOs in innovative partnerships such as the Observatory of Prostitution, which studied the World Cup's impact on Rio de Janeiro's sex industry and concluded that, in contrast to predictions of exponential growth in the numbers of trafficked women, business declined for sex workers by almost half (da Silva et al., 2014). Other sex worker-led TSOs, particularly in Latin America, have borrowed revolutionary tactics from radical labor, Indigenous, and other social movements, including hostage-taking (Abad et al., 1998) and publicly distributing invoices for sexual services provided to politicians and other public figures (Cabezas, 2019).

In sharp contrast to social justice movements for women, people of color, and queer communities that initially gathered momentum in the 1970s, the sex worker rights movement did not result in the kinds of substantive sociolegal change that its leaders had hoped to achieve. The sex worker rights movement failed to meet its goals of decriminalization, de-stigmatization, and recognition of sexual labor as work because, unlike other co-occurring identity-based social movements, it lacked financial resources, strong alliances with groups outside the movement, and received limited media attention (Weitzer, 1991). Contemporary support for sex worker rights remains extremely limited in comparison with movements that regard prostitution and trafficking as synonymous (van der Meulen, Durisin, and Love, 2013; Showden and Majic, 2014).

Despite these critical challenges, Margo St. James, a leader in the early sex worker rights movement, contends that the sheer number and diversity of sex worker rights TSOs that exist today are evidence of the movement's success (Fischer, 2013). This sheer number and diversity of sex worker rights organizations could also be read as a failure with respect to solidarity-building and the continued dominance of outlaw politics among sex worker rights TSOs in particular. It is indeed remarkable that the sex worker rights movement exists at all given that its critique is essentially anti-capitalist and pro-labor in a region that, especially in North America, lacks sizeable labor movements and tends toward political and moral conservatism relative to other countries in most of Europe. It is likewise remarkable that TSOs with a mission to assist women who want to leave prostitution exist given how little funding and general support their work has in dominant culture. Despite the significant differences and often heated denunciations that issue back and forth between ideologically opposed TSOs, the fact remains that the vast majority of people in the Americas show little concern for the issues to which sex work and prostitution TSO staff, volunteers, and advocates dedicate their lives.

Conclusion

The four unique characteristics of TSOs engaged with people involved in sex for sale throughout the Americas – the neoliberal nonprofit industrial complex, cultural values of individualism, self-help, and self-actualization, criminalization and militarization, and outlaw politics – represent a conglomeration of forces reflective of the region's historical, socioeconomic, and political struggles. All are products of the broader socioeconomic, political, and cultural contexts in which they operate as well as the global ideological and financial flows of which they are intrinsically and indisputably a part.

The violence of neoliberalism in the Americas is real and totalizing. Neoliberal efforts to spread and entrench free-market capitalism at any cost have driven almost every social disparity in the region, whether during colonialism's quest for natural resources, Cold War–era proxy conflicts, or the ongoing drug wars and associated tolls in the form of widespread human suffering, community violence, and, in the United States, mass incarceration. Yet, despite the abject failure of US mass incarceration, the country's global economic and political influence allowed for the global export of anti-trafficking strategies almost exclusively reliant on intensified criminal justice enforcement as the measure of success. These coercive measures also exist in Central and South America in addition to threats posed by military or militia forces in the form of gangs that routinely terrorize people who sell sex and further destabilize national economies and the rule of law in ways that render selling sex the only feasible option for increasing numbers of people in poverty, particularly cis- and transgender women.

The libertarian philosophical tenets of privatization and individualism have prevailed since European conquest and colonialism created the Americas as they are known today. The reach of such philosophical tenets is evident even in the terminology used to describe TSOs: Spanish-speaking Latin America and Portuguese-speaking Brazil refer to TSOs using the equivalent of the English term "nongovernmental organization", whereas in the United States "nonprofits" remain defined by their lack of capitalist productivity. The intensity and disparate impacts of relatively unregulated free-market capitalism in the Americas are likewise apparent in the extreme economic disparities within and between countries. For example, aerial photographs of the border between Haiti and the Dominican Republic throw into stark relief the privations of the former and the relative wealth of the latter, with the Haitian side of the border almost entirely deforested for use as firewood and building material, and the Dominican side lush with tropical greenery. Even the United States, which is generally regarded as the region's wealthiest nation, lacks all but the most basic social safety nets for people living in poverty and is accordingly home to a significant number of people, particularly women, who sell sex to survive and whose life circumstances have more in common with their peers in Africa than their peers in Europe.

Yet, despite these deeply rooted inequalities, the notion that individuals can determine their own destiny stems from cultural values of individualism, self-help, and self-actualization. The optimism, hope, and individualism underlying these values are pervasive among TSOs engaged with people in the sex industry across a wide spectrum of beliefs, such that in the Americas, among sex worker rights activists and abolitionists alike, microenterprise can be conceivably envisioned as a path out of poverty, as can healing of one's inner self through trauma therapy facilitated by a person with similar life experiences. Yet these cultural values may also be a key reason for the lack of progress among sex work and prostitution TSOs, as these essentially individualized forms of self-actualization may function to deter the solidarity that accompanies a shared group identity.

Yet, in spite of very limited funding, in the face of very real threats of violence both structural and interpersonal, and despite widespread sociopolitical opprobrium, people who sell sex in all 46 countries of the Americas have refused to accept a status quo in which their rights are routinely violated. People who believe that prostitution itself is a fundamental human rights violation and an act of violence against women similarly continue to struggle against dominant cultural values that sexually objectify women. These enduring realities speak to the tremendous power that regional cultural values hold in influencing all forms of political resistance in the Americas.

Notes

1 Other TSOs that provide transitional housing for women leaving prostitution include Amirah (Wenham, Massachusetts), Aspire Home (New York City), Created Women (Tampa, Florida), Dawn's Place (Philadelphia), Veronica's Voice Magdalene Kansas City (Kansas), Purchased: Not for Sale (Shreveport, Louisiana), Homestead Ministries (Manhattan, Kansas), Freedom House (San Francisco), Rahab's Hideaway (Columbus, Ohio), and Oasis House (Dayton, Ohio).

2 Among others, these TSOs include the Antiguan Resilience Collective (Antigua and Barbuda), Foko (Curaçao), Red Initiatives (Trinidad and Tobago), Quito Trans Sex Workers Association (Ecuador), Apollo Center for Trans-Identified People (Mexico City), Men in Action Collective (Monterrey, Mexico), Miluska Life and Dignity (Lima, Peru), PACE (Vancouver), Peers Victoria Resource Society (British Columbia), Stepping Stone (Halifax, Nova Scotia), the B.C. Coalition of Experiential Communities (Vancouver), the Red Umbrella Project (New York City), GLITS (New York City), SWOP, the WPN Power Company (Atlanta), and the St. James Infirmary (San Francisco).

References

Abad, A., M. Briones, T. Cordero, R. Manzo, and M. Marchán 1998. "The association of autonomous women workers, Ecuador: '22nd June'." In: *Global Sex Workers*, edited by Kempadoo and Doezema, 172–177. London: Routledge.

Allen, R. 1991. *Horrible Prettiness: Burlesque and American Culture*. Chapel Hill, NC: University of North Carolina Press.

Althaus, M. 2000. *Indecent Theology: Theological Perversions in Sex, Gender, and Politics*. London: Routledge.

Amar, P. 2009. "Operation princess in Rio de Janeiro: Policing 'sex trafficking', strengthening worker citizenship, and the urban geopolitics of security in Brazil." *Security Dialogue* 40(4–5): 513–541.

Ammar/Asociacion Mujeres Meretrices de la Argentina en Accion por Nuestros Derechos 2019. "Justicia." Accessed 6th January 2021. http://www.ammar.org.ar/-Justicia-.html.

ANAPFEH, FACSDIS, KOURAJ, SEROvie, The International Women's Human Rights Clinic at CUNY Law School, The International Gay and Lesbian Human Rights Commission, and MADRE 2014. *Fighting for Our Lives: Violence and Discrimination against Women and LGBT Persons in Haiti*. Geneva: UN Human Rights Committee 112th Session. Accessed 6th January 2021. https://www.ecoi.net/en/file/local/1201176/1930_1423567715_int-ccpr-css-hti-18153- e.pdf.

Anasti, T. 2017. "Radical professionals? Sex worker rights activists and collaboration with human service nonprofits." *Human Service Organizations: Management, Leadership and Governance* 41(4): 416–437.

——— 2018. "Survivor or laborer: How human service managers perceive sex workers?" *AFFILIA: Journal of Women and Social Work* 33(4): 453–476.

Baraka, J. 2020. "Why prostitution is slavery." Accessed 6th January 2021. https://exoduscry.com/blog/changinglaws/why-prostitution-is-slavery/.

BC Coalition of Experiential Communities 2007. "Background." Accessed 6th January 2021. https://bccec.wordpress.com/2007/12/13/background/.

——— 2019. "Documents." https://bccec.wordpress.com/category/documents/.

Bell, H., L. Sloan, and C. Strickling 1998. "Exploiter or exploited? Topless dancers reflect on their experiences." *Journal of Women and Social Work* 13(3): 352–368.

Bernstein, E. 2012. "Carceral politics as gender justice? The "traffic in women" and neoliberal circuits of crime, sex, and rights." *Theory and Society* 41(3): 233–259.

——— 2019. *Brokered Subjects: Sex, Trafficking, and the Politics of Freedom*. Chicago, IL: University of Chicago Press.

Blanchette, T., and A.P. da Silva 2012. "On bullshit and the trafficking of women: Moral entrepreneurs and the invention of trafficking in persons in Brazil." *Dialectical Anthropology* 36(1–2): 107–125.

Bliss, K.E. 2002. *Compromised Positions: Prostitution, Public Health, and Gender Politics in Revolutionary Mexico City*. University Park, PA: Pennsylvania State University Press.

Breaking Free 2019. "Women's program." Accessed 6th January 2021. https://breakingfree.net/womens-program.

Brennan, D. 2004. *What's Love Got to Do with It? Transnational Desires and Sex Tourism in the Dominican Republic*. Durham, NC: Duke University Press.

Brents, B., C. Jackson, and K. Hausbeck 2010. *The State of Sex: Tourism, Sex, and Sin in the New American Heartland*. New York: Routledge.

Brock, D. 1998. *Making Work, Making Trouble: Prostitution as a Social Problem*. Toronto, ON: University of Toronto Press.

Butler, A. 1987. *Daughters of Joy, Sisters of Misery: Prostitutes in the American West, 1865–90*. Champaign, IL: University of Illinois Press.

Cabezas, A. 2019. "Latin American and Caribbean sex workers: Gains and challenges in the movement." *Anti-Trafficking Review* 12(12): 37–56.

———— 2009. *Economies of Desire: Sex and Tourism in Cuba and the Dominican Republic.* Philadelphia, PA: Temple University Press.

Cabezas, A. and A. Alcazar Campo 2016. "Trafficking discourses of dominican women in Puerto Rico." *Social and Economic Studies* 65(4): 33–51.

Caribbean Vulnerable Communities 2019. "MACAIDS: Projects in Antigua." Accessed 6th January 2021. http://www.cvccoalition.org/content/macaids-projects-antigua.

Clement, E. 2006. *Love for Sale: Courting, Treating, and Prostitution in New York City, 1900–1945.* Chapel Hill, NC: University of North Carolina Press.

Conrad, P. 2007. *The Medicalization of Society: On the Transformation of Human Conditions into Treatable Disorders.* Baltimore, MD: Johns Hopkins University Press.

Coyote Rhode Island 2019. "What is Coyote RI?" Coyote Rhode Island 2019. Accessed 6th January 2021. http://coyoteri.org/wp/.

Created Women 2019. "Outreach." Accessed 6th January 2021. http://www.createdwomen.com/about.

CUSP/Community United for Safety and Protection 2019. "Help US gain access to our rights." Accessed 6th January 2021. http://sextraffickingalaska.com.

da Silva, A.P., G. Mitchell, L. Murray, S. Simoes, and T. Blanchette 2014. "Observatory of prostitution report on world cup sex tourism in Rio." Accessed 6th January 2021. https://redlightr.io/observatory-of-prostitution-report-on-world-cup-sex-tourism-in-rio/.

Dawdy, S. 2009. *Building the Devil's Empire: French Colonial New Orleans.* Chicago, IL: University of Chicago Press.

De Cicco, G. 2018. *The Freedom to Decide What to Do with Our Lives.* The Association for Women's Rights in Development (AWID). Accessed 6th January 2021. https://www.awid.org/profiles/freedom-decide-what-do-our-lives.

Dewey, S. 2008. *Hollow Bodies: Institutional Responses to Sex Trafficking in Armenia, Bosnia, and India.* Sterling, VA: Kumarian Press.

DISEMI (Asociacion Diversidad Sexual Milagro) 2018. "Asociacion Diversidad Sexual Milagro (DISEMI): Nueva Organizaction de Trabajadoras Sexuales en Ecuador." Accessed 6th January 2021. https://elestantedelaciti.wordpress.com/2018/04/24/asociacion-diversidad-sexual-milagro-disemi-nueva-organizacion-de-trabajadoras-sexuales-en-ecuador/.

DISEMI 2019. "Homepage." Accessed 6th January 2021. https://www.nswp.org/featured/asociacion-diversidad-sexual-milagro-disemi

Ditmore, M.H., and D. Allman 2013. "An analysis of the implementation of PEPFAR's anti-prostitution pledge and its implications for successful HIV prevention among organizations working with sex workers." *Journal of the International AIDS Society* 16(1): 17354.

Donovan, B. 2006. *White Slave Crusades: Race, Gender, and Anti-Vice Activism, 1887–1917.* Champaign, IL: University of Illinois Press.

Dorais, M. 2005. *Rent Boys: The World of Male Sex Trade Workers.* Montreal, QC: McGill-Queens University Press.

Fischer, A. 2013. "Forty years in the hustle: A Q&A with Margo St. James." Accessed 6th January 2021. https://www.bitchmedia.org/article/forty-years-in-the-hustle-sex-work-margo-st-james-interview-activism-coyote.

Fundo Brasil. n.d. "Davida project on civil rights and health in Rio de Janeiro." Accessed 6th January 2021. https://www.fundobrasil.org.br/en/projeto/davida-prostitution-civil-rights-health-rio-de-janeiro/.

Fundo Posithivo 2018. "Annual report." Accessed 6th January 2021. http://fundoposithivo.org.br/wp- content/uploads/2019/04/relatorio_2018fpenglish.pdf.

GEMS/Girls Educational and Mentoring Services 2019. "What we do." Accessed 6th January 2021. https://www.gems-girls.org/what-we-do.

Goldman, M. 1981. *Gold Diggers and Silver Miners: Prostitution and Social Life on the Comstock Lode. Women and Culture Series.* Ann Arbor, MI: University of Michigan Press.

Government of Canada 2014. "Prostitution criminal law reform: Bill C-36, the protection of communities and exploited persons act." Accessed 6th January 2021. https://www.justice.gc.ca/eng/rp-pr/other-autre/c36faq/.

Guy, D. 1991. *Sex and Danger in Buenos Aires: Prostitution, Family, and Nation in Argentina.* Lincoln, NE: University of Nebraska Press.

Hardy, K., and K. Cruz. 2019. "Affective organizing: Collectivizing informal sex workers in an intimate union." *American Behavioral Scientist* 63(2): 244–261.

Harm Reduction Coalition 2015. "Principles of harm reduction." Accessed 6th January 2021. https://harmreduction.org/about-us/principles-of-harm-reduction/.

HIPS 2019. "How we improve lives." Accessed 6th January 2021. https://www.hips.org/how-we-improve-lives.html.

Hotaling, N., A. Burris, J. Johnson, Y. Bird, and K. Melbye 2004. "Been there done that." *Journal of Trauma Practice* 2(3–4): 255–265.

Institute of Development Studies Sexuality, Poverty and Law Programme 2020. "Sex work law: Countries." Accessed 6th January 2021. http://spl.ids.ac.uk/sexworklaw/countries.

Katsulis, Y. 2009. *Sex Work and the City: The Social Geography of Health and Safety in Tijuana.* Austin, TX: University of Texas Press.

Kempadoo, K. 2001. "Women of color and the global sex trade." *Transnational Feminist Perspectives* 1(2): 28–51.

—— 2004. *Sexing the Caribbean: Gender, Race and Sexual Labor.* New York: Routledge.

—— 2016. "The war on humans: Anti-trafficking in the Caribbean." *Social and Economic Studies* 65(4): 5–32.

Kone, M. 2016. "Transnational sex worker organizing in latin America: RedTraSex, labor and human rights." *Social and Economic Studies* 65(4): 87–108.

Lam, E., and A. Lepp 2019. "Butterfly: Resisting the harms of anti-trafficking policies and fostering peer-based organizing in Canada." *Anti-Trafficking Review* 12(12): 91–107.

Lanham, M., K. Ridgeway, R. Dayton, B. Castillo, and C. Brennan, D. Dirk, D. Emmaneul, R. Dayton, B.M. Castillo, C. Brennan, D.A. Davis, D. Emmanuel, G.J. Morales, C. Cheririser, B. Rodriguez, J. Cooke, K. Santi, E. Evens 2019. "'We're going to leave you for last, because of how you are': Transgender women's experiences of gender-based violence in healthcare, education, and police encounters in Latin America and the Caribbean." *Violence and Gender* 6(1): 37–46.

Leigh, C. 2010. "Inventing sex work." In: *Whores and Other Feminists*, edited by Nagle, 223–231. New York: Routledge.

Lutnick, A. 2006. "The St. James infirmary: A history." *Sexuality and Culture* 10(2): 56–75.

MacKell, J. 2009. *Red Light Women of the Rocky Mountains.* Albuquerque, NM: University of New Mexico Press.

Mama Cash 2017. "Annual report." Accessed 6th January 2021. https://www.mamacash.org/media/publications/mc_ar2017_vdef.pdf.

McTighe, L., and D. Haywood 2017. "'There is NO justice in Louisiana': Crimes against nature and the spirit of black feminist resistance." *Souls* 19(3): 261–285.

Migrant Sex Workers Project 2019 "Report on migrant sex workers justice and the trouble with 'anti-trafficking': Research, activism." *Art.* Accessed 6th January 2021. http://www.migrantsexworkers.com/report.html.

National Sex Worker Anti-Criminalization Principles 2018. Accessed 6th January 2021. http://desireealliance.org/home/.

Nichols, J. 2008. *Prostitution, Polygamy, and Power: Salt Lake City, 1847–1918.* Champaign, IL: University of Illinois Press.

NWSP/Network of Sex Work Projects 2019. "How sex work laws are implemented on the ground and their impact on sex workers: Mexico case study." Accessed 6th January 2021. https://www.nswp.org/sites/nswp.org/files/mexico_legal_case_study.pdf.

——— 2019. "Caribbean sex work coalition." Accessed 6th January 2021. https://www.nswp.org/featured/caribbean-sex-work-coalition.

Odem, M. 1995. *Delinquent Daughters: Protecting and Policing Adolescent Female Sexuality in the United States. 1885–1920.* Chapel Hill, NC: University of North Carolina Press.

Padilla, M. 2007. *Caribbean Pleasure Industry: Tourism, Sexuality, and AIDS in the Dominican Republic.* Chicago, IL: University of Chicago Press.

Peiss, K. 1986. *Cheap Amusements: Working Women and Leisure in Turn-of-the-Century New York.* Philadelphia, PA: Temple University Press.

Pettiway, L. 1996. *Honey, Honey, Miss Thang: Being Black, Gay, and on the Streets.* Philadelphia, PA: Temple University Press.

Petrella, I. 2016. "The intellectual roots of liberation theology." In: *The Cambridge History of Religionsin Latin America,* edited by Garrard-Burnett, Freston, and Dove 359–371. Cambridge: Cambridge University Press.

Pheterson, G. 1989. *A Vindication of the Rights of Whores.* Berkeley, CA: Seal Press.

PLAPERTS 2019. "History." Accessed 6th January 2021. https://plaperts.nswp.org/historia.

——— 2019. "Homepage." Accessed 6th January 2021. https://plaperts.nswp.org.

——— 2019. "Members." Accessed 6th January 2021. https://plaperts.nswp.org/miembros.

Power/Prostitutes of Ottawa-Gatineau Work, Educate, and Resist Community Network 2019. "Bylaws." Accessed 6th January 2021. https://www.powerottawa.ca/wp-content/uploads/2019/08/POWER-Bylaws- 2014-.pdf.

Prieur, A. 1998. *Mema's House, Mexico City: On Transvestites, Queens, and Machos.* Chicago, IL: University of Chicago Press.

PROS Network & Sex Workers Project 2012. "Public health crisis: The impact of using condoms as evidence of prostitution in New York City." Accessed 6th January 2021. https://swp.urbanjustice.org/sites/default/files/20120417-public-health-crisis.pdf.

RedTraSex 2007. "A high heels movement: Women, sex workers, and activists." UNAIDS/UNFPA.

——— 2016. "Human rights situation for women sex workers in Honduras." Accessed 6th January 2021. https://tbinternet.ohchr.org/Treaties/CCPR/Shared%20Documents/HND/INT_CCPR_ICO_HND_24664_E.pdf.

——— 2017. "Human rights situation of women sex workers in Honduras." Accessed 6th January 2021. https://www.ecoi.net/en/file/local/1406698/1930_1498736096_int-ccpr-css-hnd-27561-e.pdf

────── 2018. "Human rights situation of women sex workers in Honduras." Accessed 6th January 2021. https://tbinternet.ohchr.org/Treaties/CCPR/Shared%20Documents/SLV /INT_CCPR_CSS_SLV_30315_E.pdf.

────── 2019a. "Our history." Accessed 6th January 2021. http://www.redtrasex.org/-About -Us-.html.

────── 2019b. "RedTraSex: Our achievements." Accessed 6th January 2021. http://www .redtrasex.org/IMG/pdf/Eng- RedTraSex-web.pdf.

Ritchie, A. 2017. *Invisible No More: Police Violence Against Black Women and Women of Color*. New York: Beacon Press.

Rivers-Moore, M. 2018. "We fight with god's weapons: Sex work and pragmatic penance in neoliberal Costa Rica." *Signs: Journal of Women in Culture and Society* 43(4): 851–876.

Robert Carr Fund 2019. "Sex worker networks consortium." Accessed 6th January 2021. https://robertcarrfund.org/networks/2016-2018/sex-worker-networks-consortium.

Rodriguez, D. 2007. "The political logic of the non-profit industrial complex." In: *The Revolution Will Not Be Funded: Beyond the Non-Profit Industrial Complex*, edited by INCITE!, 21–40. Durham, NC: Duke University Press.

Rosen, R. 1982. *The Lost Sisterhood: Prostitution in America, 1900–1918*. Baltimore, MD: Johns Hopkins University Press.

Ross, B. 2009. *Burlesque West: Showgirls, Sex, and Sin in Postwar Vancouver*. Toronto, ON: University of Toronto Press.

Saito, N.T. 2020. *Settler Colonialism, Race, and the Law: Why Structural Racism Persists*. New York: New York University Press.

Sardina, C. 2019. "Conference." Accessed 6th January 2021. http://desireealliance.org/ conference/.

Schlecter, K. 2019. "Sex workers unionize in Guatemala." Accessed 6th January 2021. https://nacla.org/news/2019/02/25/sex-workers-unionize-guatemala.

Sex Workers Project 2009. "The use of raids to fight trafficking in persons." Accessed 6th January 2021. https://swp.urbanjustice.org/sites/default/files/swp-2009-raids-and-traffi cking-report.pdf.

Sex Workers Project at the Urban Justice Center 2005. "Behind closed doors: An analysis of indoor sex work in New York City." Accessed 6th January 2021. https://swp.urb anjustice.org/sites/default/files/BehindClosedDoors.pdf.

Shematz, J. 2019. "Dear precious one." Accessed 6th January 2021. http://www.beau tyfromashes.org/contentpages.aspx?parentnavigationid=9825&viewcontentpageguid= f0692496-14c5-4aef-9020-7fea5a760781.

SHOP/Safe Harbor Outreach Project 2019. "Support + supplies + sex worker allies." Accessed 6th January 2021. https://sjwomenscentre.ca/programs/shop/.

Showden, C., and S. Majic, eds. 2014. *Negotiating Sex Work: Unintended Consequences of Policy and Activism*. Minneapolis, MN: University of Minnesota Press.

Silva, J.A. 2015. "Sex workers in Nicaragua break the silence and gain rights." *InterPress Services*. Accessed 6th January 2021. http://www.ipsnews.net/2015/06/sex-workers-in -nicaragua-break-the-silence-and-gain-rights/.

Smith, L. 2015. *From Congress to the Brothel: A Journey of Hope, Healing, and Restoration*. Vancouver, WA: Shared Hope International.

Sobel, A. 2018. "Transgender, queer candidates backed in runs for Colombia's senate." Accessed 6th January 2021. https://www.advocate.com/world/2018/3/09/transgender -queer-candidates-backed-runs-.colombias-senate.

St. James Infirmary 2010. "Nothing about us without us: The shared goals of the harm reduction and sex worker rights movements." Accessed 6th January 2021. https://stjamesinfirmary.org/wordpress/?p=1108.

Stroll 2019. "The fifth annual sex workers' art show: Call for entries." Accessed 6th January 2021. http://www.strollpdx.org/5th-annual-sex-workers-art-show.

SWOP Behind Bars 2019. "What is SWOP behind bars?" Accessed 6th January 2021. https://www.swopbehindbars.org/about-swop-behind-bars/why-is-swop-behind-bars/.

SWOP-USA 2016. "SWOP-USA advocacy agenda." Accessed 6th January 2021. https://www.swopusa.org/wp-content/uploads/2016/09/SWOPUSAAdvocacyAgenda2016-18TAcopy.pdf.

Timoshkina, N., and L. McDonald. 2009. *Building Partnerships for Service Provision to Migrant Sex Workers*. Toronto, ON: Wellesley Institute.

US Department of State 2003. "Belize: Country reports on human rights practices." Accessed 6th January 2021. https://www.justice.gov/sites/default/files/pages/attachments/2015/10/20/dos-hrr_2003_belize.pdf.

Valverde, M. 2008. *The Age of Light, Soap, and Water: Moral Reform in English Canada, 1885–1925*. Toronto, ON: University of Toronto Press.

van der Meulen, E.D., and V. Love. 2013. *Selling Sex: Experience, Advocacy, and Research on Sex Work*. Vancouver, BC: University of British Columbia Press.

We Are Dancers 2018. "Your rights: Legal definitions and basic FAQ." Accessed 6th January 2021. https://wadusa.org/know- your-rights/your-rights/.

Weitzer, R. 1991. "Prostitutes' rights in the United States: The failure of a movement." *The Sociological Quarterly* 32(1): 23–41.

Wolf, E. 2010. *Europe and the People Without History*. Berkeley, CA: University of California Press.

World Health Organization 2013. "Chapter 2. Addressing violence against sex workers." In: *Implementing Comprehensive HIV/STI Programs with Sex Workers: Practical Approaches from Collaborative Interventions*, 21–39. Accessed 6th January 2021. https://www.who.int/hiv/pub/sti/sex_worker_implementation/en/.

Chapter 5

Sex work and prostitution third sector organizations in Europe

Isabel Crowhurst

Introduction

The boundaries of Europe have been, and continue to be, contested and debated due to shifting notions of what count as European identities and values: "inseparable from the political and economic reality of Europe as a place is Europe as an idea and an ideal" (Kuus, 2005: 567). We can therefore "speak of multiple Europes, whose boundaries do not coincide with those of the Union or its member states" (ibid). In this chapter, our analysis of the European region includes the 27 members of the European Union (EU),[1] 6 candidate and potential candidate EU countries (also referred to as enlargement countries[2]), and Iceland, Norway, Switzerland, and the United Kingdom.[3]

The selected 37 countries, which are home to approximately 550 million people, are all democracies and most are unitary states, with the exception of four federations: Austria, Belgium, Germany, and Switzerland, and three devolved states: Italy, Spain, and the United Kingdom. National borders changed substantially in the twentieth century for most of these states, with geopolitical redefinitions taking place in the early twenty-first century in the Baltic and Balkan regions. Far from homogeneous, European countries present many cultural, demographic, economic, geographical, legal, and sociopolitical differences between and within them. Diversity and variations are also observable in relation to third sector organizations' (TSOs) establishment and development, distribution, and engagement with national and local governments. For example, in former Soviet bloc countries, the third sector remains more embryonic than in North-western Europe (Salamon and Sokolowski, 2018). Another disparity pertains to the revenue sources of TSOs, which in Scandinavia primarily derive from income from membership fees, in North-western Europe from government, and in Central and Eastern Europe from philanthropy (Salamon and Sokolowski, 2018). Whatever the explanation for such diversity, and many have been tendered,[4] the region's socioeconomic and political heterogeneity contributes to this diversification. However, an important role is also played by developments in and approaches to the specific sectors that TSOs engage in, as is indeed the case with sex work and prostitution.

Europe's regional variation remains a focus throughout this chapter, in keeping with analysis of the other two regions examined in the book. In what follows, after an overview of the contemporary landscape of sex work and prostitution in the region, we review three main clusters into which TSOs working in this area can be grouped based on their different understandings of and approaches to commercial sex and those involved in it: sex worker rights, prostitution as gendered violence, and harm reduction. We explore the ethos, claims, and demands informing organizations within these three clusters and analyze their origin, evolution, contemporary configurations, and the typologies of services they provide. The chapter's final section examines the various ways in which these organizations receive funding and how access to financial resources influences their activities and visibility.

Sex work and prostitution in contemporary Europe

Although "sex work across national boundaries is not new to the world" (Kempadoo, 1998: 14), migration within and to Europe of people involved in the sex industry have been growing steadily, albeit not homogenously, in the past four decades. In 2009, the European Network for the Promotion of Rights and Health of Migrant Sex Workers (TAMPEP) estimated that migrant sex workers accounted for 70% of the sex worker population of most of the Western and Southern European countries it mapped,[5] with notable variations: 80–90% in Austria, Luxemburg, Italy, and Spain, 60–75% in Belgium, Denmark, Finland, France, Greece, the Netherlands, and Norway, 56% in Portugal, and 40% in the United Kingdom (TAMPEP, 2009a). In some of these countries, this increase in numbers took place over a very short period of time: in Norway, for example, migrants represented 20% of the sex worker population in 2001, and by 2008 this had more than tripled to 70% (Skilbrei and Tveit, 2008; TAMPEP, 2010).

In countries that joined the EU in the 2000s, TAMPEP observed that migrants comprised a 16–18% average of sex industry workers, with notable variations: 40% in the Czech Republic, 20–30% in Hungary and Poland, 5% and 10% in the Baltic States and Romania, and as low as 2% in Bulgaria and Slovakia (TAMPEP, 2009a). The Baltic and Eastern and Central European countries are primarily places of origin for migrant sex industry workers, but they also register internal mobility (TAMPEP, 2009b). For example, after Lithuania joined the EU in 2003, a large number of Lithuanian women migrated to Western Europe to sell sex, while others relocated from the country's rural areas to bigger cities to occupy places left by those who had migrated (TAMPEP, 2007c).

In 2009, TAMPEP reported 60 different nationalities of sex workers active throughout Europe, with the largest numbers coming from Eastern and Central Europe, the Baltic countries, Africa, Latin America, and Asia (TAMPEP, 2009a). In 2008, TAMPEP's mapping reported that 87% of those working in the sex industry in Europe were cis women, 7% were cis men, and 6% were transgender

(TAMPEP, 2009a). The lack of specific service provision for male and transgender sex workers, however, results in a paucity of information on these populations, and therefore the percentages reported above are considered to be rather conservative (Grimes, 2001; TAMPEP, 2009a).

Sex markets have consistently expanded and diversified over recent decades. In 2008, just over one-third of sex workers in Europe worked outdoors (TAMPEP, 2009a), with the majority selling sexual services in a wide array of indoor settings, including brothels, massage parlors, private apartments, hotels, bondage and domination spaces, erotic phone lines, lap dancing clubs, stripping, and webcamming (TAMPEP, 2009a; Jahnsen and Wagenaar, 2018). The shift from outdoor to indoor sex work that has been taking place since the mid-2000s in response to the emergence of new commercial sex forms online and increased policing of street-based sex workers has made it more difficult for service providers to contact their target populations, although many TSOs have been developing new outreach methods to address this challenge (TAMPEP, 2009a, 2010; Sanders et al., 2018; Strohmayer, Laing and Comber, 2019). HIV prevalence rates also vary across the region from a low of 0.2% among cis-female workers in Germany to 13% in Portugal, and almost 20% in Latvia, with the limited data available suggesting that rates are higher among cis-male and transgender sex workers, at 2% in the Czech Republic and over 20% in Germany and the Netherlands (NSWP, 2014b; Reeves et al., 2017).

Prostitution policies in the 37 countries featured in this chapter can be categorized as either repressive or restrictive, using Östergren's (2017) typology mentioned in Chapter 2, with implications for TSOs' scope and reach. The goal of *repressive* policies is to eradicate the sex industry through criminal penalties and rehabilitative programs, which makes it difficult for those who sell sex to organize politically or provide harm reduction services, which "can be perceived as encouraging sex work and/or inciting crime" (Östregren, 2017: 14). Examples of repressive policies include those in Albania and Lithuania, which criminalize and regard the sale and purchase of sex as an act against morality and dignity, and Sweden, which criminalizes and regards sex purchase as a human rights violation; in these contexts, access to services may be conditional on exiting the sex industry (NSWP, 2014b; Östregren, 2017; Jahnsen and Wagenaar, 2018). The goal of *restrictive* policies is to contain, limit, and strictly regulate the sale of sex to reduce its negative consequences through criminal and administrative law, including mandatory health checks, while still permitting self-organizing and harm reduction among people who sell sex (Östregren, 2017). Examples of restrictive policies include countries that impose very specific conditions on the sale and purchase of sex, making it very difficult to do so without contravening criminal or administrative law, as in Estonia, Italy, Poland, Slovakia, and the United Kingdom, to name a few across the region. Other restrictive approaches, present in Denmark, Germany, Greece, and the Netherlands, for example, make it legal to sell and purchase sexual services, and in some instances to act as an intermediary, but only under very specific conditions that differ from other commercial activities, as in Greece, where only unmarried, cis women with citizenship status are allowed to legally perform sex work (ICRSE, 2015a).

National prostitution laws and policies, whether restrictive or repressive, are rarely applied homogeneously in each country, especially in federations and in countries with devolved regional or local administrations. For example, each of Switzerland's 26 Cantons has a different restrictive policy approach to regulating prostitution and significant variations in terms of outreach and support services for people who sell sex (Chimienti and Bugnon, 2018). Similarly, Germany's federal prostitution law applies across the country but southern states tend to put in place more repressive ordinances and bylaws than northern ones, with varying tax and trade laws likewise producing considerable disparities in working conditions and available services (Hunecke, 2018).

Legal and policy instruments that are not explicitly about prostitution also play a significant role in shaping how policing and other forms of regulation take place, as occurs with legal measures that criminalize and further marginalize trans people (ICRSE, 2015b).[6] Anti-immigration policies have also resulted in making migrants who sell sex vulnerable to arrest, abuse, and violence, especially when fear of deportation among the undocumented forces them to work in hidden spaces less visible to outreach services (TAMPEP, 2015; Vuolajärvi, 2019). Since prostitution is not recognized as part of the formal labor market of most countries, migrants with EU citizenship are often unable to provide the proof of income required to access health insurance, social assistance, and other public services (TAMPEP, 2009b). Processes of criminalization, exclusion, and marginalization are also connected to discriminatory social norms. Across Europe, and in Central and Eastern European countries in particular, Roma people's historically disadvantaged position puts them at higher risk of sexually transmitted infections, substance abuse, and sex trafficking, and makes them a particularly hard-to-reach population for TSOs (Dena et al., 2005; TAMPEP, 2007b; Finger, 2016). For example, diffused xeno-, trans-, and homophobia, combined with the absence of nondiscrimination laws, create the condition for heightened vulnerability of Roma male and transgender sex workers in North Macedonia, further aggravated by the stigma and violence they face in the public sphere and in institutional settings (NSWP, 2014b).

It is in this complex context that TSOs operate in the field of sex work and prostitution in Europe, approaching the phenomenon in different ways and with different aims, as discussed below.

Sex work and prostitution TSOs: Clusters

Variations in the composition, organization, and governance of sex for sale across Europe play an important role in shaping differences in the typologies, reach, and effectiveness of TSOs' service provision in the field. Different histories with respect to third sector service provision to people involved in commercial sex also account for a diversified picture. In some Western European countries, such as France, Italy, and the United Kingdom, women who sell sex have been the recipients of a variety of services from nonstate organizations for well over a century, and well-established sex work and prostitution TSOs and networks remain active. In most Baltic, Central and Eastern European, and Scandinavian countries, conversely, these TSOs are fewer in number, more recently formed, and confined to larger cities (TAMPEP, 2007a, 2010). Like European TSOs operating in other sectors, sex work and prostitution TSOs vary in their workforce size and composition, revenue sources, the extent and nature of their engagement with local and national policy makers and enforcers, and the type and constitution of their organization (e.g., charity, collective, committee, cooperative, or trade union). Third sector organizations relating to sex work and prostitution are however distinguished by the divergent conceptual frameworks undergirding their approaches to problems facing people in the sex industry. We identify three main clusters into which TSOs working in this area can be grouped based on their different understandings of and approaches to commercial sex and those involved in it: *Sex Worker Rights, Prostitution as Gendered Violence,* and *Harm Reduction.*

Similarly to the four-prong typology elaborated by Oselin and Weitzer (2013) in their study of prostitute-serving organizations in Canada and the United States (neutral, radical feminist, sex work, and youth oriented, see Chapter 1), the three clusters identified here tend to be aligned with the dominant theoretical paradigms elaborated in academic scholarship: empowerment, oppression, and polymorphous. Yet three important differences exist between the typology established by Oselin and Weitzer and the clusters identified here. First, our *Prostitution as Gendered Violence* is more expansive than the *Radical Feminist* category identified by Oselin and Weitzer (2013) and includes TSOs for whom prostitution is a violent and exploitative practice that reflects and reinforces gender inequality, whether they are faith-based, secular, and/or (radical) feminist. Second, instead of identifying *Youth-Oriented* programs as a separate group, TSOs that provide services to minors are included under one of the three main clusters, depending on their approach. Third, we include the additional cluster of *Harm-Reduction* organizations that provide services both exclusively to people who sell sex and to different vulnerable populations, such as injection drug users, and which might (or might not) explicitly advocate for social and legal reform on commercial sex as part of their activities, but when they do, this is not the primary focus of their remit. Doing so allows us to distinguish *Harm Reduction* TSOs from *Sex Worker Rights* and *Prostitution as Gendered Violence* TSOs, which also provide harm reduction services as part of their activities but whose primary focus is to advocate for social and legal reform with respect to commercial sex.

The ways in which TSOs across the ideological spectrum utilize harm reduction to varying degrees emphasizes how our cluster typology is a heuristic device which might not "comfortably" fit all TSOs into one of the three clusters identified, particularly when boundaries between them are blurred – although this is never the case between *Sex Worker Rights* and *Prostitution as Gendered Violence* TSOs, which could be visualized as polar opposites.

Likewise, TSOs are not static and may shift their ideological stance over time, as occurred in the 2000s when social workers at the Belgian Catholic and neo-abolitionist[7] Mouvement du Nid, which had been in existence since 1980, started rejecting the organization's approach and services "which they judged insufficient for dealing with the situations of the people they met" (David, 2019: 207). In 2006, the organization was renamed *Entre 2* and began its new activities with a harm-reduction approach directed at migrant women in the sex industry (David and Loopmans, 2018). In their study of prostitution policies in the Nordic countries, Skilbrei and Holmström (2013) note how one of the three Swedish state-supported units tasked with organizing support services for people in prostitution has transitioned over time from a strict neo-abolitionist to a harm-reduction approach. And, of course, tensions and at times overt confrontations are not uncommon between TSOs with different approaches. For example, the French neo-abolitionist Mouvement du Nid has accused harm reduction-oriented community health groups of facilitating women's exploitation by allowing them to "prostitute themselves better" (Mathieu, 2004: 158). *Sex Worker* TSOs claim that far from offering nonjudgmental services, *Prostitution as Gendered Violence* TSOs' rescue and rehabilitation efforts fail to account for the complex realities, rights, and agency of those involved in commercial sex (Hahn and Holzscheiter, 2013; FUCKFÖRBUNDET, 2019). Such deep-seated disagreements between TSOs play out in a variety of different fora, including mainstream and social media and governance initiatives, as well as in international platforms and conferences.

Sex Worker Rights organizations

Ethos, claims, and demands

Sex Worker Rights organizations hold that "people should have the right to work in the sex industry free of persecution, especially when faced with limited economic options" (ICRSE, 2016: 9). As National Ugly Mugs, a UK *Sex Worker Rights* organization, states on its website:

> We believe in and advocate for the human rights of sex workers including: the right to self-determination; the right to live free from violence; the right to live free from intimidation, coercion or exploitation; the right to work as safely as possible; the right to police protection.
>
> (NUM, 2020)

Sex Worker Rights TSOs acknowledge that sexism, misogyny, and racism pervade the sex industry (Smith and Mac, 2018) while emphasizing that criminalizing those involved in it is not the solution. As the Italian feminist sex workers' collective Ombre Rosse (Red Shadows) states:

> Often when we work as sex workers we experience forms of exploitation, discrimination and violence, which are undoubtedly also patriarchal, sexist, transphobic and racist. But we also are subjected to various forms of direct and indirect stigmatization and criminalization ... which unfortunately at times are also supported by pseudo-feminist arguments.
>
> (Ombre Rosse, 2020)[8]

The core demands of European *Sex Worker Rights* TSOs are very much in line with those of the sex workers' movement globally and include the decriminalization of sexual labor, its recognition as work, and an end to its sociolegal oppression. They campaign against violence, human rights abuse, and stigmatization, and for sex workers' improved access to health services and economic empowerment. Central to their demands is an end to criminalization, which they view as enhancing exclusion and exploitation among those who operate in the sex industry and failing to address, as the French sex worker union states, "the structural vulnerability of workers, especially migrant workers, to slavery-like working conditions" (STRASS, 2016: 32). These TSOs also advocate for an end to the conflation of sex work, migration, and trafficking, with the Sex Workers Alliance Ireland claiming that an anti-trafficking focus on criminalization, anti-immigration measures, and "awareness-raising" does not respond to "the circumstances of deep poverty, domestic violence, homelessness, and drug misuse that lead some to becoming susceptible to trafficking" (SWAI, 2019).

Sex Worker Rights TSOs emphasize that while sex workers are the people best placed to aid in the fight against sex trafficking and in developing sex work-related laws, policies and best practices for their implementation, their voices and expertise remain ignored. To challenge this status quo, they demand their meaningful involvement "in the design, development, implementation, management, and monitoring and evaluating in programming, policy and legislation" (NSWP, 2017a). Finally, these TSOs recognize that the majority of those involved in the sex industry are cis women but emphasize the growing diversity of sex workers' identities, work modes, and experiences, and the importance of advocating for and reaching out to often overlooked populations in the "sex worker communities' different sub-populations, including male and trans sex workers, (undocumented) migrant sex workers, sex workers who use drugs, or sex workers living with HIV" (ICRSE, 2015a: 10).

Origin, evolution, and contemporary landscape

We already saw in Chapter 2 that, as in most of the Americas, European *Sex Worker Rights* TSOs formed and evolved around three successive waves of collective actions led by sex workers. The first wave of sex workers' organizing comprised various ephemeral, and at times impromptu, sex workers' mobilizations over the eighteenth, nineteenth, and first half of the twentieth century, setting the precedent for a second wave of collective organizing and mobilization in the late 1970s. The first national sex worker-led collectives to emerge from the latter mobilizations were all Western European: the English Collective of Prostitutes (ECP) founded in 1975, the German Hydra founded in 1980, the Italian Committee for the Civil Rights of Prostitutes, and the Swiss Aspasie founded in 1982. Only one of these organizations has since ceased its activities: the Dutch De Rode Draad (the Red Thread), founded in 1985 and closed in 2012.

The second wave encompassed grassroots sex worker organizations formed in the mid- to late 1980s and 1990s when new funding opportunities started being channeled into HIV-related programs (Stevenson and Dziuban, 2018). Among these were the Scottish Prostitutes Education Project (SCOTPEP), founded in 1989 in Edinburgh; the community health project Cabiria, active in Lyon, France since 1993; and the Colectivo Hetaira, founded in Spain in 1995 and active until 2019, all of which combined a public health approach centered on preventing HIV/AIDS, hepatitis, and other sexually transmitted infections with advocating for sex workers' rights.

A third wave of sex worker mobilization has been taking place since the early 2000s in response to many countries' heightened criminalization of behaviors and practices related to the sale of sex, and in opposition to increasing support for the Swedish approach of client criminalization (Scoular and Sanders, 2010; Stevenson and Dziuban, 2018). During this time, Scandinavian countries have seen the formation of the majority of their *Sex Worker Rights* TSOs, including SIO in Denmark – "founded in the spring 2008, mainly as a response to the general political ambition to criminalize our profession" (SIO, 2020) – and in Sweden, where previous initiatives by sex workers had been short-lived, the Rose Alliance founded in 2010 remains active in service provision and in fighting to repeal the current prostitution law. Other countries with punitive anti-prostitution policies, for example in the Balkans and Central Europe, saw the formation of the first *Sex Worker Rights* TSOs in the 2010s which, in the process, often had to face direct state opposition. STAR-STAR in North Macedonia was able to register with the government as "Association for the Support of Marginalized Workers" in 2010, after two years of existence, but was not allowed to use "sex work" in its official name (NSWP, 2014a).

New "third-generation" organizations have also been formed since the late 2000s in countries with already well-established *Sex Work Rights* TSOs: SWARM (Sex Worker Advocacy and Resistance Movement) is a UK collective founded in 2009, PROUD, the Dutch sex worker union formed in 2015 (PROUD, 2020), and the previously mentioned Ombre Rosse, is an Italian feminist collective of sex workers and activists founded in 2016. Moreover, a number of less structured sex workers' self-support groups also organized, although not all were able to sustain their activities over a long period. The NGO Odysseus in Bratislava, Slovakia, was founded in 2004 to facilitate a bimonthly self-support group for female sex workers, and the self-support group for sex workers at the AIDS Center in Vilnius, Lithuania, was created in 2002; however, both were poorly attended and short-lived (CEEHRN, 2005).

The dynamism of this third wave of sex work rights TSOs contributed to the revitalization of the movement, expanding the breadth of its involvement in three key ways (Stevenson and Dziuban, 2018): (1) by including, representing, advocating for, and providing services to the diverse sex worker population; for example, the Romanian SexWorkCall includes "queer, trans and/or Roma" sex workers and is committed "to having an intersectional approach", including collaborations with LGBTQ+ and Roma activist groups (NSWP, 2020); (2) by becoming more attentive to the sex industry's numerous settings and associated variations in working conditions and managerial relations, as did the German BesD (the Professional Association for Erotic and Sexual Service Providers), which explicitly welcomes anyone with current or previous work experience "in a brothel or in an apartment, on the street, through an agency, in a massage parlor, in a BDSM studio, as a cam model or phone sex operator" (BesD, 2020); (3) by recognizing the increased criminalization of migrant sex workers – especially those who are undocumented – and the struggles they face (Stevenson and Dziuban, 2018).

Indeed migrant sex workers have been a particular focus for some *Sex Work Rights* TSOs; as mentioned in Chapter 2, TAMPEP, although not a TSO *per se*, was a pioneer in developing improved services for and with migrant sex workers in the 1990s, when existing services for the latter group were scarce in Europe, as further explained in Box 5.1. More recently, a number of *Sex Work Rights* TSOs have either started working with migrant sex workers specifically, are migrant sex worker-led, or they have started focusing, with targeted services and advocacy, on this population. As the Danish sex worker organization SIO states on its website:

> the struggle for sex workers' rights must begin with securing rights and good working conditions for those who are in dire need of it. … Therefore, we devote a lot of energy to raising awareness about migrant sex workers, and sex workers who work on the streets.
>
> (SIO, 2020)

Other examples include organizations such as x:talk, a sex worker-led cooperative based in London whose activities center around teaching English to migrant sex workers as a fundamental tool "to work in safer conditions, to organize and to socialize with each other" (x:talk, 2020), and Les Roses d'Acier (Steel Roses) formed in 2014 by Chinese Sex Workers in Paris, "to discuss work conditions, to better access common rights, to fight against discrimination, to try to prevent violence, to develop solidarity among sex workers, and to encourage interaction between sex workers and the rest of the society" (Les Roses d'Acier, 2016).

Box 5.1: The European Network for the Promotion of the Rights and Health of Migrant Sex Workers/TAMPEP

Originally named the Transnational AIDS/STI Prevention Among Migrant Prostitutes in Europe Project, TAMPEP was formed in 1993 through a collaboration between four TSOs: Amnesty for Women in Germany, the Committee for the Civil Rights of Prostitutes in Italy, the Mr A. de Graaf Stichting, also known as the Dutch Institute for Prostitution Issues, in the Netherlands, and later joined by LEFO, Latin American Migrant Women in Austria. Operating from a sex worker rights perspective, TAMPEP's objective was to develop "in collaboration with migrant sex workers, more effective strategies to facilitate contact with the target group, as well as new materials" (Brussa, 1998: 247). In the following years, it expanded to 25 countries in Europe (see endnote 5), and it remains active in three interdependent areas pertaining to sex workers: research on living and working conditions, intervention to reduce vulnerability to HIV and other sexually transmitted infections, and human rights advocacy (TAMPEP, 2009a: 5). With consistent European Commission funding until the late 2000s, TAMPEP coordinated numerous activities, organized meetings, and supported research among its partners, generating a wide range of resources, including manuals, multilingual training and educational materials, and detailed reports that provide insights into factors that impact service provision. TAMPEP's 2009 report "Sex Work in Europe. A Mapping of the Prostitution Scene in 25 European Countries" (TAMPEP, 2009a) remains to this day, after more than a decade, the most comprehensive mapping of commercial sex in Europe. As stressed in one of its reports, "one of the central elements in our method is the application of continuous assessment of the situation in prostitution and the techniques of the collection of data for the efficiency of outreach work" (TAMPEP, 2007c: 106). The activities that TAMPEP organized during the time of its European Commission-funded projects enabled the formation of alliances and the sharing of best practices, thus deepening existing cooperation and a shared identity among the TSOs involved – developments that due to limited, or lack of, domestic opportunity structures and resources would have otherwise proven extremely difficult (TAMPEP, 2007c). TAMPEP continues its activities today by focusing on alliance building, advocacy, and networking; however, for over a decade it has not received the scale of funding that enabled the breadth and depth of its earlier activities.

Most of the sex worker rights TSOs mentioned thus far were formed with a specific focus on sex workers' well-being and rights, yet it is equally important to acknowledge TSOs that include sex workers as part of their services to and advocacy for other communities. Maiz in Austria provides a variety of services to migrant women but a central aspect of its tasks is to work with migrant women who work in the sex industry and to fight against the stigmatization, discrimination, and criminalization of people who offer sexual services (Maiz, 2020). Other TSOs with a similar approach include LGBTQ+ organizations that provide services to LGBTQ+ sex workers, such as the Albanian Aleanca LGBT, whose mission is to enhance and protect the human rights of LGBTQ+ communities and LGBTQ+ sex workers in Albania by strengthening advocacy tools and capacities and documenting human rights abuses (Aleanca LGBT et al., 2018).

Establishing alliances between social movements has been especially important in the recent work of the International Committee on the Rights of Sex Workers in Europe (ICRSE). Stating that the "struggle for sex workers' rights intersects with many other social movements", the ICRSE has been at the forefront of promoting an intersectional approach that acknowledges that the

> struggle for sex workers' rights intersects with the fight of other social groups who have been historically marginalized and oppressed. ... Sex workers are male, female and non-binary, mothers, LGBTQ, migrants and workers. Supporting sex workers' rights means understanding the diversity and complexity of our lives and involving sex workers from diverse communities in discussions, decision and policy-making.
>
> (ICRSE, 2018: 4)

For this purpose, ICRSE created a series of briefing papers aimed at providing activists and policy makers with "the tools to explore the intersection of sex workers' rights with other rights and social struggles such as those connected with LGBT+ people, women, workers, migrants and health" (ICRSE, 2015b).

The ICRSE is also one of the two main European sex workers' networks, representing 103 organizations led by or working with sex workers – including service providers, LGBTQ+ rights organizations, and harm reduction organizations – in 32 countries in Europe and Central Asia, and more than 150 individuals including sex workers, academics, trade unionists, human rights advocates, and women's rights and LGBTQ+ rights activists. Founded in 2004 with the goal of organizing the 2005 European Conference on Sex Work, Human Rights, Labor, and Migration, it has since become an important regional network in opposing the criminalization of sex workers, raising awareness about their social exclusion, promoting their human, health and labor rights, and building alliances with (and supporting and creating training tools for) key partners, including sex workers and their organizations globally (Stevenson and Dziuban, 2018; ICRSE, 2020).

The other main European sex workers' network is the Sex Workers' Rights Advocacy Network (SWAN hereafter), which comprises 28 TSOs, both sex worker-led and non sex worker-led. Founded in 2006 and officially registered in 2012, SWAN is active in Central and Eastern Europe and Central Asia, advocating for the human rights of sex workers and building the capacities of national and local sex worker-led initiatives and their allies (SWAN, 2020a). There were some sex worker-led initiatives in the region prior to SWAN, yet in just a few years SWAN has formed a sex worker movement by "creating a platform that empowered sex workers, amplified their voices, provided practical tools and support for their work and advocated around their needs at the regional and global level" (SWAN, 2020d: 2). These transnational networks "play a crucial role in strengthening the sex worker community in the region", facilitating knowledge-sharing and inclusive self-representation (Stevenson and Dziuban, 2018, 387).

Box 5.2: Sex Worker Rights TSOs: Main activities and services provided[9]

General support services	Hotline; housing and welfare support; career guidance counseling; language classes; outreach; entrance, transition, and exit counseling; support with finding alternative employment; online forum for info, exchange, discussion, and support by and for sex workers; shelter/crisis homes; digital app to report violence; digital support via chat; fundraising for emergency situations
Health-related	Psychological support; testing for STIs; outreach work; condom and lube distribution; distribution of information material; facilitation of referrals; medical clinics; primary health care; sexual health; family planning; HIV and AIDS care
Legal and financial matters	Legal aid; litigation; migration counseling; debt counseling; tax counseling; help with filling tax returns; social security and benefits counseling
Advocacy and campaigning	Lobbying; media advocacy; engagement with local and national policy makers and politicians; organization of demonstrations, public events, conferences
Monitoring, documenting, and research	Documenting and monitoring the application and enforcement of various policies; collection of data; primary research; writing of reports
Provision of space	Meeting point; laundry services, showers, and clothes
Liaison with public institutions	Hospitals; police force; immigration officials; education bodies

---

Prostitution as Gendered Violence organizations

Ethos, claims, and demands

Prostitution as Gendered Violence TSOs approach prostitution as a fundamental obstacle to gender equality and a human rights violation against women and girls with damaging effects on their physical, psychological, and sexual integrity (CAP, 2020; Malostratos, 2020). As the Italian Association Iroko states: prostitution is "fundamentally exploitative and violent and … incompatible, in any form, with gender equality. Therefore all efforts must be made to abolish this practice" (Iroko Associazione Onlus, 2020a). Some of these TSOs explicitly point out that their approach is "not founded on morality or judgements of sex or sexuality" (Iroko Associazione Onlus, 2020a) and instead claim to adopt a rights-based approach whereby, in providing non-judgmental services, they operate by fully respecting the will of those they aim to support, even when they decide to continue their activities in prostitution. As the Danish Reden International states:

> We work to improve the conditions of women … through harm reduction, healthcare, counselling, etc. and to help them change their life situation, if that's what they want. We work from a rights-based approach and organize our offerings according to what our users themselves will say will be the best help.
>
> (Reden International, 2020a)

In other instances participation in their programs requires leaving the sex industry, as in the case of the Swedish TSO Talita's offering each woman who approaches the organization "a place in our long-term rehabilitation program. The only criteria to enter the program is the woman's motivation to leave prostitution and experience a transformed life" (Donevan, 2018: 2).

Prostitution as Gendered Violence organizations do not use the terms "sex work" and "sex worker", which they view as contributing to legitimating violence against women. Instead, they often adopt the terms "prostituted woman" or "woman involved in prostitution", and their equivalents in other languages, "so as not to accidentally further stigmatise or victimise the women and girls trapped in the sex trade" (Women@thewell, undated: 3).[10] While *Prostitution as Gendered Violence* TSOs take the position that all people involved in prostitution are victimized, they tend to focus mostly on cis women, as seen in their exclusive references to women and girls.

As mentioned previously, a recent wave of activity, since the 2000s, has seen the strengthening of what is often referred to as neo-abolitionism, "a term used to describe the more exclusive focus on clients", as compared to nineteenth-century abolitionism (Scoular, 2015: 8). This entails campaigning for criminalizing the purchase of sex acts and strengthening the criminal justice response and cooperation in the fight against traffickers and procurers (Scoular, 2015). By holding sex buyers accountable through criminal charges, neo-abolitionists claim that men who buy sex are forced to take responsibility for their actions, an approach which, as the Women's Support Project in Scotland states, "sends a clear message that it is not acceptable for women to be treated as commodities to be bought and sold for sexual use" (Women's Support Project, date n/a: 40). Neo-abolitionists regard legalization and complete decriminalization as failed policies that expand "a multi-billion pound industry which profits from violence against vulnerable women and girls" (ibid.: 37). No meaningful distinction exists between voluntary commercial sex, forced sexual exploitation, and trafficking (Scoular, 2015), with neo-abolitionists viewing prostitution as an exploitative practice believed to be at the root of, and inextricably linked to, sex trafficking. As the French Fondation Scelles (2020) notes, "the system of prostitution is a violation of human dignity and rights, a form of violence, a global organized crime that exploits the most vulnerable people and involves the unacceptable trafficking of human beings".

Origin, evolution, and contemporary landscape

In order to make sense of the emergence, influence, and expansion of European *Prostitution as Gendered Violence* TSOs throughout the twentieth century and in the last two decades, in the context of the ebbs and flows of different discourses on prostitution, we begin this section with a case study from Denmark. While acknowledging variations across and within different countries and regions, the Danish example reveals key conjunctures in the evolution of *Prostitution as Gendered Violence* TSOs, which can be observed to an extent in Europe more broadly, and which are explored in more detail after presenting this brief case study.

Danish abolitionists gained prominence during their mobilization against a new regulationist law on prostitution passed in the country in 1874, when they "campaigned against the legalization of prostitution and advocated for moral equality between men and women, arguing that both genders should be held accountable for the spreading of venereal diseases" (Spanger, 2011: 525). At this point in time, between the end of the nineteenth and beginning of the twentieth century, abolitionists, whether aligned with the women's movement or religious organizations, viewed "fallen" women as passive victims of, but also to an extent responsible for, the deprivation of the capital city, the focus of their concerns in the broader context of industrialization and urbanization (Spanger, 2011; Sevelsted, 2018). Missionaries and religious organizations, such as the Young Women's Christian Association (YWCA), set up institutions for the rehabilitation of women in prostitution in Copenhagen (Spanger, 2011; Bjønness and Spanger, 2018; Sevelsted, 2018).

Following the rise and domination from the 1920s of other discourses on prostitution, it was not until the 1990s that feminist-led abolitionists returned to assume an important role in shaping discourses about and responses to prostitution in the country, in part as a result of increased migration in and to the region (Spanger, 2011). They approached prostitution as an outcome of gendered inequality and women involved in it as victims of patriarchal violence. When a new law, passed in 1999, partially decriminalized prostitution based on the idea that "prostitution is more suitably regulated through social welfare policies" (Skilbrei and Holmström 2013: 75), public debates became increasingly emotional and centered on whether clients should be criminalized instead, as Sweden had just done. As well as feminist organizations, religious TSOs approaching prostitution as a form of gendered violence started advocating and campaigning for a policy change in the latter direction. The Reden, for example, was established in 1984 by the social work branch of the YWCA and has since had a visible presence in the country's public debate on prostitution, arguing strongly for the criminalization of buyers (Bjønness and Spanger, 2018; KFUKS Sociale Arbejde, 2020). The increasing concern for human trafficking in the early 2000s led to the foundation of Reden International, "to help foreign women in prostitution who have different needs from the Danish ones" (Reden International, 2020b). In 2008, the "8th of

March initiative", an alliance of almost 30 feminist and religious *Prostitution as Gendered Violence* TSOs and political parties, was formed to mobilize against the current prostitution law, advocating for a "Danish model" inspired by Swedish prostitution law (Moustgaard, 2010; Bjønness and Spanger, 2018). At the heart of the initiative, which lasted until 2019, was the belief that prostitution and trafficking are expressions of class divides, whereby "those paying for sex in the rich western word are exploiting other people. Those exploited are most often from poorer parts of the world and are people with hopes and dreams of escaping their poverty" (Moustgaard, 2010).

The Danish example shows, as also seen in Chapter 2, that in the nineteenth and early twentieth centuries the fight against regulationism acted as a catalyst to spark off and strengthen the feminist abolitionist movement in many Western countries. Active both at national and international levels, and often operating in alliance with Christian-inspired groups, abolitionists campaigned to eradicate prostitution and its state regulation, and started delivering services aimed at saving women in prostitution from an undignified life (Outshoorn, 2005) through a mixture of rehabilitation and redemption. Abolitionists' charitable work showed little awareness of, or concern for, inequalities related to race, class, and gender, and instead "was a one-way power relationship whereby middle-class women exerted their own definition of what was considered to be correct forms of behavior and attempted to appropriate the moral selves of the working class" (Bartley, 1998: 40). During this initial stage of the abolitionist movement, TSOs had only limited understanding of prostitution as gendered violence and did not place the issue at the forefront of their campaigning.

The second catalyst for the development of TSOs within this cluster has been the resurgence of prostitution and trafficking on the political agenda of many European countries and supranational institutions in the mid-1980s and 1990s (Outshoorn, 2005; see also Chapter 2). By this time, second-wave feminism had replaced individualistic explanations of women in prostitution as responsible for their own demise with structural gender analyses emphasizing how gender inequality supports prostitution as a form of male violence against women. *Prostitution as Gendered Violence* TSOs formed during this time were, for the most part, located in European migration destination countries and generally self-identified as feminist and/or inspired by religious (Christian) values. Examples include the Association for the Prevention, Reintegration and Care of Prostituted Women (APRAMP), founded in Spain in 1984 to help prostituted women assert "autonomy to begin a life outside of the control and abuse of their exploiters" (APRAMP, 2020); in France Fondation Scelles was created in 1993 and has since "been fighting against the system of prostitution and the exploitation of prostituted persons" (Fondation Scelles, 2020), and Ruhama emerged in Ireland in 1989 "in response to a lack of any support services available to women in prostitution, and was small, inconspicuous and quiet in its initial stages" (Ruhama, 2018: 7).

Finally, the increasing political support for criminalizing the purchase of sex at the beginning of the new millennium can be identified as the third and most recent set of events that have spurred the development and, arguably, strengthening of European *Prostitution as Gendered Violence* TSOs. Decades-old organizations adapted their mission to support this policy approach and, when successful, to help monitor its implementation. The French Fondation Scelles made a major contribution to having the 2016 law criminalizing the purchase of sexual acts adopted, and has since been dedicating parts of its effort to monitoring its implementation and contributing to the repression of perpetrators (Fondation Scelles, 2017). Similarly, Ruhama took an active role in the Irish "Turn Off the Red Light" campaign,[11] which resulted in the passing of the Criminal Law (Sexual Offenses) Act 2017, which makes it a criminal offence to purchase, but not to sell, "sexual access to another person" (Ruhama, 2018: 7).

New TSOs were also formed in the 2000s and 2010s to support women victims of prostitution and advocate for criminalizing the purchase of sex. Inspired by Christian values, Talita was established in Stockholm in 2004 by two trauma therapists "offering both emergency assistance and long-term support to women exploited in prostitution, pornography or human trafficking for sexual purposes" (Donevan, 2018: 179). As one of Talita's managers writes:

> Talita sees Sweden's prostitution laws as a hugely facilitating factor in achieving [its] mission and assisting women in exiting prostitution. The Swedish Model protects society's most vulnerable, extending support, protection and resources to all individuals bought and sold for sex, regardless of what sort of coercion has brought them into the sex industry. As we see in our daily work, criminalizing the buyer, and not the seller, sends a clear message to our target group about whose side the police and other authorities are on.
>
> (Donevan, 2018: 193)

Since its foundation Talita has expanded its activities to opening safe houses in Stockholm and Gothenburg, collaborating with partner organizations in Romania and Kenya, and founding a new Talita organization in Mongolia. Talita's internationalization can be viewed as part of a growing trend among Western European *Prostitution as Gendered Violence* TSOs to partner with or set up "sister" TSOs in countries, in and beyond Europe, where migrant prostitution originates.

As of 2005, the Italian Iroko Association has been working in Nigeria to support potential victims, survivors, returnees, and vulnerable women, girls, and families in Edo State by providing scholarships and other basic needs, and in 2019, it opened its first dedicated office in Benin City (Iroko Associazione Onlus, 2020b). The French Mouvement du Nid has a delegation in Martinique. Initiatives supported by transnational organizations are also worthy of note, such as the Coalition Against Trafficking in Women (CATW) and the European Women's Lobby (EWL),[12] which have been campaigning with local TSOs in the Baltics, the Balkans, and Eastern Europe to promote the criminalization of clients. Bringing together *Prostitution as Gendered Violence* TSOs across countries, albeit not just within Europe, is also the aim of the Coalition for the Abolition of Prostitution

(CAP International), "an advocacy vehicle for frontline NGOs and a global convener for change" comprising 23 organizations based in Europe, North America, Latin America, Asia, the Middle-East, and Africa, whose main objective is

> to advocate for the adoption of 1) domestic legislation and 2) international standards that: eliminate sexual exploitation of women and girls; deliver effective protection, support and exit options to prostituted persons and victims of trafficking; empower frontline services and survivors of prostitution.
> (CAP, 2017: 3)

Similar to TSOs in the first cluster, the *Prostitution as Gendered Violence* organizations mentioned so far specifically address prostitution as the main focus of their activities. There are others, however, that address a variety of issues related to women and/or exploitation and vulnerability, including exploitation in prostitution. Médicos del Mundo, for example, is a Spanish humanitarian and social health association founded in 1990 to promote "the fundamental right to health and a decent life for all people, denouncing situations of injustice and violation of human rights" in 19 countries across Asia, America, Africa, the Middle East, and Europe, and it has introduced programs on prostitution "guaranteeing and protecting human rights of victims of trafficking for sexual exploitation and women in prostitution" (Mundos, 2020). In Iceland, Stígamót, the Education and Counseling Center for Survivors of Sexual Abuse and Violence, is a grassroots organization founded in 1990 to fight against sexual violence and to provide assistance to "survivors of rape, sexual molestation, sexual harassment, pornographic exploitation and prostitution" (Stigamot, 2020).

As indicated previously, an analogous understanding of the phenomenon of commercial sex does not preclude disagreements, as was evident in the 1971 split between the French abolitionist TSOs Mouvement du Nid and Amicale du Nid, which occurred over differences regarding what abolitionist-informed activities and services would be more beneficial to women in prostitution, whether advocacy or the provision of shelter and rehabilitation by professional social workers (Mathieu, 2013). More recently, *Prostitution as Gendered Violence* TSOs have begun to differ with respect to their focus on the criminalization of clients approach; the UK-based Beyond the Wall, for example, emphasizes the need to support women in prostitution as opposed to dwelling on unproductive debates "on whether the Nordic approach is the right way or not", which, it claims, are "creating a polarisation where any common ground that there was is being lost. Lines are being drawn and there is little attempt to listen to what is often perceived as 'the other side'". Trying to move beyond this conflict, the organization encourages its peer TSOs to "look at ways of working together to reduce the real-life horror that many sadly live with" (Beyond the Streets, 2014). Similarly, fieldwork with Italian TSOs in the 2000s carried out by this chapter's author revealed a plurality of views among Catholic TSOs, which otherwise shared an understanding of prostitution as violence. The staff of some of these organizations expressed discomfort over the equation of prostitution with slavery and trafficking embraced by some TSOs, and perceived them as simplistic and as neglecting the plurality of experiences amongst migrant women in prostitution they witnessed on a daily basis (Crowhurst, 2007).

Box 5.3: Prostitution as Gendered Violence TSOs: Main activities and services provided

General support services	Hotline; rehabilitation; safe housing; trauma therapy; planning for the future; transition and integration into society; housing and welfare support; career guidance; language classes; outreach to support, motivate and build relationships with target population
Health-related	Psychological support; distribution of information material; facilitation of referrals; (in few cases) provision of condoms, lube, personal alarm
Legal and financial matters	Legal aid; immigration advice; help with applying for social welfare benefits; opening a bank account; managing budgets
Advocacy and campaigning	Lobbying; media advocacy; engage with local and national policy makers and politicians; awareness raising; develop partnerships to pursue and implement common strategies; change attitudes
Monitoring, documenting, and research	Documenting and monitoring the application and enforcement of various policies; collection of data; primary research; writing of reports
Education in schools	Educational activities in schools (e.g., on the harms of prostitution and pornography); prevention activities
Liaise with public institutions	Hospitals; police force; immigration officials; training of professionals

---

Harm-Reduction organizations

Ethos, claims, and demands

Our third cluster comprises *Harm-Reduction* TSOs, which have at their core harm-reduction principles designed to reduce negative health consequences and improve the quality of life of people who use illicit drugs, sell sex, or engage in other behaviors deemed "high risk" (Collins et al., 2012). Harm-reduction service providers do not pass judgment on the behavior of their target populations and instead work with those affected to reduce the risks associated with such behaviors (Ward and Day, 1997). "Meeting people where they are at" rather than holding them to a standard that may cause them to avoid health care altogether is at the core of *Harm-Reduction* TSOs' ethos. As the Antwerp-based Boysproject, an organization that "works for the wellbeing of male and transgender sex workers", states:

> Our main aim is harm reduction and we work pro-actively. In practice, harm reduction is about minimizing risks in different areas, like sexuality, sex work and health. We give them [sex workers] support in different areas to improve their situation and minimize their risks. But we always respect their choices and we never make them do anything they don't want to!
>
> (Boysproject, 2020)

Where possible, *Harm-Reduction* TSOs advocate for their clients and to improve the services available to them. As the Hamburg-based TSO ragazza!, which works with women who sell or exchange sex for drugs, states, "through lobbying we call attention to the situation of these women and take joint political action. ragazza! and its field of work, drugs and prostitution, is represented on various committees and working groups, both within and outside our district" (ragazza!, 2020). Similarly, the UK-based MASH (Manchester Action on Street Health) works locally to "challenge other agencies" to improve their services, liaising with them, local authorities, and enforcement agencies "to ensure coordinated provision which meets our clients' needs" (MASH, 2020), and POW Nottingham, which "seeks to affect larger societal change through advocacy and training, increasing public awareness and providing the tools needed to engage the local and national communities around issues of sex work and sexual exploitation" (POW Nottingham, 2020).

In order to ensure that the services they provide are better targeted, some *Harm-Reduction* TSOs, like Boysproject and ragazza!, only reach out to specific groups of people who sell sex. Others reach out to all sex industry workers and where possible they have sub-projects tailored for specific populations. Still others reach out to many different vulnerable and at-risk populations, including sex workers, and may or may not have services specifically targeting them.

Origin, evolution, and the contemporary landscape

Melissa Ditmore (2006) explains that harm minimization approaches date back centuries, as shown in the writings of Saint Augustine and Thomas Aquinas who advocated tolerance of prostitution to prevent the spread of greater "evils", including sodomy and unfettered lust. Similarly, the type of regulationism implemented in many nineteenth-century European countries can also be viewed as an approach aimed at reducing the harms inherent in prostitution. As Skilbrei and Holmström write in relation to the regulationist system applied in the Nordic countries during this time, "this approach to prostitution was a harm reductive one as it was an attempt to control the spread of STIs, especially syphilis" rather than to eradicate the sale of sex (Skilbrei and Holmström 2013: 73). Yet the implementation of such policies was primarily for the benefit of society, as opposed to being based on any concern for the women who sold sexual services (Ditmore, 2006). In contrast, contemporary harm reduction emerged in the 1980s as a public health response to concerns about HIV/AIDS and injecting drug use aimed at improving the health and well-being of populations at risk (Cusick, 2006).

Throughout the 1980s and 1990s, *Harm Reduction* TSOs started to develop in Europe with the aim of minimizing health risks for people in the sex industry, who were identified as a particularly vulnerable population in the context of the HIV/AIDS pandemic. Here we focus in particular on TSOs that, at least at their inception, had a specific/unique public health focus and emerged in parallel to and distinctly from harm reduction initiatives developed by sex worker organizations during this same time.

The development and evolution of *Harm Reduction* TSOs were, and continue to be, shaped by context-specific prostitution policies and politics; the status and organization of public health provisions; and levels of engagement, or lack thereof, with relevant public bodies including the police, local authorities, sex worker collectives, and national health care providers. In France, for example, the government's delayed response to the HIV/AIDS crisis allowed time and space for grassroots harm-reduction TSOs to develop and grow in numbers, challenging in turn the monopoly of abolitionist rescue-based services targeted at those involved in prostitution (St Denny, 2016). Similarly, as Marion David (2019) notes, in Belgium, a contributing factor to the spread of harm reduction TSOs during the last two decades of the twentieth century was traditional abolitionist groups' refusal to address health-related aspects of prostitution, partly to avoid practices they were against in principle, such as distributing condoms, but also for fear that any type of prostitution-related health monitoring might facilitate a return to regulationism.

Indeed, concerns that harm reduction services might increase health monitoring, surveillance of, and stigma attached to sex workers have been acknowledged and addressed by many of those involved in their delivery. As Netta Maciver and colleagues asked themselves before setting up a health care service for women selling sex in Glasgow in 1989: "Would the service offer something positive or simply contribute to further control?", but also, "would the women be exposed to publicity and risk to their family and community lives?" and "could this service contribute to further scapegoating of an already much scapegoated group?" (Maciver, 1992: 87). The danger of medicalizing sex workers and of reducing the responsibility and control they can have over their health by making them feel that "they cannot be 'healthy' without the approval of a doctor" (Ward and Day, 1997: 162) was also considered. One way of addressing these issues has been for harm-reduction initiatives, whether governmental or not, to work with sex workers as peers, educators, and experts in the field. The project coordinated by Maciver in Glasgow, for example, started with the understanding that it "could only proceed as a partnership with the women concerned [... and] it has become a well-used service because its main architects are the women who use it" (Maciver, 1992: 87, 94–95).

Similarly, the French Agency for the Fight Against AIDS helped set a participatory agenda whereby people with sex industry experience could work on an equal footing with health care professionals, based on the understanding that they would be "better placed to deliver a message promoting safer sex and better health [and] assisting service users in accessing mainstream services and infrastructure" (David, 2019). In the United Kingdom, the 1990s were a "golden age" when considerable financial resources were available to third-sector-led projects and to health clinics and sexual health outreach services within the national health care system. Research shows that information gathered about the complex and intersecting vulnerabilities of sex workers during this time meant that in order to achieve their aims, most of these initiatives adopted a collaborative multi-agency approach to support sex workers with sexual health as well as housing, violence, addiction, financial issues, and more (Phoenix, 2009). This in turn facilitated fruitful relationships with some local police constabularies in the country, especially in relation to interventions aimed at helping sex workers against violent clients and at prosecuting the latter (Maciver, 1992; Phoenix, 2009, 2017). An example of this is the SAFE Project, which pioneered the "Ugly Mugs Scheme" in Birmingham, UK, through the setting up a system of intervention by the police, not aimed at prosecuting sex workers but at protecting them from violence and exploitation. This same template was streamlined in many other British major cities, resulting in a scaling down of the punitive hardline policing previously in place and especially targeted at street sex workers (Phoenix, 2008). In this sense, Phoenix argues, "these projects played an important role in shifting the mode of regulation. … As a result, coercive state-centered responses were displaced as formal criminal justice interventions gave way to a public health and welfare agenda" (Phoenix, 2008: 40).

As the UK case presented here indicates, while the initial priority of many *Harm Reduction* TSOs was reducing the risk of HIV and other infectious diseases, they soon started utilizing a more holistic approach following a "biopsychosocial" model. This moves away from an exclusive focus on the absence of disease and emphasizes the importance of access to sexual health education, health care and decision-making, aiming to minimize a complexity of interlinked health, psychological, social, and structural harms (Ditmore, 2006; Stevenson and Petrak, 2007). This is the case for Pro-tukipiste, a Finnish TSO founded in 1990 providing specialist health and social services aimed at the promotion of "participation and human rights of people who work in sex or erotic industry and of those who are victims of trafficking" (Pro-tukipiste, 2020). At its three drop-in centers, one in each of the largest cities in the country, it provides health and psychological counseling, testing and vaccinations, free condoms, lubricants, clean needles, syringes and other equipment associated with safer injecting, as well as guidance and advice on how to access services such as "applying for benefits, employment, education opportunities, housing and residence permits", help with legal advice, and accompanying their clients to other offices when needed (Pro-tukipiste, 2020).

Harm Reduction TSOs for the most part take a proactive approach that usually entails outreach work to provide their services in different spaces where commercial sex takes place. The organization ROZKOŠ bez RIZIKA (Bliss without Risks), active since 1992 in the Czech Republic, carries out its outreach programs in 12 regions directly in clubs, private homes, and outdoor locations (RIZIKA, 2020). Since 2010, Médecins du Monde, French-based TSO, has been working on different issues, including the promotion of sexual and reproductive health, harm reduction, and fighting HIV. Among its projects is Funambus, a risk-reduction program for people in the sex industry that it has been carrying out since 2010 with outreach services in the French city of Nantes. Through its mobile unit working in prostitution on the streets of the city during its biweekly outings,

> [i]t offers a welcoming, listening and exchange space conducive to health education, prevention material with appropriately translated information on risks linked to STIs, HIV, hepatitis, information on social rights, rights to health and existing services, guidance based on the needs expressed by target population on social structures, care, accommodation, legal aid, integration, assistance. … This program is mainly aimed at migrants who are unaware of the healthcare system and their rights to health insurance and for whom its complexity undermines effective access to healthcare.
>
> (OSCARS, 2010)

Harm Reduction projects in some instances result from collaboration between *Sex Worker Rights* and other TSOs. In Switzerland, the Boulevards bus, a reception space established in 1996 for those operating in the sex industry, emerged from a collaboration between the Geneva AIDS Group and the *Sex Worker Rights* TSO Aspasie to "prevent and reduce the risks associated with the practice of prostitution and the consumption of drugs. … It offers information and prevention as well as materials (condoms, lubricants, intimate wipes) with a needle exchange program for drug users" (Aspasie, 2020). In Denmark, since 2017 the organization Minoritet, a "voluntary association that works to create dignified conditions and solutions for street minorities" (Minoritet, 2020), and the Danish *Sex Worker Rights* organization SIO launched the project Sexelance, "harm reduction on four wheels", aimed at making "street-based sex work more safe" in Copenhagen.

> Sexelance is an ambulance car that can be used by street-based sex workers to see clients. Inside the car there are banners saying that the volunteers will call the police if there are signs of violence. The banners also encourage sex workers to inform the authorities if they are victims of trafficking.
>
> (NSWP, 2017b)

Its clinical looking interior, Plambech (2018) explains, is to avoid the risk of being seen as encouraging prostitution.

In the example above, we have mostly considered *Harm-Reduction* TSOs that specifically focus on sex workers, but there are many more operating in different fields of intervention, including commercial sex. Medicines de Monde was an example, and others in different European regions are *JAZAS*, founded in Bosnia in 1991, "the first NGO which was active in the field of AIDS prevention in the territory of the former Yugoslavia (then the Yugoslav Association Against AIDS)" working with different vulnerable populations but especially sex workers (SWAN, 2020c); and the Romanian Association Against AIDS (ARAS), a "non-governmental, apolitical, voluntary-based, not for profit organization, founded in Bucharest in 1992" (SWAN, 2020b). Since then it has been running the first program targeting sex workers in Romania, and in 2001, it opened a specific project for sex workers who are intravenous drug users (ibid.). In its reports on service provision organizations for sex workers in Europe, TAMPEP praised ARAS for being one of the relatively few organizations to successfully integrate multiple vulnerabilities within their harm reduction services, in particular by establishing communication and partnership between sex work and drug harm reduction services that took into account the specific needs and context of Roma sex worker drug users (TAMPEP, 2007b).

As with TSOs in the other two clusters, *Harm Reduction* TSOs are part of national and transnational networks and coalitions. Some are members of sex worker networks such as the ICRSE, SWAN, and the Global Network of Sex Work Projects (NSWP), and others form part of drug harm reduction organizations such as the Eurasian Harm Reduction Association (EHRA), a "non-for-profit public membership-based organization uniting harm reduction activists and organizations from Central and Eastern Europe and Central Asia" (EHRA, 2020), and Correlation, the European Network on Social Inclusion and Health, whose "activities connect harm reduction services, grassroots organizations, community-based services, research institutes, and health facilities from all over Europe" (Correlation, 2020).

Box 5.4: Harm Reduction TSOs: Main activities and services provided

Health-related	Psychological support; testing for STIs; outreach work; condom, lube, and syringe distribution; distribution of information material; facilitation of referrals; medical clinics; primary health care; sexual health, family planning, HIV, and AIDS care; needle exchange; outreach
Legal and financial matters	Legal aid; help with filing tax returns; social security and benefits counseling
Advocacy and campaigning	Lobbying; media advocacy; engage with local and national policy makers and politicians
Liaise with public institutions	Hospitals; police force; immigration officials; welfare services

Funding issues

Sex work and prostitution TSOs in Europe are funded from a variety of sources, including statutory ones (national governments, local authorities, supra-national institutions such as the EU), external donors (e.g., Aidsfonds, the Global Fund to Fight AIDS, TB and Malaria, Mama Cash, the Open Society Foundations, and the Robert Carr Fund), donations, fundraising, and membership fees. Many of these income sources need to be sought and/or applied for regularly to ensure continuity of projects and activities pursued and the very sustainability of the organizations. To respond to the time-limits established by funding bodies, which often grant small pots of money with a yearly duration, TSOs have to design short-term projects. The threat of losing funding and the risk of interrupting or downsizing their interventions are some of the main barriers identified by TAMPEP (2007b) to TSOs' delivery of quality services that respond appropriately to the needs of their target populations. When the Global Fund to Fight AIDS, TB and Malaria suspended funding to North Macedonia in 2017, the activities of many TSOs dependent on those funds, including the *Harm Reduction* TSO Healthy Options Project Skopje (HOPS), were jeopardized. A coalition of TSOs was subsequently formed and some support was received through an Open Society Foundations grant, but the activities of HOPS and others had to be downscaled, resulting in overall reduced service provision (NSWP, 2017c; Open Society Foundations, 2017).

The alternating availability of external funds is linked to ever-changing political environments, including those of governments' orientations and agendas, that play a role in dictating who can access funding and for what purpose. David (2019) cites the example of Francophone Belgium, where the *Sex Worker Right TSO* Espace B denounced the politicization of regional funding visible in the munificent grants awarded to the abolitionist Mouvement du Nid in the 1990s. In the Netherlands, the *Sex Worker Rights TSO* De Rode Draad was subsidized for many years by the state and city governments and participated as a key actor in local and national policy making. From the 2000s, however, the new focus of the national discourse on trafficking in the sex industry and on sexual exploitation led to a political rollback with state subsidies redirected to exit and anti-trafficking programs. De Rode Draad was defunded and lost support from politicians and ministers, filing for bankruptcy in 2012 (Gilges, 2018). Similar developments have taken place at the EU level. As a TAMPEP report claims, the preoccupation with sex trafficking since the early 2000s increased funding initiatives from the EU and other donors to anti-trafficking and abolitionist efforts, "yet rarely to sex worker-led groups or service providers with a human rights-based approach to the issue" (TAMPEP, 2015: 3). In the second year of the EU-funded DAPHNE project – an initiative that lasted from 1997 to 2013 and was aimed at funding NGO projects that support victims of violence against women, children, and young people – some members of the European Parliament demanded more transparency after noting that "monies went to only those anti-trafficking measures that did not address prostitution" (Elman, 2007: 101). TSO networks and coalitions that are embedded within EU institutions and are acknowledged by them as legitimate interlocutors can also act as gatekeepers that mobilize influence to ensure that funding is directed at "their" organizations and not at others. Joyce Outshoorn claims that European Women's Lobby "adherents have made several attempts to exclude from funding those NGOs that are seen as promoting the legalization of prostitution, including researchers taking a similar position" (2018: 370). These examples show that funding exclusions tend to apply in particular to organizations that support sex worker rights. This has on occasion raised suspicion over where the funds they manage to access originate, with some unfoundedly accused of being financed by pimps, traffickers, and clients (Grundell, 2015). More recently crowdfunding initiatives by *Sex Worker Rights* TSOs to support sex workers who have been financially severely affected during the coronavirus pandemic have been criticized by neo-abolitionist groups which took the opportunity to accuse these TSOs of normalizing the exploitation of women in prostitution (see for example, Il Manifesto, 2020, Pasionaria, 2020).

Conclusion

This chapter has evidenced the great variety in sex work and prostitution TSOs' typology of services and approaches, and the changes that these organizations have navigated and responded to over time in Europe. In the past three decades in particular, rapid shifts in sex industries' composition, organization, and location in the context of international migrations, geopolitical reconfigurations, internal mobilities, public health crises, and technological advances meant that TSOs already active in the field have had to adjust their service provision, goals, and the breadth of their advocacy. New TSOs have also emerged more recently in response to these developments.

Whether more or less established in time, these organizations subscribe to different views of what prostitution is and how it should be responded to, both politically and in terms of service provision. These views, which served to identify three main clusters of TSOs in the region, might be aligned with or in opposition to dominant political agendas and discourses, and this determines the extent to which they can access funding and contribute to shaping local and/or national policy interventions. Indeed, as this chapter has shown, TSOs are not merely reactive to prevailing political frameworks and dynamics, but they can play an important role in defining them. This was visible in a number of examples presented, including that of the British context in the 1990s when a conducive political environment favored the formation of new and better targeted harm-reduction services and their engagements with public institutions, which in turn contributed to changing how prostitution was governed, albeit for a relatively short time. The contribution of the Dutch De Rode Draad to local and national policy making in the Netherlands in the 1990s is one of the very few cases where an organization within the *Sex Worker Rights* TSO cluster has been actively involved in policy making and benefitted from a political climate that made it possible to apply for and receive state funds. The chapter thus indicated different "golden ages" for TSOs in this field, making it clear that what is a favorable time for some TSOs can be experienced as a time of obscurantism and political exclusion by others.

In Europe, *Sex Worker Rights* TSOs have been struggling, more than organizations in the two other clusters identified, for recognition, for inclusion in policy making decisions, for funding, and to have meaningful discussions, at national government levels, about the policy approach they advocate for – with this state of affairs being particularly acute at the current conjuncture. The conflation of trafficking and prostitution is a dominant framework, and the policy model that is built around it and on an understanding of prostitution as gendered violence is increasingly popular and gaining traction across the region and beyond. TSOs that support and are helping give prominence to this approach have more active roles in policy consultations and policy making and are facilitated in their activities by better access to funding. It is however within *Prostitution as Gendered Violence* TSOs in particular that we observed fractures and disagreements with some "breaking ranks" to pursue typologies of service provision that might not have been in line with their original goals and others calling for a move away from policy model-centered advocacy. The demand for the "best model" of prostitution regulation is also driving many of the current national and transnational debates in Europe, where prostitution has become one of the most controversial areas of political contention (Crowhurst and Skilbrei, 2018). The contemporaneous popularity and contentiousness of the so-called Nordic model, and the political battles that have been unfolding around it, have contributed to intensifying conflicts and disagreements between TSOs. The divisiveness in the field has not spared *Harm Reduction* TSOs, which have been the target of strong criticism, including that of facilitating prostitution and therefore the exploitation of those involved in it. Nevertheless, their activities have received funding more steadily by local, regional, or/and national governments and continue to be embedded in structures of welfare provision.

Lastly, the chapter shed light on the roles that TSOs can have in mapping and data collection on the fast-changing European sex industries. Localized efforts are engaged in by TSOs towards these ends, and coalitions and transnational organizations play a role in expanding the geographical reach and coverage of such activities. However, as noted in a recent overview of prostitution policies in Europe,

> prostitution policy takes place in a largely evidence-free environment. ... Not a single country can boast a precise and reliable statistics. In many countries ..., with the exception of an occasional study by a local NGO, there simply is no data.
>
> (Wagenaar, 2018: 13)

The depth and breadth of the mapping, analysis, and development of best practices that was enabled by the sustained and substantial European funding of the

TAMPEP project in the late 1990s and 2000s remains unparalleled. The current nature of oppositional politics around prostitution, played out at local, national, and supra-national levels, is proving to be an insurmountable impediment to the realization of similar projects and TSO collaborations.

Notes

1 Austria, Belgium, Bulgaria, Croatia, Republic of Cyprus, Czech Republic, Denmark, Estonia, Finland, France, Germany, Greece, Hungary, Ireland, Italy, Latvia, Lithuania, Luxembourg, Malta, Netherlands, Poland, Portugal, Romania, Slovakia, Slovenia, Spain, and Sweden.
2 Albania, Bosnia and Herzegovina, Montenegro, the Republic of Kosovo, the Republic of North Macedonia, and Serbia.
3 The decision to include these countries and exclude others (for example, Belarus, Georgia, Moldova, Turkey and Ukraine) is motivated by the need to contain the scope of the study which, being already broad, would not allow to expound on the socioeconomic, political, and cultural specificities of countries whose belonging to the "idea and ideal" of Europe remain especially contested (see Parker, 2008; White and Feklyunina, 2014).
4 Explanations for such diversity include differences in welfare state regimes (Archambault, 2009), varying heterogeneity in national populations (Weisbrod, 1977), values and sentiments rooted in religion (Putnam, Leonardi, and Nanetti, 1994; Putnam, 2000), and social origins theory, which examines relations established between social groupings and institutions during industrialization and modernization (Salamon, Sokolowski, and Haddock, 2017).
5 Published over a decade ago, TAMPEP's 2009 report *Sex Work in Europe* and others by the network are the most recent and comprehensive mapping "of the prostitution scene" in Europe, based on the collection of empirical data carried out through the collaboration of TSOs in 25 European countries (see also Box 5.1). These are, in the North Region: Denmark, Estonia, Finland, Germany, Latvia, Lithuania, Norway, and the United Kingdom; in the East Region: Austria, Czech Republic, Hungary, Poland, Slovenia, and Slovakia; in the West Region: Belgium, France, Luxemburg, the Netherlands, and Switzerland; and in the South Region: Bulgaria, Greece, Italy, Romania, Spain, and Portugal.
6 For example, in Italy, a law that criminalizes "so-called cross-dressing", when applied, is used to prosecute trans sex workers (ICRSE, 2015b).
7 In research that crosses national, societal, and linguistic boundaries, "the definition and understanding of concepts and the relationship between concepts and contexts are of critical concern" (Hantrais, 2009, 72). An example of the pertinence of this important point in our cross-regional analysis is the use and meaning ascribed to the terms abolitionism and neo-abolitionism. In the Americas, proponents of the approach that view prostitution as a form of violence against women chose to call themselves neo-abolitionists because of this term's roots in the original abolitionism among the nineteenth-century activists who fought to abolish the transatlantic slave trade. In Europe, abolitionism in this field generally refers to the nineteenth-century movement, which used this appellative because they wished to abolish the regulation of prostitution while also drawing parallels between the American campaign against slavery and their own crusade against the "white slave trade" (Gibson, 1986). However, the "neo" in neo-abolitionism in Europe is generally used to identify a more recent alliance formed since the 2000s between radical feminists, social democrats, and moral and religious conservatives who consider prostitution a modern-day slavery, aim to decriminalize the

sell and to criminalize the purchase of sex, and thus distinguish themselves from earlier European abolitionists' activists on prostitution (Scoular, 2015). We use the term "neo-abolitionist/neo-abolitionism" in the European context specifically to refer to TSOs, which since the 2000s have been advocating for the criminalization of the purchase of sex based on the understanding that prostitution is always a form of violence, and "abolitionist/abolitionism" with TSOs who preceded them in time. Organizations that have been in existence for many decades, such as the Mouvement du Nid in France and Belgium, are referred to here as neo-abolitionists because they have embraced and actively advocate for the criminalization of clients.

8 Author's translation.

9 In this box, and in the two similar ones included in the next two sections, we list many, but by no means all, of the services that TSOs provide, based on a review of their websites, and therefore reflecting the language they use.

10 See also (Malostratos 2019).

11 Established in 2009 in Ireland, the Turn Off the Red Light campaign was an alliance of over 70 civil society organizations, unions, and individuals aimed at lobbying for a change in the national law on prostitution, which it achieved in 2017.

12 Founded in 1990s at the initiative of EU civil servants, the European Women's Lobby is the largest umbrella organization of women's association in the EU, with the aim to support the latter and lobby EU institutions on women-related issues. It considers prostitution as a form of violence against women and has been campaigning for its abolition for a "Europe free of prostitution" (EWL, 2020).

References

Aleanca LGBT, PINK Embassy Albania, Pro LGBT, Streha, ERA—LGBTI Equal Rights Association for Western Balkans and Turkey, and I. World 2018. "Written contribution on the position of LGBTI persons to the 3rd cycle of the universal periodic review of the Republic of Albania." Accessed 5th May 2020. https://www.lgbti-era.org/sites/default/files/pdfdocs/Written%20Contribution%20to%20the%203rd%20Cycle%20of%20UPR%20Review%20of%20Albania.pdf.

APRAMP 2020. "Misión, visión, valores." Accessed 1st June 2020. https://apramp.org/quienes-somos/.

Archambault, E. 2009. "The third sector in Europe: Does it exhibit a converging movement." In: *Civil Society in Comparative Perspective*, edited by Enjolras and Sivesind, 3–24. Bingley, UK: Emerald Books.

Aspasie 2020. "Association boulevards." Accessed 8th June 2020. https://www.aspasie.ch/activites/bus-boulevards/.

Bartley, P. 1998. "Preventing prostitution: The ladies' association for the care and protection of young girls in Birmingham, 1887–1914." *Women's History Review* 7(1): 37–60.

Bes, D. 2020. "Become a member." Accessed 8th May 2020. https://berufsverband-sexarbeit.de/index.php/join-us/?lang=en.

Beyond the Streets 2014. "The wrong question?" Accessed 25th May 2020. https://beyondthestreets.org.uk/2015/10/31/hello-world/.

Bjønness, J., and M. Spanger 2018. "Denmark." In: *Assessing Prostitution Policies in Europe*, edited by Jahnsen and Wagenaar, 153–168. Abingdon, UK: Routledge.

Boysproject 2020. "Professional methodologies intro." Accessed 6th May 2020. http://www.boysproject.be/en/professional-2/methodologies/intro-6.

Brussa, L. 1998. "The TAMPEP project in Western Europe." In: *Global Sex Workers*, edited by Kempadoo and Doezema, 246–259. New York: Routledge.

CAP 2017. "Coalition for the abolition of prostitution." Accessed 2nd June 2020. http://www.cap-international.org/wp-content/uploads/2016/02/CAP-Plaquette-ENV3-WEB.pdf.

——— 2020. "Human-rights based approach." Accessed 19th May 2020. http://www.cap-international.org/campaigns/human-rights/.

CEEHRN 2005. "Sex work, HIV/AIDS, and human rights in Central and Eastern Europe and Central Asia." Accessed 24th July 2020. https://www.unodc.org/documents/hiv-aids/publications/CEEAndCAsiaharm_05_sex_work_east_eur_0408.pdf.

Chimienti, M., and G. Bugnon 2018. "Switzerland". In: *Assessing Prostitution Policies in Europe*, edited by Jahnsen and Wagenaar, 136–150. Abingdon: Routledge.

Collins, S.E., S.L. Clifasefi, D.E. Logan, L.S. Samples, J.M. Somers, and G.A. Marlatt 2012. "Current status, historical highlights, and basic principles of harm reduction." In: *Harm Reduction: Pragmatic Strategies for Managing High-Risk Behaviours*, edited by Marlatt, Larimer and Witkiewitz, 2nd edition, 6–10. New York: Guildford Press.

Correlation 2020. "Who we are." Accessed 8th June 2020. https://www.correlation-net.org/who-we-are/.

Crowhurst, I. 2007. "The 'foreign prostitute' in contemporary Italy: Gender, sexuality and migration in policy and practice." PhD, Sociology. United Kingdom: London School of Economics and Political Science.

Crowhurst, I., and M.-L. Skilbrei 2018. "International comparative explorations of prostitution policies: Lessons from two European projects." *Innovation: The European Journal of Social Science Research* 31(2): 142–161.

Cusick, L. 2006. "Widening the harm reduction agenda: From drug use to sex work." *International Journal of Drug Policy* 17(1): 3–11.

David, M. 2019. "The moral and political stakes of health issues in the regulation of prostitution (the cases of Belgium and France)." *Sexuality Research and Social Policy* 16(2): 201–213.

David, M., and M. Loopmans 2018. "Belgium." In: *Assessing Prostitution Policies in Europe*, edited by Jahnsen and Wagenaar, 77–91. Abingdon, UK: Routledge.

Ditmore, M.H. 2006. *Encyclopedia of Prostitution and Sex Work 1*. Boston, MA: Greenwood Publishing Group.

Donevan, M. 2018. "Talita's 15-year experience working with women exploited in prostitution, pornography and human trafficking for sexual purposes." In: *Prostitution Heute*, edited by Angelina, Piasecki and Schurian-Bremecker, 179–196. Baden-Baden: Tectum Verlag.

EHRA 2020. "About us." Accessed 8th June 2020. https://harmreductioneurasia.org/about-us/.

Elman, R.A. 2007. *Sexual Equality in an Integrated Europe*. Basingstoke, UK: Palgrave.

EWL 2020. "Together for Europe free from prostitution." Accessed 23rd July 2020. https://womenlobby.org/-Together-for-a-Europe-Free-From-Prostitution-?lang=en.

Finger, S. 2016. "Sex-work and mobility as a coping strategy for marginalized Hungarian Roma women." *ACME: An International Journal for Critical Geographies* 15(1): 104–128.

Fondation Scelles 2017. "Activity report 2017." Accessed 1st June 2020. http://www.fondationscelles.org/pdf/Scelles_Foundation_ACTIVITY_REPORT_2017_FormatLetter.pdf.

———— 2020. "Our convictions, our objectives." Accessed 19th May 2020. https://www
.fondationscelles.org/en/about-us/convictions-objectives.

Fuckförbundet 2019. "Twenty years of failing sex workers." Accessed 21st May 2020.
http://www.sexworkeurope.org/sites/default/files/userfiles/files/FF19%20-%20INTE
RACTIVE%20%281%29.pdf.

Gibson, M. 1986. *Prostitution and the State in Italy, 1860–1915. Crime, Law, and Deviance
Series*. New Brunswick, NJ: Rutgers University Press.

Gilges, G. 2018. "Activism for sex workers in the Netherlands: Interview with Jan Visser
about foundation and end of de rode Draad, 1985 to 2012." *Moving the Social* 59:
13–24.

Grimes, T. 2001. *Such a Taboo: An Analysis of Service Need and Service Provision for
Males in Prostitution in the Eastern Region*. Dublin: Irish Network Male Prostitution
& East Coast Health Board.

Hahn, K., and A. Holzscheiter 2013. "The ambivalence of advocacy: Representation and
contestation in global NGO advocacy for child workers and sex workers." *Global
Society* 27(4): 497–520.

Hantrais, L. 2009. *International Comparative Research*. Basingstoke: Palgrave Macmillan.

Hunecke, I. 2018. "Germany." In: *Assessing Prostitution Policies in Europe*, edited by
Jahnsen and Wagenaar, 107–121. Abingdon, UK: Routledge.

ICRSE 2015a. "Nothing about us without us." Accessed 18th May 2020. http://www.sexw
orkeurope.org/sites/default/files/userfiles/files/ICRSE_10years%20report_Decemberr2
015_photo_final.pdf.

———— 2015b. "Underserved. Overpoliced. Invisibilised. LGBT sex wokers do matter."
Accessed 10th March 2020. https://www.sexworkeurope.org/sites/default/files/resou
rce-pdfs/icrse_briefing_paper_october2015.pdf.

———— 2016. "Surveilled. Exploited. Deported. Rights violations against migrant sex
workers in Europe and Central Asia." Accessed 6th January 2021. https://www.sex
workeurope.org/sites/default/files/resource-pdfs/icrse_briefing_paper_migrants_righ
ts_november2016.pdf.

———— 2018. "Diverse, resilient, powerful. Intersectional activism toolkit for sex workers
and allies." Accessed 26th May 2020. http://www.sexworkeurope.org/sites/default/files
/userfiles/files/ICRSE_Intersectional_Activism_Toolkit_final.pdf.

———— 2020. "About us." Accessed 28th May 2020. http://www.sexworkeurope.org/
about-us.

Il Manifesto 2020. "Lettera in merito all'articolo sul 'lavoro sessuale'." Accessed 24th July
2020. https://ilmanifesto.it/lettera-in-merito-allarticolo-sul-lavoro-sessuale-pubblica
to-su-il-manifesto/?fbclid=IwAR2AfD_PQxnx9CcvSC97HHi9ndeXLNmO9AmU
AekZlOF03Tff7VoGqai6Ljg.

Iroko Associazione Onlus. 2020a. "Abolitionism." Accessed 4th May 2020. http://www
.associazioneiroko.org/abolitionism/.

Jahnsen, S.Ø., and H. Wagenaar 2018. *Assessing Prostitution Policies in Europe*.
Abingdon, UK: Routledge.

Kempadoo, K. 1998. "Introduction: Globalizing sex workers' rights." In: *Global Sex
Workers: Rights, Resistance, and Redefinition*, edited by Kempadoo and Doezema,
1–28. New York: Routledge.

KFUKS Sociale Arbejde 2020. "Prostitution." Accessed 15th May 2020. https://kfuksa.dk
/viden-om/prostitution.

Kuus, M. 2005. "Multiple Europes: Boundaries and margins in European Union enlargement." *Geopolitics* 10(3): 567–570.

Les Roses d'Acier 2016. "What gives them the right to judge us?" In: *Sex Workers Speak. Who Listens?*, edited by Macioti and Geymonat. OpenDemocracy. Accessed 14th December 2020. https://www.opendemocracy.net/en/beyond-trafficking-and-slavery/what-gives-them-right-to-judge-us/

Maciver, N. 1992. "Developing a service for prostitutes in Glasgow." In: *Working with Women and AIDS: Medical, Social, and Counselling Issues*, edited by Bury, Morrison and Mclachlan, 85–98. London: Routledge.

Maiz 2020. "Maiz sex & work." Accessed 8th May 2020. https://www.maiz.at/en/node/18.

Malostratos 2019. "Leguaje recomendado papa referirse a la trata y la explotacion sexual de prostitucion en el marco del derecho internacional." Accessed 6th January 2021. https://malostratos.org/wp-content/uploads/2019/03/LenguajeRecomendado-A4-Impresion.pdf.

——— 2020. "What is prostitution?" Accessed 19th May 2020. https://malostratos.org/asociacion-contra-la-prostitucion/que-es-la-prostitucion/.

MASH 2020. "Who we are." Accessed 20th May 2020. http://www.mash.org.uk/about-mash/who-we-are/.

Mathieu, L. 2004. "The debate on prostitution in France: A conflict between abolitionism, regulation and prohibition." *Journal of Contemporary European Studies* 12(2): 153–163.

——— 2013. "Genèse et logiques des politiques de prostitution en France." *Actes de la recherche en sciences sociales* 3: 5–20.

Minoritet 2020. "Minoritet." Accessed 8th June 2020. http://www.minoritet.dk.

Moustgaard, U. 2010. "Prostitution of poverty or sexual self-determination?" www.Kvinfo .dk. Accessed 15th May 2020. https://kvinfo.dk/prostitution-of-poverty-or-sexual-self-determination/?lang=en.

Mundos, M.D. 2020. "Quienes somos." Accessed 2nd June 2020. https://www.medicosdelmundo.org/quienes-somos.

NSWP 2014a. "Global report: Good practice in sex worker-led HIV programming." Accessed 11th March 2020. https://www.nswp.org/resource/global-report-good-practice-sex-worker-led-hiv-programming.

——— 2014b. "Good practice in sex worker-led HIV programming in Europe." Accessed 10 April 2020. https://www.nswp.org/sites/nswp.org/files/Regional%20Europe.pdf.

——— 2017a. "Briefing note: Meaningful involvement of sex workers." Accessed 6th January 2021. https://www.nswp.org/sites/nswp.org/files/meaningful_involvement_document_en.pdf.

——— 2017b. ""Sexelance" van available in Denmark for street-based sex work." Accessed 8th June 2020. https://www.nswp.org/news/sexelance-van-available-denmark-street-based-sex-work.

——— 2017c. "HOPS calls on macedonian government to support harm reduction programmes." Accessed 24th July 2020. https://www.nswp.org/news/hops-calls-macedonian-government-support-harm-reduction-programmes.

——— 2020. "SexWorkCall Romania." Accessed 27th April 2020. https://www.nswp.org/members/sexworkcall-romania.

NUM 2020. "About." Accessed 18th May 2020. https://uglymugs.org/um/about/.

Ombre Rosse 2020. "Chi siamo." Accessed 25th May 2020. https://ombrerosse.noblogs .org/chi-siamo/.

———— 2020b. "Iroko Nigeria." Accessed 2nd June 2020. http://www.associazioneiroko .org/iroko-nigeria/.

Open Society Foundations. 2017. "Three case studies of global fund withdrawal in south Eastern Europe." Accessed 24th July 2020. https://www.opensocietyfoundations.org/u ploads/cee79e2c-cc5c-4e96-95dc-5da50ccdee96/lost-in-translation-20171208.pdf.

OSCARS 2010. "Le Funambus: Programme de réduction des risques et de promotion de la santé auprès des personnes se prostituant à Nantes." Accessed 6th January 2021. https:/ /www.oscarsante.org/pays-de-la-loire/action/detail/19369.

Oselin, S.S., and R. Weitzer 2013. "Organizations working on behalf of prostitutes: An analysis of goals, practices, and strategies." *Sexualities* 16(3–4): 445–466.

Östergren, P. 2017. "From zero-tolerance to full integration: Rethinking prostitution policies." *DemandAT Working Paper*. Accessed 24th February 2020. http://www.dema ndat.eu/sites/default/files/DemandAT_WP10_ProstitutionPoliciesTypology_June 2017_0.pdf.

Outshoorn, J. 2005. "The political debates on prostitution and trafficking of women." *Social Politics: International Studies in Gender, State and Society* 12(1): 141–155.

———— 2018. "European Union and prostitution policy." In: *Assessing Prostitution Policies in Europe*, edited by Jahnsen and Wagenaar, 363–392. Abingdon: Routledge.

Parker, N., ed. 2008. *The Geopolitics of Europe's Identity: Centers, Boundaries, and Margins*. New York: Palgrave Macmillan.

Pasionaria 2020. "Sex worker rispondono alle abolizioniste": "Esistiamo e Prendiamo Parola." Accessed 24th July 2020. https://pasionaria.it/ilmanifesto-prostituzione-ab olizioniste-femminismo/.

Phoenix, J. 2008. "Be helped or else! Economic exploitation, male violence and prostitution policy in the UK." In: *Demanding Sex: Critical Reflections on the Regulation of Prostitution*, edited by Munro and Della Giusta, 35–50. Aldershot, UK: Ashgate.

———— 2009. *Regulating Sex for Sale: Prostitution Policy Reform and the UK*. Bristol, UK: Policy Press.

———— 2017. "Prostitution and sex work." In: *The Oxford Handbook of Criminology*, edited by Leibling, Maruna, and McAra, 6th edition, 685–703. Oxford: Oxford University Press.

Plambech, S. 2018. "The sexelance: Red lights on wheels." Accessed 8th June 2020. https ://www.opendemocracy.net/en/beyond-trafficking-and-slavery/sexelance-red-lights-on -wheels/.

POW Nottingham 2020. "About us." Accessed 20th May 2020. http://pow-advice.org.uk/ about-pow-nottingham/.

Pro-tukipiste. 2020. "Pro-tukipiste." Accessed 6th January 2020. https://pro-tukipiste.fi/en /pro-tukipiste-en-translation/.

PROUD 2020. "Welkom bij PROUD." Accessed 8th May 2020. https://www.wijzijnproud .nl.

Putnam, R.D. 2000. "Bowling alone: America's declining social capital." In: *Culture and Politics*, 223–234. New York: Springer.

Putnam, R.D., R. Leonardi, and R.Y. Nanetti 1994. *Making Democracy Work: Civic Traditions in Modern Italy*. Princeton, NJ: Princeton University Press.

Ragazza! 2020. "Public relations." Accessed 20th May 2020. http://ragazza-hamburg.de/ public-relations.

Reden International 2020a. "On reden international." Accessed 19th May 2020. https:// kfuksa.dk/reden-international/om-reden-international.

———— 2020b. "Reden Internationals histories." Accessed 1st June 2020. https://kfuksa.dk /reden-international/om-reden-international/reden-internationals-historie.

Reeves, A., S. Steele, D. Stuckler, M. McKee, A. Amato-Gauci, and J.C. Semenza 2017. "National sex work policy and HIV prevalence among sex workers: An ecological regression analysis of 27 European countries." *The Lancet HIV* 4(3): e134–e140.

ROZKOŠ bez RIZIKA 2020. "About us." Accessed 4th June 2020. https://rozkosbezrizika .cz/en/about-us/.

Rubio Grundell, L. 2015. "Sex workers organisations and EU policy-making: Explaining an institutional and ideational exclusion." *4th European Conference on Politics and Gender.*

Ruhama 2018. "Annual report." Accessed 1st June 2020. https://www.ruhama.ie/wp-conte nt/uploads/Ruhama-Annual-Report-2018.pdf.

Salamon, L.M., and W. Sokolowski 2018. "The size and composition of the European third sector." In: *The Third Sector as A Renewable Resource for Europe*, edited by Enjolras, Salamon, Sivesind and Zimmer, 49–94. Cham: Palgrave Macmillan.

Salamon, L.M., S.W. Sokolowski, and M.A. Haddock 2017. *Explaining Civil Society Development: A Social Origins Approach.* Baltimore, MD: Johns Hopkins University Press.

Sanders, T., J. Scoular, R. Campbell, J. Pitcher, and S. Cunningham 2018. *Internet Sex Work: Beyond the Gaze.* London: Palgrave MacMillan.

Scoular, J. 2015. *The Subject of Prostitution: Sex Work, Law and Social Theory.* Abingdon, UK: Routledge.

Scoular, J., and T. Sanders 2010. "Introduction: The changing social and legal context of sexual commerce: Why regulation matters." *Journal of Law and in Society* 37(1): 1–11.

Sevelsted, A. 2018. "Protestant ethics-in-action: The emergence of voluntary social work in Copenhagen 1865–1915." *European Journal of Sociology/Archives Européennes de Sociologie* 59(1): 121–149.

SIO 2020. "About SIO." Accessed 24th April 2020. http://www.s-i-o.dk/english/about-sio/.

Skilbrei, M.-L., and C. Holmström 2013. *Prostitution Policy in the Nordic Region: Ambiguous Sympathies.* London: Ashgate.

Skilbrei, M.-L., and M. Tveit 2008. "Mangfoldig marked: Prostitusjonens omfang, innhold og organisering." www.fafo.no/pub/rapp/20085/20085.pdf.

Smith, M., and J. Mac 2018. *Revolting Prostitutes: The Fight for Sex Workers' Rights.* London: Verso Trade.

Spanger, M. 2011. "Human trafficking as a lever for feminist voices? Transformations of the Danish policy field of prostitution." *Critical Social Policy* 31(4): 517–539.

St Denny, E. 2016. "Explaining the emergence and gradual transformation of policy regimes: the case of contemporary French prostitution policy (1946–2016)." PhD. Nottingham Trent University.

Stevenson, C., and J. Petrak 2007. "Setting up a clinical psychology service for commercial sex workers." *International Journal of STD and AIDS* 18(4): 231–234.

Stevenson, L., and A. Dziuban 2018. "Silent no more: Self-determination and organisation of sex workers in Europe." In: *Assessing Prostitution Policies in Europe*, edited by Jahnsen and Wagenaar, 376–392. Abingdon, UK: Routledge.

Stigamot 2020. "Stigamot." Accessed 2nd June 2020. https://www.stigamot.is/is/language s/english.

STRASS 2016. "The French state against sex workers: A security and racist logic." In: *Sex Workers Speak. Who Listens?*, edited by Macioti and Garofalo Geymonat, 30–35.

Accessed 14th December 2020. https://www.opendemocracy.net/en/beyond-trafficking
-and-slavery/french-state-against-sex-workers-security-and-racist-logic/

Strohmayer, A., M. Laing, and R. Comber 2019. "Justice-oriented ecologies. A framework
for designing technologies with sex work support services." In: *Routledge International
Handbook of Sex Industry Research*, edited by Dewey, Crowhurst, and Izugbara. 544–
555. Abingdon: Routledge.

SWAI 2019. "Press release: Sex workers could be allies in sex trafficking if we were
allowed." Accessed 18th May 2020. https://sexworkersallianceireland.org/2019/07/
press-release-sex-workers-could-be-allies-in-sex-trafficking-if-we-were-allowed/.

SWAN 2020a. "About SWAN." Accessed 28th May 2020. http://swannet.org/en/about.

——— 2020b. "ARAS—Romanian association against AIDS." Accessed 8th June 2020.
http://www.swannet.org/en/members/aras---romanian-association-against-aids.

——— 2020c. "JAZAS—Association against AIDS." Accessed 8th June 2020. http://
www.swannet.org/en/members/jazas-association-against-aids.

——— 2020d. "Strategic plan 2018–2022." Accessed 28th May 2020. http://www
.swannet.org/files/swannet/SP'18-22%20ENG%20single%20pages%20CORRECTED
_21.NOV%20(1).pdf.

TAMPEP 2007a. "Final report." Accessed 6th January 2021. https://tampep.eu/wp-content
/uploads/2017/11/report_tampep_7.pdf.

——— 2007b. "Gap analysis of service provision to sex workers in Europe." Accessed
8th June 2020. https://tampep.eu/wp-content/uploads/2017/11/Gap-Analysis-of-Serv
ice-Provision-to-Sex-Workers.pdf.

——— 2007c. "TAMPEP final report 7." European Commission for Health and Consumer
Protection. Accessed 2nd April 2020. https://tampep.eu/wp-content/uploads/2017/11/
report_tampep_7.pdf.

——— 2009a. "Sex work in Europe." Accessed 6th January 2021. https://tampep.eu/wp-
content/uploads/2017/11/TAMPEP-2009-European-Mapping-Report.pdf.

——— 2009b. "Sex work migration health." Accessed 10th April 2020. https://tampep.eu
/wp-content/uploads/2017/11/Sexworkmigrationhealth_final.pdf.

——— 2010. "TAMPEP national mapping reports 8." Accessed 10 April 2020. https://we
bgate.ec.europa.eu/chafea_pdb/assets/files/pdb/2006344/2006344_d4_deliverable_t8
_annex_10_d_national_reports_mapping.pdf.

——— 2015. "TAMPEP on the situation of national and migrant sex workers in Europe
today." Accessed 6th January 2021. https://tampep.eu/wp-content/uploads/2017/11/
TAMPEP-paper-2015_08.pdf.

Vuolajärvi, N. 2019. "Governing in the name of caring—The Nordic model of prostitution
and its punitive consequences for migrants who sell sex." *Sexuality Research and
Social Policy* 16(2): 151–165.

Wagenaar, H. 2018. "Introduction: Prostitution policy in Europe—An overview." In:
Assessing Prostitution Policies in Europe, edited by Jahnsen and Wagenaar, 1–28.
Abingdon, UK: Routledge.

Ward, H., and S. Day 1997. "Health care and regulation: New perspectives." In: *Rethinking
Prostitution: Purchasing Sex in the 1990s*, edited by Scambler and Scambler, 139–163.
London: Routledge.

Weisbrod, B.A. 1977. *The Voluntary Nonprofit Sector: An Economic Analysis*. Lexington,
MA: Lexington Books.

White, S., and V. Feklyunina 2014. *Identities and Foreign Policies in Russia, Ukraine and
Belarus*. New York: Palgrave Macmillan.

Women's Support Project. n.d. "Women and power." Accessed 19th May 2020. http://www.womenssupportproject.co.uk/userfiles/file/uploads/WSP%20-%20Money%20&%20Power%20-%20pack%202.pdf.

Women@thewell. n.d. "Mind your language." Accessed 21st May 2020. https://gnb-user-uploads.s3.amazonaws.com/cnb/website/watw/d7bcf59eda1ff8a9a1a19ea003063ab4.pdf.

x:talk 2020. "About X:Talk." Accessed 28th April 2020. http://www.xtalkproject.net/about/.

Chapter 6

Conclusion

Isabel Crowhurst, Susan Dewey,
and Chimaraoke Izugbara

Introduction

This book has addressed third sector organizations' service provision and advocacy activities for people who sell sex in Africa, the Americas, and Europe. We set out to widen the scope of limited existing research on these organizations by looking at how the values they embrace and the approaches that underpin their understandings of sex for sale inform their activities and relationships with other TSOs, the donor community, with governmental institutions, and with their target populations. Starting from the premise that, as historically situated social actors, sex work and prostitution third sector organizations (TSOs) are an inseparable dimension of social relations, socioeconomic and political processes, and are embedded in, continuously shaped by, and redefining them, our analysis has shown different ways in which these organizations produce and define the subjects they aim to support and represent, and in so doing influence their lives and well-being while also reinforcing, challenging, and/or resisting local and global discourses on sex work and prostitution.

The focus on three vast and diverse geosocial regions has inevitably entailed a loss of context-specific details, including those pertaining to the cultural politics of more contained units of analysis, such as individual countries or TSOs. The globality (Therborn, 2004) of a cross-continental outlook, however, has enabled us to observe the connectivity and variability of these TSOs and of the social phenomena, structures, and discourses they operate within, beyond national boundaries. While recognizing the socially constructed and contested nature of the geosocial regions we explored, our analysis allowed us to identify patterns that reveal specificities and continuities within these regions, as we further tease out and elaborate in the next sections.

This concluding chapter elaborates on some of the continuities, differences, themes, and issues that emerged from our analysis of sex work and prostitution TSOs in the three regions. First, it discusses how third sector organizations have variously mobilized the enduring political capital of prostitution. It then illustrates disconnects between abstract debates regarding the essential nature of sex trade and the on-the-ground realities facing TSOs. Next, it examines how interactions between dominant and oppositional groups mutually shape encounters between one another as well as each group's understanding of its own identity. The chapter then explores the credibility deficit that has historically faced sex worker rights TSOs and continues to shape their activism. It concludes with an exploration of future directions for sex work and prostitution TSOs.

The political capital of prostitution

We began our exploration in Chapter 2 with an overview of shifting understandings and responses to prostitution across the three regions over the past two centuries, revealing, in so doing, how organized nonstate actors have contributed to constituting the (gendered) prostitute subject, *her* social function, and *her* needs. This historical outlook showed the role played by the construction and regulation of prostitution in building modern nation states and empires, in expanding control over colonized territories and their inhabitants, and in turn, in condemning colonial rulers and their legacies by brandishing prostitution as an evil imported from morally negligent Europe. As a ductile signifier, the prostitute subject has served as a vehicle for the construction and reinforcement of norms – in the shape of social mores and laws – underpinned by gendered, racialized, and classed constructions of who should be punished for breaking them, of who might need to be rescued instead, and of who can be in the rightful position to be a legitimate rescuer. The prostitute subject has also continued to raise questions about the boundaries of acceptable work based on economic opportunities or the lack thereof, notions of human dignity, legislation, choice, and perceived occupational risks.

The political capital of prostitution and the power that comes with it have not waned with time; if anything, prostitution remains an important and contested signifier of values and norms around which nations are meant to coalesce, gain strength, and even become ideal models to be emulated. TSOs, with the different configurations they have assumed over time and across different places, have had (and continue) to negotiate these norms and the political and legal instruments they subtend: in some instances championing and influencing them, and in others acting as vocal opposers or as detached outliers mostly concerned with providing practical support. The politics of prostitution however is inescapable: all sex work and prostitution TSOs are value-driven political actors.

Even when TSOs purport to offer non-judgmental or neutral charitable services, they position their goals and activities vis-à-vis specific understandings of their "constituents", construct and circulate particular imageries of them, make sense of how they relate to and share, or not, the life experiences of their target populations, and engage in processes of negotiations with various economic and political agents, other citizens, their own members, and dominant discourses around prostitution that might facilitate or impede their work and goals.

Social constructions of sex work and prostitution do not emerge in a vacuum, and analysis presented throughout this book has demonstrated how cultural and historical forces help to co-construct the political capital of prostitution. Chapter 3 examined the African historical paradox through which the existence of prostitution was both a response to and a justification for colonial rule. In contemporary African nations, neo-colonial forces in the form of dependency on aid from the Global North set the agenda for many sex work and prostitution TSOs, resulting in irreconcilable policy and programmatic models that hinder the emergence of workable blueprints for promoting equity and well-being for the sex worker in Africa.

Chapter 4 likewise located colonialism as central to the creation of the sex industry in the Americas while also noting how the practice of settler colonialism created societies stratified by race and class in ways that remain apparent in the contemporary sex industry. In the present-day Americas, the political capital of prostitution is evident in the intensity and scope of criminalization and militarization mobilized to regulate disorder, as is apparent in police efforts to "clean up" red light areas, as occurred in Brazil prior to the Olympics when officials ordered police to remove sex workers and other disorderly citizens from public view.

Colonialism's legacy is apparent in all three regions through the whitewashing evident in depictions of sex work and trafficking as social problems detached from the deeply rooted structural inequalities that enable their existence in the first place. Such whitewashing and the concealing of lived lives that come with it are processes that some TSOs participate in by leveraging the political capital of prostitution to strategically engage with dominant cultural norms in order to meet their broader political goals. Chapter 4, for instance, examined how anti-trafficking groups in the Americas adhere to discourses that represent prostitution as modern-day slavery while failing to acknowledge how the enduring legacy of the trans-Atlantic trade in human beings continues to manifest in the over-policing of Black people. Likewise, we see the myth of individualism that undergirded settler colonialism at the forefront of the neoliberal nonprofit industrial complex through which capital tightly controls the types of already very limited social safety nets available to people in poverty.

Such whitewashing was also evident in Chapter 5's observations regarding how some TSOs recast the high prevalence and difficult living and working conditions of migrants relative to local people in the sex industries of Western Europe as a problem of trafficking rather than of global socioeconomic inequalities, penalizing immigration laws, exclusions from otherwise robust socioeconomic safety nets, and diffused anti-migrant xenophobia. Migrants' cross-border movements are part of an enduring socioeconomic neo-colonialism that is also evident in the circulation of ideologies which are in part exported by TSOs in Europe and the Americas to Africa, and from Western Europe to Eastern Europe. Yet, as was discussed in Chapter 4, nowhere is ideological neo-colonialism more apparent than in the US dominance of anti-trafficking efforts both regionally in the Americas and globally through the 2000 Victims of Trafficking and Violence Prevention Act, which authorizes significant financial resources for TSOs that oppose prostitution and threatens sanctions to countries that do not comply. In all these instances, TSOs and the political agents that dominate their agendas and activities recast prostitution as a problem in need of solutions that often serve a very different, and sometimes much more insidious, purpose.

Conflicting views and understandings

The landscape that this book has addressed is one of great complexity, with sex work and prostitution TSOs representing, reinforcing, and playing out divisions that have deep historical roots. Whatever the position embraced by these organizations, whether historically or currently, they all share an understanding that something is wrong with prostitution and that it demands urgent attention – but what they identify as the "problem" with prostitution and the cause of and solution to this "problem" differ substantially. Yet the shared belief exists, among all TSOs studied, that their approach offers unique insights into social problems associated with the sale of sex.

In the region-focused Chapters 3, 4, and 5, we found numerous examples of the different frameworks of understanding of prostitution upon which TSOs base their goals, activities, claims, and demands. The tapestry of sex work and prostitution TSOs that our analysis documented is multiform and their approaches cannot be reduced to the two polarized perspectives – sex work as work vs. prostitution as violence against women – that have emerged as the most dominant in public discourses and debates in Europe and North America in particular. Across the three continents, we have seen TSOs, some in the past, others in current times, that identify prostitution with sin, vice, degeneration, a social problem and/or public health risk, sexual exploitation, sexual labor, and in some instances, with a combination of these and other factors. At the basis of these perspectives are explanations that focus on one hand on pathologies and abnormalities, whether individualized or viewed as traits of particular groups of people, and on the other on broader social forces and structures, including patriarchy, racism, the feminization of poverty, economic precariousness, organized crime, retrenchment of welfare, privatization of health services, legacies of colonialism and slavery, and postcolonial economic extractivism.

The extent to which these frameworks of understanding are more or less complex matters a great deal. As Jane Scoular states in relation to the aporia that stifles feminist approaches to prostitution, "viewing accounts of sex workers' rights and exploitation as antithetical, [...] not only serves to paralyze feminism, but also denies the lived reality of those involved in sex work who, in their everyday lives, have to integrate both perspectives" (2015: 152). While feminist and other debates about prostitution can and often take place on abstract planes and in contexts that are far removed from the realities of sex work, for example in academia, in political institutions, or in the media, the vast majority of the TSOs we have looked at engage in the unspectacular, challenging, and often contradictory realities of the everyday lives of people who sell sex. In this way, they have to grapple with what prostitution, and the myriad different contexts, subjectivities, and structures that shape the way it is experienced, materially does to people. These messy empirical realities are a far cry from abstractions, stripped of complexity, about what prostitution is meant to symbolize. As the previous chapters have shown, however, there are different degrees to which TSOs are willing to acknowledge complexity, messiness, and contradictions in the field. Some are very much committed to abstract and symbolic meanings ascribed to prostitution that often entail a top-down, rigid, one-model-fits-all type of response. Others are and have been responsive to and driven by their interpretations of the changing needs and preferences of the individuals they encounter.

For example, TSOs have been increasingly addressing the diversity of people who sell sex and their multiple and intersecting experiences of exclusion and vulnerability, with some of them specifically targeting sex workers who are from ethnic and racial minoritized groups, who identify as LGBTQ+, who are migrants, who are undocumented, homeless, addicted, etc. An intersectional perspective that accounts for complex experiential identities has directed TSOs' advocacy to question policies that are not necessarily prostitution-related but nevertheless negatively affect those who operate in the sex industries, including those that regulate immigration and access to public health services, and those that address homophobia and transphobia. Intersectional perspectives have also stimulated solidarity and collaborations with other social justice and human rights movements, or at least they have mobilized initiatives to pursue such engagements.

Intersectional perspectives also affect funding which is often more easily found in fields other than prostitution, unless this is attached to other more "fund-worthy" issues/problems, such as HIV/AIDS or exploitation in trafficking. As we saw, however, linking prostitution to other vulnerabilities has resulted in creating frameworks of understandings that permanently and rather simplistically conflate them. This emerged in particular from the chapter on Africa, where TSOs sex work-related funding is almost exclusively attached to HIV/AIDS, and so is the general perception of sex workers. Yet African TSOs distinguish themselves from their counterparts in Europe and the Americas through their much clearer acknowledgment of poverty as a central antecedent to their involvement in the sex industry in ways that make TSOs in Africa more readily able to receive funding that addresses sex work through the lens of economic marginalization. Theorizing by African TSOs about the nature of the sex trade remains somewhat limited in comparison to TSOs in Europe and the Americas, which we attributed to the prominence of received ideologies as a legacy of colonialism.

African TSOs are also distinguished from their peers in Europe and the Americas due to the prominent role taken by neo-abolitionist African women's rights TSOs that also address a range of other issues, such as women's equal political and economic representation. This is sharply distinguished from contemporary anti-prostitution movements in the Americas, where the second-wave feminists who regarded the sale of sex as a political issue on par with other socioeconomic justice issues for women are nearing retirement or are no longer active in the field. In the waking of waning feminist interest in sex work and prostitution, the contemporary anti-prostitution movement in the Americas is dominated by evangelical Christians.

In Europe, conversely, neo-abolitionist critiques of prostitution and sex work are rooted much more deeply in secular arguments for women's rights than in conservative moral crusades derived from religion, as in both Africa and the Americas, or essentialist notions that position sex trade as antithetical to culture, as is the case in Africa. Similar to how HIV/AIDS and poverty dominate TSOs' conceptualizations of sex work and prostitution in Africa, discourses on trafficking take center stage in the Americas and Europe. The prioritization of sex trafficking funding in the Americas and Europe has contributed to strengthening TSOs which focus on this phenomenon, as well as the perspectives which view it as equal to prostitution.

Dialectical dance

The landscape presented throughout this book is one in which interactions between dominant and oppositional TSOs mutually shape encounters between one another. TSOs engage with one another's respective ideological stances and actions as part of this mutually constitutive process and, in so doing, shape understandings of their organizational identities as distinct, aligned, or in opposition to the work of other TSOs as well as dominant cultural and politico-economic forces. Following Hoang (2015: 179), we draw on political scientist and historian William Sewell's notion of the dialectical dance, which describes the dynamic interplay between groups. Sewell argues that:

> The official cultural map may, of course, be criticized and resisted by those relegated to its margins. But subordinated groups must to some degree orient their local systems of meaning to those recognized as dominant; the act of contesting dominant meanings itself implies a recognition of their centrality. Dominant and oppositional groups interact constantly, each undertaking its initiatives with the other in mind. Even when they attempt to overcome or undermine each other, they are mutually shaped by their dialectical dance.
>
> (Sewell, 2005: 173)

This dialectical dance is apparent across our three regions, whether in the form of coalition-building among ideologically like-minded TSOs, the adoption of ideologies about the exchange of sex that circulate globally, or, perhaps most notably, the frequency with which TSOs define themselves through their opposition to particular beliefs or practices.

This dialectical dance has, at times, taken the form of effective and durable collaborations between TSOs and sometimes also between TSOs and national and transnational state and non-state institutions. In Chapter 5 on Europe, we already elaborated on the unique work that TAMPEP as a network was able to carry out through a collaboration between TSOs in 25 countries. This facilitated mapping of the sex industry across the region, training, sharing of best practices, the creation of manuals for service providers, and more. Continuous and sustainable funding from the European Commission was essential to enable this unique work, which produced a wealth of resources and reports that are still widely used. Indeed, it was through TAMPEP's report that we were able to provide details about the composition of the sex industry in Europe. Similar depth and width of data are not available for the Americas or Africa. Published in the 2000s, TAMPEP's mappings and reports are becoming outdated, and it is very unlikely that similar initiatives will be funded to the same extent in the near future. Effective service provision by TSOs, however, as TAMPEP itself has evidenced, can only take place where an accurate mapping of the phenomenon, one which is not just localized but geographically broad, provides enough knowledge of the target population, its changes, and movements, and therefore of its needs.

We have also seen examples of TSOs which, by reflecting on their practice and engagements with sex workers, changed the typology of their service provision, in some instances breaking away from partnerships and collaborations with other TSOs despite the risk of losing financial and political support. In other cases, the encounters between TSOs have been more antagonistic with considerable resources invested in challenging each other's perspectives, with conflicts at times becoming vicious and entailing attacks to the integrity and professionalism of counterpart TSOs. The formation of coalitions and networks of TSOs which share core values and approaches around sex work and prostitution has contributed to supporting individual TSOs in these fraught encounters and to manage the fatigue they entail. At the same time, it has created alliances that can exert powerful influence by excluding others, thus ending up escalating ideological conflict in the field.

This dialectical dance also takes place between dominant cultural norms and rights-based movements for those who sell sex, as people who sell sex face widespread stigma and discrimination throughout the world. Yet such stigma and discrimination manifest in different ways depending on cultural and geographic context. Chapter 3 provided examples of the dominant cultural tensions that TSOs navigate in contexts that depict sex work and prostitution as essentially contrary to African cultural values as a product of decadent Western influence. Chapter 4 emphasized how, in the Americas, a strong regional cultural focus on individualism results in an emphasis on peer-to-peer support and microenterprise as alternatives to selling sex as part of broader cultural norms that regard individual responsibility as a feasible route of out poverty.

There is also a powerful financial component to the performance of the dialectical dance in each of the three regions. Chapter 3 emphasized the key role that funders largely based in the Global North play in shaping African TSOs' priorities, language, and approaches. The dialectical dance surrounding sex work and prostitution TSOs in Africa and the Americas, as detailed in Chapters 3 and 4, stops short of providing largescale funding or widespread support to such initiatives. For example, sustained funding is unavailable to support regional collaboration and knowledge-sharing in Africa and the Americas, even when these collaborations exist. In sharp contrast, the scope of pan-European organizing for sex worker health and human rights, including national and EU support for these rights and even government funding made available to support them at various times in some countries is impressive. Equally impressive, when compared to Africa and the Americas, is the extent of sex worker-led organizing and the instances, albeit localized and mostly short-lived, of incorporation of sex workers into legal- and policy-related decision-making. As noted in Chapter 4, Canada's alignment with Western Europe and unique status in the Americas as a secular democracy with strong socioeconomic safety nets and support for human rights and harm reduction makes its approach closely resemble Europe; hence, it is unsurprising that the only TSOs providing services to migrant sex workers in the Americas are located in Canada.

Resistance is a key aspect of the dialectical dance, as is evident in the prevalence of outlaw politics in the Americas, wherein TSOs envision themselves as fighting a righteous battle against dominant cultural norms in order to achieve their vision of freedom from oppression. As noted in Chapter 4 with respect to Latin America, these outlaw politics are in part a legacy of the liberation theology ethos that helps these organizations to flourish and inspires their radical politics and solidarity, even when these politics diverge. Sex worker rights TSOs in Africa, like their peers in the Americas, continue to face significant challenges with respect to garnering widespread support. These challenges also exist in Western Europe, where sex worker TSOs face less open hostility and have access to greater resources than in Africa or the Americas but nonetheless experience stigma and discrimination.

Sex workers and testimonial injustice

The historical overview presented in Chapter 2 highlighted in particular the perspectives of those who took it upon themselves to organize with the aim to rescue, reform, and contain women in prostitution. Acts of resistance, mostly by women in prostitution over the 19th and until the second half of the 20th century were mentioned, but we know far less about them and about other support and advocacy initiatives, more or less organized, that they might have put in place. The lack of historical accounts about the lives and voices of those who have operated in prostitution partly explains this omission which in turn reflects the long-held belief that, for their own good, these individuals should be acted upon, whether through rescue, containment, or detention by others who know better. In this respect, historian Judith Walkowitz writes:

> One problem has been the paucity of historical sources that allow entry into the inner life of the prostitute. Illiterate women rarely left ego documents, while their personal statements extracted from legal testimonies were heavily mediated "through the discourse of those doing the recording". Legal evidence, even police notes, may include a striking description of a prostitute's milieu or a short first-person statement from the woman herself. But such evidence rarely summons up a streetwalker's complex thinking about her social world and embodied self.
>
> (Walkowitz 2016: 192)

Although these points refer to historical research on prostitution in England, they have a much wider resonance and highlight the long history of dismissing, and therefore silencing, the voices and experiences of those involved in prostitution, including (and perhaps especially) by those who take it upon themselves to "help" them. It was only in the 1970s in the Americas and Europe, and over a decade later in Africa, that organized sex workers' demand to be identified and treated as rights-bearing subjects as workers started being documented and gained visibility and consideration at national and global levels. By insisting on agency and prostitution as sexual labor, they have since been challenging narratives of victimization and dishonor that informed many TSOs' interventions and activities until then.

In such a fraught terrain, TSOs that hold a minoritized position on prostitution that challenges the dominant framework of understandings often struggle to gain recognition as legitimate actors. We have observed notable differences across and within the three regions we looked at; however, we can generalize in saying that difficulties in gaining access to funds and in engaging in collaborative governance with local, national, and supranational institutions are experienced more by organizations whose members advocate for themselves as rightful subjects as opposed to those whose members advocate for others as powerless victims. Thus, while we have shown that some sex work and prostitution TSOs have had and continue to have an important role in putting pressure on authorities and even in shaping prostitution-related legislation, most of them have been unable to gain and exert political influence consistently. In addition to this, previous chapters have shed light on the unique obstacles that sex workers encounter in their TSO-related support and advocacy activities. Being "out" as a sex worker, advocating for sex workers' rights, and working to provide support to sex workers can pose real threats to one's life; it can lead to arrest, stigma, violence, and harassment, including by public authorities. These threats can operate to curtail the activities and collaborative opportunities of TSOs, where even getting together to discuss common issues and challenges can risk arrest and conviction, as was evident in Chapter 4's example of the sex worker rights TSOs' Desiree Alliance canceling its 2019 annual conference due to concerns that then-newly introduced US legislation could be used to arrest and prosecute attendees.

We found the concept of testimonial injustice elaborated by philosopher Miranda Fricker (2007) useful in making sense of these diffused exclusionary processes. Testimonial injustice, she explains, occurs when identity prejudice, i.e. "prejudices against people *qua* social type" (Fricker, 2007: 4) "causes a hearer to give a deflated level of credibility to a speaker's word" (ibid.: 1). Sex workers, to this day, suffer from a credibility deficit that limits their recognition and value as human beings and social actors, whether as individuals or as collectives in organized formations. This credibility deficit is enforced in law and policy as well as being enshrined in many neo-abolitionist TSOs' perspectives that, because no one would voluntarily choose to sell sex, those who claim to do so must be suffering from undiagnosed mental or psychological problems.

Testimonial injustice that excludes the voices of sex workers as authorities on their own lives is globally pervasive. Yet constitutional challenges to law and policy that violate sex worker rights are rare but do occur, such as when the US Supreme Court ruled that the practice of excluding sex worker rights groups from funding was unconstitutional or when the Superior Court of Canada temporarily decriminalized the sale of sex on the same grounds. However, as is the case in Europe, even when these exclusionary practices are less explicit and formal bans do not exist, the growing strength of neo-abolitionist TSOs and coalitions of TSOs at both national and European Union level means that sex worker rights TSOs do not get funding.

The credibility deficit that accompanies testimonial injustice also leads to lack of inclusion of sex workers in decision-making about the best policy and practical approaches to issues that most directly impact their lives. Consider the example of microenterprise programs designed to provide women who sell sex with alternative sources of income. Women who sell sex are rarely consulted in Europe, Africa, or the Americas regarding what types of work might constitute a viable alternative and, as a result, microenterprise programs reflect a context-specific "one-size-fits-all" approach to poverty. For example, microenterprise in the Americas takes a "welfare to workfare" approach in which work is the way to individual salvation from poverty. Such programs in the Americas focus exclusively on low-threshold, poorly paid service sector occupations, and ignore the difficulties associated with starting a small-scale business in countries with requirements for licensure and related permits as well as the fact that many women are in the sex industry because they cannot meet these requirements and also because service industry jobs pay so poorly. In Africa, small-scale businesses such as market trading, clothmaking, or hairdressing do not require elaborate registration formalities. Such businesses may create real opportunities for women but microenterprise is not often designed to address the significant stigma that sex workers who venture into them may continue to face in the community.

Yet despite the testimonial injustice that has historically shaped and continues to influence sex worker rights activism, our analysis indicates the existence of a vibrant sex work and prostitution TSO sector. These TSOs have diverse agendas and many have equally diverse leadership, with some including both sex workers and professionals in relevant fields as part of a community-wide coalition-building approach. Given such longstanding diversity and vibrancy among sex work and prostitution TSOs, it is helpful to conclude with some discussion of potential future directions for TSOs and researchers interested in their work.

Future directions

The 2020 coronavirus pandemic has indisputably changed the scope of advocacy and service provision work for all TSOs, irrespective of their mission. At the time of writing, a majority of people across the world are now significantly poorer, sicker, and more socially disconnected than they were just a few months earlier in late 2019. The beneficiaries of the essential healthcare and social services that some TSOs provide were already among the poorest, sickest, and most socially isolated and these conditions have only worsened given that the pandemic preys on those who are already in poor health and lack access to healthcare. Most TSOs operated on very limited budgets prior to the coronavirus outbreak, and the current global health and economic crisis will inevitably force some of the most vulnerable TSOs to cease their operations entirely. TSOs that relied heavily on volunteer support to conduct their everyday work now find that their former volunteer base has too many critical problems of their own that they must attend to, including looking for work or (for those fortunate enough to have a job) balancing work from home with homeschooling or full-time childcare. The fact that many TSO volunteers are women due to the feminization of care-work only compounds this problem.

It is difficult to ascertain what the future may hold for sex work and prostitution TSOs in this bleak scenario. People throughout the world have historically supported conservative leaders during times of crisis, and such leaders rarely champion the causes of the marginalized and stigmatized. The widespread social and economic suffering wrought by the pandemic has increased social isolation to levels that most people have never before experienced, and with that isolation has come a dramatic rise in depression, anxiety, and disregard for others, as is evident in the refusal by many people, including the former US President Donald Trump's entire presidential cabinet, to engage in basic public health precautions designed to protect others.

The future of sex work and prostitution TSOs, even those aligned with dominant cultural beliefs and norms, is at best uncertain in a climate fraught with pandemic-generated socioeconomic anxieties. In what follows, we attempt to identify some potential future trends for sex work and prostitution TSOs in each of the three regions. We then conclude with directions for future research.

In Africa, where sex work persists despite perceptions that it is antithetical to local culture and where most sex workers face devastating risks, stigma, discrimination, and mistreatment, some future trends regarding TSOs can be anticipated. First, given how sex work and prostitution TSOs in Africa have evolved in the recent past, their future will be closely tied to discourses and policies regarding sex work in the Global North. Second, the typologies of TSOs identified in the region will continue, at least in the immediate future, to both assert their local relevance and fight each other for supremacy. However, it is the professed operational strategies of these TSOs, the region's evolving policy and political and economic climate, and the nature of Global North investments in prostitution-related matters that will ultimately shape TSOs' continued ability to function and generate the resources, funding, public goodwill, and critical partnerships that they require to be successful in their activities related to sex work.

In the Americas, the totalizing violence of neoliberalism does not appear to be declining, and with it the continued heavy state intervention to which sex workers have been historically subjected. TSOs' reduction to being the "welfare arm" of the state, dependent on its funding priorities and needing to adjust to required practices of professionalization might end up expanding the gap between the lived experiences of those in the sex industry and abstract conceptualizations about what is best for them. Hegemonic discourses and practices however have historically been the generative spark of resistance and the outlaw activities and politics of those presently marginalized hold promise that disruption to the current state of affairs is not impossible.

In Europe, contestations around prostitution are played out, significantly more than in Africa and the Americas, around different policy approaches the support or opposition to which are often viewed as key factors in establishing core distinctions between TSOs and who among them should receive funding and legitimacy. Europe has observed various ebbs and flows in its approaches to prostitution over the past two centuries, and it has exported shifting values and systems of regulation over time to different parts of the world. This trend is continuing to this day, and it is likely to continue in the future with TSOs playing an important part in transplanting prostitution policy models and the dissent and controversy that come with them.

In light of these possible future trajectories for TSOs in the three regions, great potential remains for future research with sex work and prostitution TSOs. This is especially the case given that TSOs are often critical gatekeepers for researchers in terms of making introductions and facilitating trust-building with people who operate in the sex industry. Researchers often rely on TSOs so heavily for these purposes that some TSOs have developed processes and/or guidelines for working with researchers due to the widespread perception that research is an extractive industry that generally offers limited benefits to its participants (Stella, 2006). Yet TSOs remain curiously overlooked as sites of research themselves and, when they are studied at all, are often dismissed as examples of inadequate or misguided service provision.

We conclude with a brief discussion of key areas for exploration in future research by answering four questions. (1) How do sex work and prostitution TSOs understand their own and one another's work across ideological divides? (2) What factors influence TSOs' strategic choices to support their organizational goals? (3) In what ways do legal and regulatory frameworks and dominant cultural norms surrounding race, gender and sexuality influence TSOs' forms and purposes? (4) How do TSO staff and volunteers manage the everyday stress and courtesy stigma that accompanies their work?

First, little is known about the nuances of how TSOs understand their own and one another's work, especially within and across deep ideological divides. The field would benefit tremendously from analyses of how the dialectical dance described in this chapter takes place across and among TSOs, particularly in the course of their everyday operations. How, for example, do neo-abolitionist TSOs reconcile their belief that prostitution is a form of violence against women with the reality that people from a range of gender identities work in the sex industry? How do TSOs, particularly those working at the interstices of services provision and activism, make difficult decisions about how and with whom to collaborate? How do theory, ideology, and identity politics translate into practice in the resource-scarce environments in which most operate, and what motivates TSO staff and volunteers to do this work? Ethnography, with its keen attention to the minutiae that constitute the human experience, would be a particularly relevant method with which to explore these questions.

Second, we know that sex work and prostitution TSOs take a wide range of advocacy and service provision approaches, but very little is known about how they make strategic choices to support their organizational goals. Certainly, the availability of activist energy, community and volunteer support, and funding all influence these choices, but what other forces are at work? Using some combination of large-scale survey methods combined with in-depth interviews would help to examine how TSOs make these choices in response to their understandings of the sex industry, and would also shed light on potential for TSOs to work together by moving beyond a half-century of debates about the nature of the sex industry.

Third, in what specific ways do legal and/or regulatory frameworks and dominant cultural norms surrounding race, gender and sexuality influence the forms and purposes of sex work and prostitution TSOs? We have noted how sex worker rights TSOs have successfully partnered with local and national governments in Western European societies and, in the case of pre-Bolsonaro Brazil, how sex workers were considered equal partners in public health efforts. Mapping TSOs by geographic location, type of legal/regulatory framework, and then correlating that information with existing research on local cultural norms regarding race, gender and sexuality could potentially illustrate how context matters for TSOs.

Finally, courtesy stigma and burnout are well-documented phenomena among front-line service professionals whose jobs bring them into regular contact with people who use illicit drugs, break the law, or otherwise deviate from dominant social norms. Researchers should consider exploring how the "guilt by association" of courtesy stigma and associated likelihood of burnout impacts TSO staff and volunteers, including (and perhaps particularly) those who have sex industry experience. Surveying large numbers of sex work and prostitution TSOs, as domestic violence researchers have done with front-line service provision staff, would potentially provide insights into how these TSOs manage the everyday stress of their work. These research directions could be pursued on many different levels, from the very localized to the national to the transnational, and it is our hope that this book has shown what engaging in the latter and large-scale analyses can contribute to understandings of complex social dynamics and phenomena.

TSOs are fascinating research sites because they operate as zones of contestation as they translate their understandings of sex work and prostitution into practice. Their influence and activities co-constitute and are co-constituted by interconnected and historically configured global forces. Our analysis has demonstrated how these organizations are not external to normative power but participate in it and are subject to it, conditioning how they can exist, who they can reach out to, where, and whether they can achieve their goals.

References

Fricker, M. 2007. *Epistemic Injustce*. Oxford: Oxford University Press.

Hoang, K.K. 2015. *Dealing in Desire*. Berkcley, CA: University of California Press.

Scoular, J. 2015. *The Subject of Prostitution: Sex Work, Law and Social Theory*. Abingdon, UK: Routledge.

Sewell, H. 2005. *Logics of History: Social Theory and Social Transformation*. Chicago, IL: University of Chicago Press.

Stella, by and for Sex Workers in Montreal 2006. *Sex Workers and Research Ethics*. Montreal, QC: Stella. Accessed 6th January 2021. www.chezstella.org/docs/ConsSI DArechEthiA.pdf.

Therborn, G. 2004. *Between Sex and Power: Family in the World 1900–2000*. London: Routledge.

Walkowitz, J.R. 2016. "The politics of prostitution and sexual labour." *History Workshop Journal* 82(1): 188–198.

Index

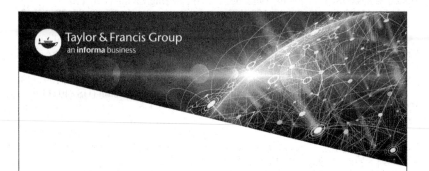

Printed in the United States
By Bookmasters